THE PRESIDENTS & THEIR FAITH

FROM GEORGE WASHINGTON TO BARACK OBAMA

Boise, Idaho

Published in Boise, Idaho, by Russell Media Web:
http://www.russell-media.com

This book may be purchased in bulk for educational, business, ministry, or promotional use.

For information please email customerservice@russell-media.com.

ISBN (hardcover): 978-1-9374989-4-8
ISBN (paperback): 978-1-9374989-8-6
ISBN (e-book): 978-1-9374989-5-5

Printed in the United States of America.

DEDICATIONS

My portions of this labor are dedicated to my wife, Cynthia, who believes that I can write something that others might be interested in reading. Thank you.

Darrin Grinder

For my wife, Kiley Ruwe Shaw, and our two daughters, Maddison Grace Shaw and Eleanor Rosa Shaw. Their encouragement, enthusiasm, and humanity help sustain me.

Steve Shaw

TABLE OF CONTENTS

INTRODUCTION

At the center of the political system of the United States is the office that the United States Constitution refers to simply as "President of the United States of America." During the Constitutional Convention of 1787 in Philadelphia, delegates such as George Washington, James Madison, Benjamin Franklin, James Wilson, Alexander Hamilton, and others struggled for over six weeks to construct this office that today is seen alternately as the nation's Chaplain-in-Chief or the nation's fire hydrant. As one leading contemporary scholar of the American presidency contends, "Familiar as it is, the American presidency has never been easy to understand. The institution has a protean character that defies fixed descriptions or settled explanations. Its history is riddled with eminence and embarrassment, proficiency and paralysis."[1]

We have had forty-four presidencies and forty-three presidents. The oddity, of course, is caused by Grover Cleveland, the only president to be elected to two non-consecutive terms in U.S. history. All have been white, males, save for President Barack Obama, and all have been Protestant (more or less), save for President John Kennedy, our country's first and to this point only Catholic president. In the words of Howard Fineman of *Newsweek*, "Every president invokes God and asks His blessing. Every president promises, though not always in so many words, to lead according to moral principles rooted in Biblical tradition."[2]

All of our presidents have spoken of (and most claimed to have spoken to) a higher power of some sort, from Supreme Being or Divine Legislator to a more personal Lord or Savior. Almost all quoted from or claimed to have read the Bible (either regularly or when Congress perhaps was in session). Some presidents were religiously devout; others, apparently not. Some presidents attended church services with utmost consistency; others, seldom, if at all. Some presidents were convincingly orthodox in their religious thought and practice; others were held either in high suspicion or low esteem because of questions or misperceptions or downright unfounded conclusions about their faith. Almost all of our presidents have viewed the United States as having some kind of special (they may or may not use covenantal language) relationship with God and yet few were deep or disciplined students of religion and theology, or perhaps even our own national history. In short, most presidents reflect what Alexis de Tocqueville concluded about Americans in the early nineteenth century during his brief but highly consequential trek across the young Republic: we embrace religion and try to keep theology at arm's length.

In his masterful account of the presidential election of 1960, in which the Catholicism of Senator John Kennedy of Massachusetts figured prominently, Theodore White concluded, "The Presidency hovers over the popular American imagination almost as a sacerdotal office, a priestly role for which normal political standards are invalid."[3] Similarly, Michael Novak argues, "Every four years Americans elect a king—but not only a king, also a high priest and prophet." Novak adds that the election "of a president is an almost religious task; it intimately affects the life of the spirit, our identity."[4] The Constitution prohibits, as we all know, any religious test for holding political office in the United States; however, it clearly is (or at the least appears to be) the case that no serious candidate for the White House can even run the risk of violating our religious/political norm that one be (or to the cynic, at least appear to be) religious. And moreover, the candidate should be not just religious, but acceptably religious, for it does appear to be the case that we do have a religious litmus test concerning the American presidency.

The last Unitarian president was William Howard Taft, who faced allegations of heresy during the 1908 campaign. Reverend Timothy Dwight, president of Yale University, warned Americans, "If Jefferson is elected, the Bible will be burned, the French 'Marseillaise' will be sung in Christian churches, and we may see our wives and daughters the victims of legal prostitution; soberly dishonored; speciously polluted."[5] Some in the American electorate still question the religious bona fides of President Obama, in spite of his numerous and public statements about his Christian beliefs and religious journey. And the presidential election of 2012 already has engendered at least a conversation about the prospects of the country having as president a member of The Church of Jesus Christ of Latter-Day Saints.

Randall Balmer, professor of American religious history and student of the American presidency, cautions against seeing the election of any candidate (especially our own) as a harbinger of the Second Coming. "The introduction of religious language and faith claims into presidential politics," Balmer argues, "raises an important question: So what?" Does a candidate's faith or even his moral character make any substantive difference in how he governs?"[6] Does ethical earnestness translate into an effective presidency? Do spiritual disciplines make one a great president? According to Balmer, "If we persist in vetting the faith of our presidential candidates, we must find a way to reinvest both religion and the political process with a profundity befitting the importance of both."[7]

That is the challenge facing us as authors of this brief and so we hope (and pray?) informative book on presidents and their religious faiths. And we think it is the challenge facing you, the reader, especially if you vote, or are thinking about voting in the race for the White House. On the eve of another presidential election, we find ourselves once again confronting questions about our national identity and national purpose. We hope this book persuades you to think carefully about the connection between faith and presidential leadership.

GEORGE WASHINGTON
1789-1797

How does one begin to talk about the first President of the United States, especially with respect to his beliefs regarding the human condition, about the afterlife, and how we shall treat one another, about who even qualifies as being human? We think we know Washington, the father of our country, of his integrity, of his slave ownership, of his Deism. But knowing the man's heart is, of course, impossible, since he is so far removed from us in time and culture. Furthermore, Washington has become Washington the cultural icon, living in the rarefied air of heroes, minor deities, and saints. In this chapter on the faith of George Washington, we seek not to tell a new story, nor to dash busts of the sculpted man, but instead to allow his own words and the words of those closest to him to show a clear and integrated picture of what he believed about humanity's relationship with deity and how he then acted upon those beliefs.

When trying to understand Washington's faith from more than two hundred years away, we must remember his religious context. From the founding of Jamestown well into the eighteenth century, there was but one official religion, one denomination (though that term was not in use at the time), one church in Virginia—Anglican. A land-holding man and leader in the community could only be a member of the Anglican Church, regardless of his personal beliefs or even his public behaviors. Education was religious, though it could still be broad and excellent, taking in the Greek and Roman classics as well as biblical studies. Later in the eighteenth century there would be room for Presbyterian communities and schools, but these were certainly the exceptions. Therefore, George Washington was reared as an Anglican, most likely learning the creeds and catechism determined by Canterbury. Just because there was one dominant church and Virginians did not have many choices does not mean that those calling themselves Anglican were not sincere or devout. However, one must remember when viewing an individual's religious choices from our perspective of current American denominationalism, in which there are hundreds of choices concerning where and how and when to worship, that we must not look at the decision to attend church as a definitive answer to the question of a man's faith.

What we know for certain is that Washington was very comfortable using the language both of the church and of the Bible. In all his writings (private and public) and in his many speeches, Washington quoted from the Bible more than from any other work.[1] What this tells us is that Washington knew the Bible very well (at least the Old Testament, since that was most often his source of allusion), and he also knew his audience. It is interesting to think about political speeches and writing in the context of time and experience. Today's political leaders often quote from previous leaders, from the Declaration of Independence, from Supreme Court Justices, from American authors; Washington and his contemporaries had none of these resources. Rejecting the national tales of England and Europe, Washington drew from the stories and cadences of the most accessible and recognizable text available to him and to his audiences—the Hebrew Old Testament.

We know that George Washington was a vestryman at the Anglican Church near Mount Vernon, which means that he was involved in helping to run the business of the local parish. For instance, the Virginian churches owned property (given to them by the colonial government), and the property was used to raise tobacco, the sale of which helped support the churches and the priests. The vestrymen would arrange for the growing, harvesting, drying, and selling of the tobacco. Interestingly, one could be a vestryman without being particularly religious or spiritual; it was seen as the duty of every leading citizen to serve at some time as a vestryman.

Washington's attendance at church services was quite casual, especially when he was at home. According to his diary, he went to church no more than about once a month from 1760 to 1773. Paul F. Boller, author of *George Washington and Religion*, writes, "Washington, we know, also transacted business on Sundays, visited friends and relatives, traveled, and sometimes went fox-hunting instead of going to church. Washington wrote in his diary that frequently during the 1760s, on Sundays he stayed 'at Home alone all day.'"[2] With the eyes of the country on him while he was president, Washington attended services nearly every Sunday at St. Paul's Chapel or Trinity Church while in New York and Christ Church when in Philadelphia.[3]

Most interestingly, and perhaps most telling, is what Washington did and did not do while attending church services on Sundays both at home and in the roaming United States capital. Apparently, Washington chose not to be a communicant during his times at church, chose not to partake in the central sacrament of the Christian Faith. This struck one of his parish priests as both inappropriate and unacceptable, so from the pulpit the priest stated that those in positions of leadership should take communion when offered, to be good examples to the other parishioners. At a later time, Washington seemed to have told a friend that he agreed with the priest, and therefore would no longer go to church on those Sundays when communion was being served. Washington's step-granddaughter, Nellie Park Custis (with whom he was apparently close) remembered that the great president never knelt in church but "always stood during the devotional parts of the service."[4] So while Washington was respectful enough not to remain seated while everyone stood, he did not seem to feel the need to lower himself to the floor through devotion to God. We do not know why Washington chose not to participate fully in services—if this was some way to keep himself separate and above the fray of religious battles rampant at that time, or if he had so much integrity that he did not wish to participate in something he did not fully believe. Inferring from what we know of his church attendance, of his public speeches, of his private writings, it is plausible that Washington did not believe in the divinity of Jesus, or in the efficacy of particular sacraments, and thus chose not to take what was supposed to be the body and blood of Christ. We could speculate that Washington took religion seriously enough that he did not wish to belittle central sacred practices by treating them as if they meant nothing at all.

In his work *George Washington and Religion*, Boller summarizes Washington's relationship with religion the following way: "If Washington was a Christian, he was surely a Protestant of the most liberal persuasion. He was . . . more of a 'unitarian' than anything else in his apparent lack of convictions."[5] James Madison agreed. He wrote:

> [I do] not suppose that Washington had ever attended to the arguments for Christianity, and for the different systems of religion, or in fact that he had formed definite opinions on the subject. But he took these things as he found them existing, and was constant in his observance of worship according to the received forms of the Episcopal Church in which he was brought up.[6]

Boller also relates that, during Washington's time as president, Philadelphia clergy often tried to draw Washington's personal beliefs into the open, to get him to state unequivocally whether or not he was a "Christian." One of the clergy wrote of their collective failure, noting, "The old fox was too cunning for us."[7] To his contemporaries, then, to those who knew Washington best (his secretary, his friends, his priests, his relatives), Washington was a man who seemed to believe in a Deity, some sort of divine, beneficent being who somehow ordered the world, but Washington seems never to have written or spoken about Jesus, about personal sin (though he would talk of national sins and shortcomings), or about the need for redemption.

In contrast to what his contemporaries knew of Washington's faith, there grew up after his death a burgeoning enterprise for story-tellers who could relate the saintliness of this first president. The same writer who gave us the fictional story of Washington's chopping down the cherry tree and his subsequent truth-telling also wrote of his being "Christ's faithful soldier and servant" and of Washington's saintly death ("Father of mercies, take me to thyself")—stories that have helped build the myth of George Washington. But Washington's secretary, Tobias Lear, recounts Washington's last few days of life very clearly, and records his last words as:

"I am just going! Have me decently buried; and do not let my body to be put into the vault less than three days after I am dead." I bowed assent, for I could not speak. He then looked at me again and said, "Do you understand me?" I replied, Yes! "'Tis well!" said he.[8]

This personal account of Washington's last moments do not prove that Washington was not a Christian, but its breath of fear does not much tempt those who remain to canonize the adored and respected. As far as death-bed confessions and saintly visions go, Washington only left us with the most human of statements, "Wait to make sure I am really dead before you bury me."

Without question, though, the first United States President was concerned about religion, about its place in the new republic, in the lives of its citizens. From his public speeches and writings, it is clear that Washington thought one of the critical aspects of this constitutional government was the standard of keeping churches safe from the persecution of other churches, and from the persecution of the government.

JOHN ADAMS
1797-1801

★ ★ ★ ★ ★ ★ ★ ★ ★ ★ ★ ★

"The longer I live, the more I read, the more patiently I think, and the more anxiously I inquire, the less I seem to know . . . Do justly. Love mercy. Walk humbly. This is enough."[1] John Adams offered this advice to his granddaughter, Caroline, just prior to his death on July 4, 1826, and only a few hours after Thomas Jefferson passed away. In the words of David McCullough, "Adams was a devout Christian and an independent thinker, and he saw no conflict in that."[2]

John Adams was born on October 19, 1735, in Braintree (later Quincy), Massachusetts, into a family whose roots go back to the early seventeenth century and the Puritan migration to the New World. His forebears were pious Puritans; his father, Thomas, was a deacon at the Braintree meeting-house, which had been built three years before John's birth and where he was baptized. The Adams family had a pew to the left of the pulpit, and attended Sunday services twice each Sabbath. Once when Adams was young his father took him to a heresy trial at the church where the minister was charged with Arminianism; he was found guilty and dismissed.[3] Protestant, Calvinist Christianity permeated Adams' early years, and in addition to the United First Parish Church, Adams also was schooled in Puritan orthodoxy at Dame Belcher's school in town. His parents wanted Adams to study for the ministry, and he thought carefully albeit briefly along those lines, but instead, after attending Harvard, where his days started with morning prayers and scripture readings beginning at 6:00 a.m. and ended with evening prayers at 5:00 p.m., Adams turned to teaching and then a few years later, the law, where he would establish himself as one of the leading attorneys in Boston.[4]

"His principal preoccupations," during these early years, according to Page Smith, an Adams biographer, "were theology—the nature of the universe and God's relation to it, . . . In theology he was bent on steering a course between skepticism and Deism on one side and Calvinist orthodox on the other."[5] During these years Adams was a self-described "church-going animal,"[6] not only attending Congregationalist services but almost all other Protestant denominations as well: Baptist, Methodist, Anglican, Presbyterian, Quaker, and German Moravian. After attending services, often twice or three times on Sunday, he would comment on their singing and especially the preaching he encountered. He especially disliked "indifferent" ministers who were or appeared to be lukewarm in their convictions. As the Pulitzer Prize-winning Adams biographer David McCullough writes, "Indifference was a quality Adams found difficult to tolerate."[7] As with almost all others of his day, he was suspicious of Roman Catholicism. In Philadelphia he would attend his first Catholic Mass, accompanied by George Washington and others, at St. Mary's Catholic Church on Fifth Street.[8] "For the first time," Smith tells us, "Adams was confronted with so much that generations of his people had abhorred and rebelled against, and he found himself both distressed and strangely moved."[9] He writes to his wife, Abigail, "The dress of the priest was rich with lace—his pulpit was velvet and gold. The altar-piece was very rich—little images and crucifixes about—wax candles lighted up. But how shall I describe the picture of our Savior in a frame of marble over the altar at full length upon the Cross, in the agonies, and the blood dropping and streaming from his wounds?"[10]

Adams carried on an interior dialogue with himself about such matters, as revealed in his capacious diary that he kept for over three decades. The diary illustrates his critical self-examination, including his struggles with a variety of religious and theological issues, such as life after death, the Trinity, and the nature of God. As Adams once put it, "I hate polemical politics and political divinity. My religion is founded on the love of God and my neighbor; on the hope of pardon for my offenses; upon contrition; upon the duty as well as the necessity of [enduring] with patience the inevitable evils of life; in the duty of doing no wrong but all the good I can; to the creation of which I am but an infinitesimal part."[11]

Over the course of his life Adams came to question, as many do, the religious beliefs and practices of his youth and early adulthood. His skepticism about various theological matters would increase, and he would come to find Congregationalist orthodoxy too rigid, dogmatic, and confining. According to Smith, "He rejected the notion of the Trinity as superstition and with it the idea of the divinity of Christ."[12] In 1810 in a letter to Dr. Benjamin Rush, a leading figure of the Revolutionary era and early American republic, Adams would write, "The Christian religion, as I understand it, is the brightness of the glory and the express portrait of the eternal, self-existent, independent, benevolent, all-powerful and all-merciful Creator, Preserver and Father of the Universe . . . Ask me not then whether I am a Catholic or Protestant, Calvinist or Arminian. As far as they are Christian, I wish to be a fellow disciple with them all."[13]

On so many theological matters, such as the divinity of Jesus or life after death, Adams came to believe, as Joseph Ellis argues, "such questions were inherently unanswerable, but he had presumed that God would afford him the opportunity to debate [Benjamin] Franklin in heaven."[14] As Adams wrote in an 1816 letter, "If it should be revealed or demonstrated that there is no future state, my advice to every man, woman, and child would be . . . to take opium."[15] Beyond his letters to Abigail, the likes of which in terms of content and volume we are likely never to see again, his letters to Jefferson are instructive as well. After the death of his beloved Abigail, Adams wrote to Jefferson, "I do not know how to prove physically, that we shall meet and know each other in a future state; nor does Revelation, as I can find it, give us any positive assurance of such a felicity . . . If I did not believe in a future state, I should believe in no God. This Universe, this all would appear, with all of its swelling pomp, a boyish firework."[16]

Adams was the first president to live in what later became known as the White House. During his administration, however, the home was known simply as the Executive Mansion, which Adams moved into on November 1, 1800. Upon doing so, Adams would write, "Before I end my letter, I pray Heaven to bestow the best of blessings on this house and all that shall hereafter inhabit it. May none but wise and honest men ever rule under this roof."[17] These wise words would be carved into the mantle of the State Dining Room in the administration of a fellow president from Massachusetts, John F. Kennedy. (In the year before his death, Adams also wrote, "No man who ever held the office of President would congratulate a friend on obtaining it".[18])

As noted earlier, Adams died on the same day as Thomas Jefferson: July 4, 1826. For John Quincy Adams, the death of these two patriots on the same day a few hours apart demonstrated the work of Divine providence. Adams' funeral was held at the First Congregational Church in Quincy. His life constantly was occupied by thoughts about religion and theology. For most of his adult life, "He was a Unitarian who privately confessed a weakness for the beauty of Episcopal liturgy."[19] About Adams, McCullough concludes, "His faith in God and the hereafter remained unshaken. His fundamental creed, he had reduced to a single sentence: 'He who loves the Workman and his work, and does what he can to preserve and improve it, shall be accepted of Him.'"[20]

THOMAS JEFFERSON
1801-1809

★ ★ ★ ★ ★ ★ ★ ★ ★ ★ ★ ★

Hide the Bibles in the yard. Sew the prayer books into the comforters. And pray that we make it unscathed through this tribulation brought on by godless men. This cry was, of course, heard during the height of the Cold War when the communists from either within or without would jeopardize our freedom of religion (and most particularly our freedom to be Christian). Lately, in some more feverish communities, we may have heard this echoed with the Obama presidency, but it is nothing new, and the president who first sparked such fear today has a monument in Washington, D.C.

Based partly on his strong support for church and state separation, and based mostly on his refusal to discuss his personal beliefs in public, Thomas Jefferson stated that he did not care if his neighbor worshipped

21

one god or twenty. The Federalist clergy of New England (supporters of John Adams) "seized on this remark as conclusive evidence that Jefferson was some combination of pagan, infidel, atheist and heretic. Editorials throughout New England played on the theme that the most Christian country in the world was now headed by a man who denied the central tenets of Christianity."[1] According to another account, "When news reached New England [of Jefferson's election to the presidency], farmwives buried family Bibles in the gardens to protect them from Jefferson's minions who, they were told, would confiscate the Scriptures after he took office."[2]

During Jefferson's presidency, he chose to help Thomas Paine return to America from France, but many Americans found fault with the president for his friendship with the author of *The Age of Reason,* an argument for "free-thinking" and Deism. As a result, President Jefferson was called an "arch infidel," "a defiler of Christian virtue," and "'a companion of the most vile, corrupt, obnoxious sinner of the century.' All Americans who took Christianity seriously now had to make a choice, said one editor, between 'renouncing their savior, or their president.'"[3] Yet this was also the president who helped a Christian missionary school attain federal funding in order to educate and "civilize" frontier Native Americans. Jefferson called himself a Christian. He believed in and supported religion (especially Christianity as he understood it) as a means of solidifying a shaky nation, and he believed strongly that religion was freest and purest when it was not, in any way, connected to government.

Like George Washington, Thomas Jefferson, a son of Anglican Virginia, was reared as an Anglican and supported the church monetarily throughout his life. While there are no surviving records of Jefferson's baptism in the church, it is reasonable to assume he was baptized, since we do know there were two clergymen presiding over his marriage in 1772.[4] We do know, by contrast, that out of good conscience, Jefferson declined to be a godparent for the children of a French friend, since "the person who becomes sponsor for a child, according to the ritual of the church in which I was educated, makes a solemn profession before God and the world, of faith in the articles, which I had never sense enough to comprehend, and it has always appeared to me that comprehension must precede assent."[5] As a man who owned more books than probably any other American during his lifetime, Jefferson still chose to record family births, deaths, and marriages in his father's *Book of Common Prayer*, and he gave generously to St. Anne's Church in Charlottesville, Virginia.[6] Even after the state's role in supporting the church had ended (partly by the work of Jefferson), Jefferson chose to give support to an important cultural institution, and this is significant. Since he continued to support the church after his presidency, one might assume that Jefferson did not give monies purely out of political expediency in order to make himself more palatable to those who had called him an infidel. Further, it is reasonable to assume that using his father's prayer book to record meaningful life events was a way to connect with a familial and spiritual heritage of Anglicanism.

While it is certain that Jefferson thought and wrote a great deal about religion in general, when it came to talking to those other than his closest friends about his personal views of God and religion, Jefferson chose to keep his opinions private. This inclination toward privacy is at least partly to blame for the fear some felt regarding Jefferson's "godlessness," for certainly, if he were a godly man, then one could assume that his faith would show in his conversations. But in a letter to Benjamin Rush (an orthodox Christian), Jefferson wrote, "I never told my own religion, nor scrutinized that of another. I never attempted to make a convert, nor wished to change another's creed."[7] To Jefferson, there was a role for religion in the public realm—that of encouraging public virtues and providing positive structure to societies—but what one experienced in private should remain private. Jefferson did, however, openly share his religious theories and beliefs to those he counted as intimates.

In a letter to his nephew, Peter Carr, Jefferson encouraged the young man to test every religious expression against the standard of reason:

> "Fix reason firmly in her seat, and call to her tribunal every fact, every opinion. . . . Question even the existence of God," Jefferson wrote. Because if such a being existed, he would "certainly more approve the homage of reason than of blindfolded fear. . . . Your own reason is the only oracle given you by heaven, and you are answerable not for the rightness but uprightness of the decision."[8]

One specific example Jefferson gave Carr about a biblical story that seemed to fail the test of reason was that of Joshua's commanding the sun to stand still in the sky (Joshua 10:12-13). Jefferson reasons that this story is worth exploring just because so many believe it to be true, but "'you are astronomer enough to know how contrary it is to the law of nature that a body revolving on its axis, as the earth does, should have stopped.' And by that sudden halt in its rotation, would it not have 'prostrated animals, trees, buildings?'"[9] Jefferson suggested to Carr that it was more reasonable to believe that those recording the biblical account were in error than to believe that so many laws of nature were broken without any apparent consequences.[10]

One significant religious tenet that troubled Jefferson was the issue of the Trinity, which seemed to him to be improbable and unbiblical. Further, he did not believe in the divinity of Jesus, for Jefferson did not see in the Gospels that Jesus even claimed divinity for himself. In the famous correspondence between the two friends and rivals John Adams and Thomas Jefferson, Jefferson confides to his friend that before too long reason would win in America and that most Americans would become Unitarians, rejecting Trinitarian doctrine and Christ's divinity.[11] Jefferson held on to this "hope" in American rationalism, the hope that the "rational" rejection of the Trinity would win out over "superstition," despite the religious fanaticism he witnessed throughout the country, which he believed was threatening to religious freedoms and democratic values.[12] Jefferson struggled with the desire to see himself as some sort of Christian (for he greatly respected the "true" teachings of Jesus) but had often felt as though he could not consider himself as such since he held such heterodox views. Edwin Gaustad, in his work *Sworn on the Altar of God: A Religious Biography of Thomas Jefferson*, asserts that Jefferson learned much from Joseph Priestly's lectures on *History of the Corruptions of Christianity* (1782), arguing that this work altered Jefferson's views on Christianity more than any other book in his vast library: "He [Jefferson] thought that he had utterly rejected Christianity; now he found, to his relief, and perhaps to his delight as well, that he had only rejected a hopelessly corrupted form of Christianity. Somewhere underneath all that dross, pure gold could yet be found,"[13] and Priestly's lectures had pointed toward a way in which Jefferson could accommodate his reasoning to his desire for faith in some sort of religious system.

Encouraged by Priestly's work, and, of course, by his own intellectual curiosity and interest in religion, Jefferson went on to create two of his most famous works: his version of the Gospels (often known as *The Jef-*

ferson Bible) and his book *The Morals and Life of Jesus of Nazareth*. Jefferson began a project similar to *The Morals* in 1802, completing the "wee-book" in 1816, a "'document in proof that I am a real Christian, that is to say, a disciple of the doctrines of Jesus . . .' What he really meant was that he admired the moral values embodied in the life of Jesus but preferred to separate 'what is really his [Jesus'] from the rubbish in which it is buried' much in the way 'as the diamond from the dunghill.'"[14] Jefferson's basic idea was that the Bible as it was printed (written by men who did not quite understand Jesus, who wanted to reshape him, or who were not privy to the lights of reason and science, but rather slaves to superstition) was a seriously flawed work, but that the real teachings of Jesus were the most "sublime" of all philosophies, and that true Christianity (that is following what Jefferson understood to be Jesus' teachings) was, perhaps, the greatest religion in history. However, one had to perceive what the actual teachings were, and to do that one had to start from the presupposition that Jesus was not divine, did not claim to perform miracles, and that any miraculous happenings attributed to Jesus were merely the fantasies of his followers. So Jefferson saw himself as a Christ-follower, a disciple of the Jesus he created by literally cutting from the Gospels all references to the supernatural, so that the nativity story is stripped of angels, wise men, and the virgin birth. In Jefferson's version, when John baptizes Jesus, there is no dove from heaven. Upon seeing a man who was blind from birth, Jefferson's tale does have the disciples asking whose fault it was that this man suffered, and Jesus does answer that it was no human's fault. But Jesus does not go on to heal the man. Most significantly, Jefferson's Gospel ends with these words:

> Now, in the place where he was crucified, there was a garden; and in the garden a new sepulchre, wherein was never man yet laid. There laid they Jesus, and rolled a great stone to the door of the sepulchre, and departed.[15]

Jefferson was not a godless man, nor was he a man without faith in some sort of after-life (reward or punishment), but he did see Jesus as an example of a man whom it was actually possible to imitate, since he was just that, a man and nothing more.

Regardless of his personal beliefs regarding orthodox Christianity or any other religion, Jefferson did respect the power of religion to shape culture and to help maintain a civil society. There is a contradictory side to Jefferson regarding religion (and many other things, such as slavery and marital fidelity); he was strongly opposed to an established church of any kind, and he refused to use his platform as president to promote one religion over another, or even to appear to adhere to one religion, faith, or denomination over another. On the other hand, Jefferson did allow for the allocation of federal monies to a Christian mission to western Native-American tribes who sought to educate and "civilize" these tribes. We could argue that since Jefferson had a sort of faith in the power of religion to build and maintain the social order, he saw no problem with supporting religious education for those with "savage" traditions, since church groups were the only providers of formal education in the young United States. At the same time, however, Jefferson refused to call for a national day of prayer during an extreme cholera epidemic, stating that religious actions and their promotion is the realm of the church, not the state. So there seems to be a pragmatic side to the ways in which Jefferson chose to draw the lines of separation between church and state. According to Thomas E. Buckley in his essay "Religion and the Presidency of Thomas Jefferson," "Jefferson took religion so seriously that while in important respects a passion for religious freedom defined his life, he also laid the foundation of a religion for the republic that would support the country's national identity in its most formative years and that sustains it today."[16]

Thomas Jefferson not only was a church-going man who attended services regularly throughout his time as president, but he also supported the Anglican Church monetarily throughout his life. He thought deeply and often about religion, about its role in the lives of individuals and in the life of the new United States of America. To his friend Benjamin Rush, Jefferson made assurances that he was a follower of Jesus, and when a rumor arose that he had become an orthodox Christian and was soon to write a testimonial book, Jefferson felt "dismay and disgust . . . [and] did his best to quell those rumors."[17] Jefferson often thought about the moral problems of slavery, yet he failed to free any of his slaves (unlike Washington) and even fathered children by at least one of his slaves. So even though Jefferson, like many in his class and culture, equated religion with moral behavior, rather than with right beliefs, neither Jefferson's behaviors, nor his beliefs would strike Evangelical Christians of yesterday or today as being particularly

Christian. A flawed man in many ways, a brilliant man in many others, Thomas Jefferson, the unbeliever, significantly shaped the United States, helping to balance the new nation's identity as a nation under a supreme being, yet a nation that was not in any way a Christian nation.

JAMES MADISON
1809-1817

★ ★ ★ ★ ★ ★ ★ ★ ★ ★ ★ ★

James Madison and his lifelong devotion to and advocacy of "the sacred principle of religious liberty" are one of the greatest success stories in American history. We revere Madison (or should) for his historic work on behalf of religious liberty, and for the documents (his 1785 "Memorial and Remonstrance Against Religious Assessments," the U.S. Constitution, and the Bill of Rights of 1791) that are a testament to his devotion to the fundamental cause of conscience. Despite serving two terms in the presidency, Madison has been ranked by scholars of the presidency as no more than "average." However, with respect to what Madison called "the divine right of conscience,"[1] no other American, not even Jefferson, ranks above Madison when it comes to protecting religious freedom and thereby adding, as Madison put it, "lustre to our country."[2] In the words of one leading Madison biographer, "There is no principle in all of Madison's wide range of private opinions and long public career to which he held with greater vigor and tenacity than this one of religious liberty."[3]

We know very little, however, about the personal religious faith of Madison. According to Ralph Ketcham, a leading Madison scholar, "The subject of Madison's religion has seldom been addressed by scholars, largely because he recorded so little of his religious sentiments."[4] This is especially true in Madison's life from roughly 1774, when he was twenty-two years old, until his death in 1836. "All we know for certain," according to Notre Dame professor and Madison expert, Vincent Munoz, "are basic facts pertaining to Madison's religious life."[5] Scholars long have been bedeviled by the true nature of his religious beliefs, in large measure because after the mid-1770s, "he kept his mouth shut"[6] about these beliefs. If there is any conclusion bordering on consensus about Madison and religion, it is that "[W]e can say that his argument for the right to religious freedom is built upon a political theology of religious individualism consistent with many forms of Protestant Christianity."[7]

James Madison was born on March 16, 1751, into a prominent, land-holding, slave-owning, Anglican family in Virginia. His mother was a devout member of the Church of England, which was the sole established church in the colony, and his father was a vestryman at the church in St. Thomas Parish. The church was erected in 1750, the year before Madison's birth, and where he was baptized. As a youngster Madison's paternal grandmother was his tutor until he reached the age of twelve when he left home to attend a boarding school led by the Scottish minister Rev. Donald Robertson. At the age of sixteen Madison returned home to be tutored by Rev. Thomas Martin, rector of the Brick Church in Orange County where the family worshipped.[8]

Madison was sent for his college education to the College of New Jersey (Princeton), whose president, Dr. John Witherspoon, was a leading Scottish Presbyterian Calvinist, and the only clergyman to sign the Declaration of Independence. Madison completed his four-year curriculum in thirty months, graduating in the class of 1771. Upon his graduation, Madison remained at Princeton for an additional six months of graduate study, which included Hebrew, divinity, and theology.[9] When Madison wed Dolly Payne

Todd, they were married by an Episcopalian priest in an Episcopalian ceremony. (She was Quaker, but became an Episcopalian nine years after Madison's death in 1836; she worshipped at St. John's Church in Washington, D.C.) Madison was buried in an Episcopalian service, according to the *Book of Common Prayer,* but according to biographer Lance Banning, Madison never identified himself as an Episcopalian and we have no record of Madison being a full communicant in the church.[10]

In his adult years, among other things, Madison liked to read books on religion and theology, apparently for relaxation. When Thomas Jefferson was establishing his "little academical village" otherwise known as the University of Virginia, he asked Madison to provide a "Theological Catalogue" to help build the library on campus.[11] Before his White House years, when Madison was a member of the House of Representatives from Virginia, he often attended the public services held in the House chamber, as was the custom in those days before any real roster of churches existed in the District of Columbia.

As far as we know, Madison never made a public profession of faith. According to biographer James Hutson, Madison "is such a commanding figure in the founding period's controversies over religion's relation to government that a knowledge of his personal religious convictions is sought as a key to his public posture on church-state issues."[12] However, Hutson continues, "Seeking evidence of his faith quickly leads to the conclusion that there is, in the words of the poet, no there there, that in the mature Madison's writings there is no trace, no clue as to his personal religious convictions."[13] Nonetheless, one scholar of Madison, William Lee Miller, argues that Madison is "probably America's most theologically knowledgeable President."[14] According to retired federal judge John Noonan, Jr., "To suppose that James Madison had only a political religion because he did not publicly display his piety is to miss the genius of the man: his modesty. He followed Jesus," Noonan argues, "as a true follower will."[15]

Noonan and others rely heavily on the fact that Madison's personal life, in the words of one of Madison's contemporaries, was "without stain or reproach."[16] Crucial to his argument are Madison's efforts on behalf of religious liberty, especially in the contentious circumstances in Virginia in the 1770s and 1780s. In the 1770s, for instance, Madison engineered one of the most crucial political-theological accomplishments after the break from England when he secured the adoption of "free exercise of religion" as the operative language rather than mere "toleration." In the 1780s Madison produced one of the most significant documents in American political-religious history; his "Memorial and Remonstrance Against Religious Assessments" of June, 1785, helped defeat the Virginia legislature's attempt to tax citizens to support their ministers' salary. Madison's chief culprit was religious persecution, which he had personally witnessed toward non-established Baptists in Virginia. His principal remedy was a political-social-legal environment in which the individual believer (or non-believer) would live in a zone beyond political authority, where one's conscience would be exempt from state-sponsored compulsion to believe or act as if one believed.[17] As expressed in a January 24, 1774, letter to fellow Princeton alum, William Bradford, Madison wrote, "That diabolical Hell conceived principle of persecution rages among some and to their eternal infamy the clergy can furnish their Quota of Imps for such business. This vexes me the most of any thing whatsoever."[18]

Madison's thesis concerning religious liberty was even more pronounced and developed in his 1785 "Memorial." He wrote:

> The Religion then of every man must be left to the conviction and conscience of every man; and it is the right of every man to exercise it as these may dictate. This right is in its nature an unalienable right. It is the duty of every man to render to the Creator such homage and such only as he believes to be acceptable to him. This duty is precedent, both in order of time and in degree of obligation, to the claims of Civil Society. Before any man can be considered as a member of Civil Society, he must be considered as a subject of the Governor of the Universe.[19]

The import of this approach cannot be overstated; in the words of Noonan, Madison was "the first statesman who, himself a believer, and not knowing any persecution himself, had enough empathy with the victims of persecution to loathe the idea of enforced religious conformity and to work to produce law that would forever end it.[20] It is easy," Noonan points out, "to be tolerant if you don't believe. To believe and to champion freedom—that is Madison's accomplishment."[21]

We know more about Madison's religious practices and political efforts on behalf of religious liberty than we know about his religious principles and convictions. Even when in the White House he often was asked to commit to writing his religious views. His response, beyond silence, was to observe, "The letters and communications addressed to me on religious subjects have been so numerous, and of characters to various, that it has been an established rule to decline all correspondence on them."[22] What Madison did do as president, among other things, was to oppose (unsuccessfully) the appointment of a congressional chaplain, and he vetoed in 1811, on establishment of religious grounds, an act of incorporation of an Episcopal Church in the District of Columbia.[23]

Madison died on June 28, 1836. There's a fascinating, and given Madison's consistent reticence to reveal his core religious beliefs in public or even in his private writings, fitting account of his final words that fateful morning at Montpelier, the family estate in Virginia. His body servant, Paul Jennings, who shaved Madison every other day for sixteen years, recounts that near the end, Madison's favorite niece asked him, "What is the matter, Uncle James?" According to Jennings, Madison mysteriously replied, "Nothing more than a change of *mind*, my dear."[24] With that, the life of America's foremost proponent of religious freedom came to an end.

JAMES MONROE
1817–1825

★ ★ ★ ★ ★ ★ ★ ★ ★ ★ ★ ★

Throughout the more than two hundred years of the United States' existence, Americans have had some inclination as to the religious leanings and identities of the sitting president. In fact, during some of the nation's most distressing periods, Americans have demanded to know about their presidents' or candidates' religion. Some of these men have left little record of their personal faith, whether because they did not serve for long, died too young, refused to speak on the subject, or simply had no faith of which to speak. President James Monroe, however, is particularly interesting because we do know much about his life, especially his life as president (he served as president for two terms). We know about his friends, mentors, and peers. Those who knew Monroe well respected him and saw him as a man with a great deal of personal integrity, although most were silent about his religious faith. When scholars wish to understand those who have been reticent to reveal their personal lives, they oftentimes delve into the individual's private letters. Through these writings, biographers are able to eavesdrop on the dead's conversations with their loved ones about life's most significant events. But Monroe, unlike so many other presidents and public personalities, burned all of his correspondence with his wife after her death, and his other correspondence reveals nothing about Monroe's faith life. We therefore are left to speculate about his faith.

There are a few facts regarding Monroe's life that are at least marginally religious. Since Monroe was from an established Virginian family, he was, at some level, a participant in the established church before the Revolution—the Anglican Church. Monroe began attending the College of William and Mary at sixteen years of age, so he would have attended chapel where Anglican theology and ideals would have been saturated into the nature of the place at that time. It should also be noted, however, that some of Monroe's contemporaries saw William and Mary as a place that tested one's faith. Virginian Episcopalian Bishop William Meade, for example, stated in his work *Old Churches, Ministers and Families of Virginia* that "The College of William and Mary was regarded as the hotbed of infidelity and of the wild politics of France."[1] So Monroe's religious education may have been "tainted" by the French, as was Jefferson's before him.

Regardless of whatever Monroe's personal feelings and experiences with religion were, we know his decisions about faith would have been well informed. In other words, no matter his faith (in God, or in himself), he would have chosen that faith. We also know that, like so many other American Presidents, Monroe regularly attended St. John's Episcopal Church in Washington, D.C., while he was president. Monroe also was married and buried with Anglican and Episcopal religious rites.[2] Further, Monroe was apparently a vestryman for St. John's, and the rector of that church officiated when Maria Hester (Monroe's daughter) was married at the White House in 1820.[3]

While Monroe was serving as Virginia's governor, his only son, John Spence, died when sixteen months old, and apparently Monroe was deeply distraught. The funeral was held at St. John's Episcopal Church in Richmond, "But the letters Monroe wrote to others about his little son's death include no references to the consolation of religion."[4] Similarly, when Elizabeth, his wife, died in 1820, Monroe was not reticent to express to his friends in writing how devastated he was by his loss of her. But again, he did not give any indication about religious faith, faith in an afterlife, or any comfort he received from religion.[5] Even Jefferson would mention eternal rewards and the hope in some sort of afterlife. This absence of religious language in Monroe's heartfelt letters does not prove he had no religious faith, but it is perhaps a telling omission.

We also do not know whether or not Monroe would fall into the fraternity of Deists that came into prominence during the Age of Reason, but we do know that he, like Jefferson, kept close company with the most prolific, respected, and hated of American Deists, Thomas Paine. During his time as United States minister to France, Monroe and his wife helped to nurse the expatriate Paine back to health at their own home. David L. Holmes, in his essay "The Religion of James Monroe," states that Paine and Monroe formed a close relationship during this time and that "It is inconceivable that Paine and Monroe did not discuss religion during this period."[6] According to this same source, Paine wrote parts of his infamous work *The Age of Reason* during his time in France with the Monroes, even borrowing their King James Bible to write the second part of this work. To many orthodox American Christians, Paine became known as an infidel (and Holmes adds that to these same Christians, all Deists became known as infidels). To some, Monroe would have been guilty of at least aiding an infidel, but more than likely Monroe and his wife were simply aiding another American, another intellectual for whom they had great respect.

A significant thing we do know about Monroe's affiliations is that he was a Free Mason, and there are many in the United States, especially among modern Evangelical Christians, who view the Masonic Order as being a cult, a religion of its own. In their own literature, the Masons state that a belief in God is a requirement of membership, but in the literature it also is made clear that men of all faiths are welcome. Much speculation and many writings exist that seek to show how Free Masonry is a demonic, ancient group, and there are even strange conspiracy theories swirling in the ether regarding world leaders, Masonry, and domination. Regardless, many men who have by all other evidence been considered

Christian (or Jewish) have also been Free Masons, so to say that Monroe was a Mason and therefore not a Christian would be at best fallacious.

When we look to one's words to determine one's religious faith, most world religions point to one's actions as being the evidence of orthodoxy and faith. Perhaps it is because our hearts are far more complex than even our minced words could ever be. And, because our actions are hopelessly divided into the seen and unseen, the admirable and the despicable, that we turn to words to see if an individual like Monroe is "one of us," one who knows and says the right code words. For those who knew James Monroe, there was no doubt that he was a spectacularly good man, one who gave of himself to others, and in this sense, his actions were Christian. Like other presidents, however, he not only owned slaves, but even had some slaves executed when they planned an uprising. Monroe was, like many of his peers, absolutely confounded by the slavery issue, knowing it was an evil institution, yet participating in it fully.

One man who likely knew Monroe better than any other was his legal and political mentor, Thomas Jefferson. Jefferson was unequivocal in his praise for Monroe's character: "Turn his soul wrong side outwards and there is not a speck on it."[7] Another close friend of Monroe's, John Quincy Adams, gave him the highest praise, and the characteristics Adams attributes to Monroe certainly are those which Christians would desire for themselves. Adams gave praise "of a mind, anxious and unwearied in the pursuit of truth and right, patient of inquiry, patient of contradiction, courteous even in the collision of sentiment, sound in its ultimate judgments, and firm in its final conclusions."[8] Yet another friend of Monroe's, Judge Egbert R. Watson, spoke of Monroe's gentleness and thoughtfulness toward others.[9] Granted, these praises of Monroe were written by men who enjoyed the soft glow of remembrance and affection, not by Monroe's political adversaries, or even by his children or wife, so they are not proof of Monroe's character. But there is, nevertheless, a remarkable consistency of praise for Monroe by his peers.

To his young nephew, Monroe wrote a fairly typical piece of advice, devoid of religious language, but full of encouragement for virtuous living:

> You may by your industry, prudence, and studious attention to your
> business, as well as to your books, make such exertions as will advance
> your fortune and reputation in the world, whereby alone your happi-

ness or even tranquility can be secured. Not only the reality of these virtues must be possessed, but such an external must be observed as to satisfy the world you do possess them, otherwise you will not enjoy their confidence.[10]

Monroe seems to have been interested in how others viewed his actions, not just his words, and this is perhaps key to why we see no references to faith in his own words; his actions are the evidence. Throughout both his inaugural addresses, Monroe points to economic, political, and cultural gains as being evidence that the nation was on the right track, and he referred to an active, though often impersonal, god "Providence" only a very few times. The positive actor in the nation's fate, to Monroe, was simply the powerful U.S. Constitution, not the church, and not Providence. In an address to a joint session of Congress, Monroe spoke clearly of the Constitution's role in American success, not God's:

It is unnecessary to treat here of the vast improvement made in the system itself by the adoption of this Constitution and of its happy effect in elevating the character and in protecting the rights of the nation as well as of individuals. To what, then, do we owe these blessings? It is known to all that we derive them from the excellence of our institutions. Ought we not, then, to adopt every measure which may be necessary to perpetuate them?[11]

Elsewhere in his first inaugural address, Monroe praises Americans themselves for the nation's survival: "Had the people of the United States been educated in different principles; had they been less intelligent, less independent, or less virtuous can it be believed that we should have maintained the same steady and consistent career or been blessed with the same success?" In his second inaugural, Monroe closes with attributing his calling to the presidency to the American people, not to God (as we will hear from later presidents): "I shall forthwith commence the duties of the high trust to which you have called me."[12]

David L. Holmes summarizes the faith of James Monroe as that of an Episcopalian "of deistic tendencies who valued civic virtues over religious doctrine." Holmes goes on to claim that Monroe may have been "the most skeptical of the early presidents of the United States."[13] A friend to deists and doubters, Monroe was silent about his personal religious beliefs, at least in the extant records. But there also is no evidence proving that

Monroe was not a man of some religious faith: he went to church regularly, he supported the church monetarily, and ancient religious rites accompanied the significant events in his life. Perhaps Monroe did not speak of his religion either because he did not think it was relevant, or because neither his religion nor his character had ever been challenged during this presidential era of good feelings. (Monroe was elected to his second term as president with a vote one-shy of unanimous.) He simply may not have felt the need to protest or prove his Christianity. John Sutherland Bonnell leaves Monroe's ambiguity intact and lends it a positive atmosphere when he writes, "neither in his public addresses nor in private correspondence does he lift the veil."[14] Today, as then, Monroe's veil remains fully in place.

JOHN QUINCY ADAMS
1825-1829

★ ★ ★ ★ ★ ★ ★ ★ ★ ★ ★ ★

"Make no mistake about it, the four most miserable years of my life were my four years in the presidency."[1] John Quincy Adams, one of our most highly educated and experienced chief executives, won the same office and suffered the same fate as his father, serving only one term in an era of two-term and fairly popular presidents. Born into one of the most famous political families in American history, Adams was raised as an independent Congregationalist, and upon his father's death in 1826, joined a Unitarian church near the family homestead in Quincy, Massachusetts. He was the only son of a president also to be elected to the presidency until George W. Bush's election in 2000. He is also the only president to serve in Congress after leaving the presidency, which Adams did with great distinction, especially with respect to his role in debating (or trying to debate) slavery in the House of Representatives in the 1830s and 1840s. And, Adams often exercised on the Sabbath in a manner we're not likely to see again: "John Quincy Adams liked to read the Bible in the mornings and would plunge naked into the Potomac for a swim before attending his weekly Sunday church service."[2]

According to Adams' principal biographer, Paul C. Nagel, "Adams rarely moved beyond a rational approach to questions involving religious faith, although he always claimed to be a Christian and to acknowledge an afterlife."[3] A great portion of what we know about the religious faith of Adams can be gleaned from his personal journal that he started, as an eleven-year-old, on January 12, 1779. Throughout his life, as Fred Kaplan tells us, Adams' "first concern was to master his soul, seeking discipline, modesty, tolerance, calmness of spirit, and religious faith—all virtues in which he was woefully weak, as he was the first to acknowledge."[4] In this diary that he kept virtually his entire life, Adams reveals his struggles to believe and act upon his philosophical, political, and religious principles, and to impart those not only to his family (especially his children) but to the fledgling nation itself. For instance, for decades in his journal, and in other settings, Adams inveighed against slavery, referring to it as "that outrage upon the goodness of God," and also writing, "The world, the flesh, and all the devils in hell are arrayed against any man who now in this North American Union shall dare to join the standard of Almighty God to put down the African slave-trade."[5]

John Adams once described himself as "a church-going animal," and his son traveled a similar road. When he was Secretary of State under President Monroe, on Sundays in Washington Adams would often attend three services (morning, afternoon, and evening) at three different churches, and often would write critiques of the sermons afterwards. As President he often followed the same practice of attending several different religious services for Sunday worship; once with a rather unusual if not amusing result. In his first year in the White House he returned one Sunday evening from his third church service of the day to find the mansion's doors all locked with no key to be found.[6]

Adams viewed religion as more than merely a system of morals yet he was left mystified and often troubled by the supernatural elements of orthodox Christian theology. He believed that the life and teachings and death of Jesus clearly deserved close scrutiny, and that the ethics of Jesus were beyond compare. He "preferred to emphasize the sublime moral beauty of Christ's teachings."[7] He had fears about Unitarianism, even though he was raised in and identified with the liberal wing of Congregationalism, and he was equally rankled at times by Evangelicalism, although he enjoyed sermons that were delivered by a not-indifferent minister. His concerns centered on his conclusions about the connections between religion and republicanism, for Adams argued that morality was essential for the survival of the Republic, and he worried deeply (as he did about most things) about "genial Unitarianism" and "intolerant Fundamentalism." He was most offended by what he viewed as intolerant Calvinism, and he wrote and spoke about the need for a more "modest faith" with respect to the various theological mysteries. These concerns even led Adams to become president of the American Bible Society during a time when he also was president of the American Academy of Arts and Sciences.[8]

What Adams especially desired was a moral people who would practice humility and humane behavior. Religion served not only as a source of personal solace for Adams (he and his wife Louisa Catherine Johnson Adams experienced great sorrow with almost all their children) but it also performed a vital function of social utility, not unlike what Jefferson, Madison, de Tocqueville and others pointed out. As Jon Meacham writes, "Adams represented a particular breed of believer, one who takes solace in scripture but does not necessarily think the Bible is the only field of battle in life's wars."[9] What Adam wanted was for him and his country to be thought of highly and treated well by history. Reputation and standing mattered greatly to Adams; hence, his consistent mixing of praise and criticism of himself, his family, friends, and fellow Americans. We see this especially in political terms with his opposition to slavery, as evidenced by his diary entries, public speeches, behavior in Congress, and legal argument before the United States Supreme Court in the *Amistad* controversy. In his consistent opposition to slavery, and as he recoiled at the sectional divisiveness threatening the Union, we see "the view of a man who, as the shadows lengthened, not only felt but thought that the right thing to do, however unpopular, would win him treasure in heaven if not on earth."[10]

Befitting a man of his unflagging devotion to public service, coupled with his views about slavery's injurious impact on individuals, communities, and countries, Adams collapsed at his desk in the House of Representatives chamber as he tried to rise to speak in the afternoon of Monday, February 21, 1848. He was carried to the Speaker's private chambers and died in the evening of February 23. Near the end of his long and eventful life, Adams had written, "I reverence God as my creator. As creator of the world. I reverence him with holy fear. I venerate Jesus Christ as my redeemer; and, as far as I can understand, the redeemer of the world. But this belief is dark and dubious."[11]

"Old Man Eloquent," as Adams was known, would deliver no more speeches or write any more letters exhorting family, friends, and fellow citizens to seek the best in themselves and others. His life was one in which he always sought personal improvement, a pursuit fueled in part by his brooding nature and self-examination. "His was a nature," Nagel writes, "ordained to be darkened by worry."[12] And he often sought relief, among other things, in reading the New Testament in Greek, reading sermons for relaxation, and turning to Biblical commentaries and theological treatises following sermons, discussions with colleagues, and probably most interesting of all, provocative arguments with himself alone in his study, where he was perhaps most content of all.

ANDREW JACKSON
1829-1837

★ ★ ★ ★ ★ ★ ★ ★ ★ ★ ★ ★

It is difficult to write about Andrew Jackson kindly, with the progression of 170 years. All of our presidents, if not all humans, are more contradictory than unified, but this seems especially true of Jackson and his legacy. The first subjective reactions of critics and scholars of Native-American culture to Jackson, however, stem from the knowledge that Jackson played a major role in the slaughter of Native Americans, and that he is considered to be the most dreaded American President in Native-American consciousness. There is a saying that Native Americans would rather have four five-dollar bills or two ten-dollar bills, than a twenty-dollar bill, which bears Jackson's likeness. We have attempted to show the complexities of each man's faith in each of these presidential vignettes, and we have tried to communicate that no president seems to be just one thing: a Christian, a non-Christian (since there have not been presidents from any other religious backgrounds). And, yet, there is Jackson, a devout Presbyterian Christian (the nation's first Presbyterian president), a devoted husband, a powerful leader, and a man who was complicit in cultural (if not actual) genocide—certainly a complex portrait.

Andrew Jackson was born on the frontier, of Scots ancestry, and the mark of rigid Calvinistic Presbyterian was on him his entire life. The Bible was available to young Jackson as he was growing up, with few other books in the home. The story of this young hero's life is a profound tale of frontier hardiness and independence, his father dying while Jackson was young, and his mother dying as a result of illness contracted while she was trying to free Andrew's older brothers from British captivity when Jackson was only fourteen years of age. His mother reared him in a Christian manner, but he remembered most particularly her last advice to him, calling him to honor, to honesty, "'But sustain your manhood always.' Gentleman, her last words have been the law of my life."[1] And it seems that he lived them out, so much so that this idea of "manhood" became incredibly powerful in his life, leading him to participate in duels brought on by slights against his character. The major rules of Jackson's life, then, were to uphold his own dignity, his own superiority, ignoring any rule of religion, especially the Golden Rule.

While Jackson left a record of powerful leadership and strong-armed tactics wherever he went in life, thus giving truth to his motto of sustaining his "manhood" always, there also is plenty of evidence that he took his religion, his Christianity, seriously, at least as seriously as any other American. More than most presidents before him, Jackson was clear about his personal beliefs, though also, like his predecessors, he worked to keep religion and government separate. During a time of regional crisis (another cholera epidemic), President Jackson was asked to call for a national day of prayer. His response could not have been clearer:

> I am constrained to decline the appointment of any period or mode as proper for the manifestation of this reliance. I could not do otherwise without transcending those limits which are prescribed by the Constitution for the President, and without feeling that I might in some degree disturb the security which religion now enjoys in this country

in its complete separation from the political concerns of the General Government.[2]

And again, like his predecessors, Jackson, this rugged frontiersman from low places, saw that government's involvement with religion hurt religion, degraded it, and even compromised it. Not only did Jackson refuse to bring religion into government, he also strove to keep government from imposing on religion, even to the point that he split his church attendance between churches of two different denominations while he was in Washington (Episcopal and Presbyterian) so that no one could accuse him of sectarianism. However, like Jefferson before him, Jackson did understand the acculturating power of religion, thus supporting religious education (Sunday Schools) for frontier Native Americans and whites. Rebutting an accusation that he had favored one religious sect over another while supporting Western religious education, Jackson responded by saying:

> I am no sectarian, though a lover of the Christian religion. I do not believe that any who shall be so fortunate as to be received to heaven, through the atonement of our blessed Saviour, will be asked whether they belonged to the Presbyterian, the Methodist, the Episcopalian Baptist or Roman Catholic [church]. All Christians are brethren, and all true Christians know they are such because they *love* one another. A true Christian loves *all*, immaterial to what sect or church he may belong.[3]

Jackson obviously knew Jesus' statement to his disciples regarding loving one another, though given Jackson's treatment of Native Americans and African Americans, a twenty-first century observer would have to question either Jackson's integrity, his definition of *love*, or his definition of *all*.

While one may find Jackson's choices as a Christian troublesome, there is little doubt that he knew the Bible and that he chose to follow the faith of his Presbyterian forebears, especially after his marriage to Rachel. In his diary, Jackson recorded he read from three to five chapters of the Bible a day and that he read the Bible through at least once a year—more than most American Christians spend in the sacred text. Jackson wrote his son-in-law to "Go read the Scriptures, the joyful promises it contains will be a balsam to all your troubles."[4] Back at his beloved Hermitage (the Tennessee home that meant more to him than anything, save his wife, Rachel), Jackson built a chapel so that Rachel would not have to miss any services, though he, himself, attended the chapel frequently. While in

Washington, Jackson paid pew rent to both St. John's Episcopal and First Presbyterian churches, where he alternated attendance, according to biographer H. W. Brands.[5] As a Presbyterian, Jackson's theology would have been recognizable to both Americans of his day and of ours. He believed God had a definite plan for the world and for each individual's actions in that world, though God's ways were mysterious. As a Calvinist, Jackson would likely have viewed the Bible as being the inherent Word of God, basically infallible, and so, like some American leaders before him, he may have viewed God's commands to destroy the enemies of Israel literally, and that understanding of God could possibly have made Jackson's views and actions toward his enemies (and especially toward Native Americans) consistent with how he understood God to act in the world. Compared to the kings of Israel and Judah whose actions are recorded in Second Kings (especially the ones carrying out the words of the prophets Elijah and Elisha), Jackson can seem merciful and tolerant.

As with so many larger-than-life historical figures, we often turn to their deathbeds to attempt to hear from their own mouths what they believed in and hoped for as they faced the unknown. It is not surprising, though, that deathbed reports by the survivors are often contradictory, depending on the legacy they believed the dying hero deserved. But we do have Jackson's diary and the words he left with his children, secretary, and friends, and it seems that as he became more and more frail, his thoughts turned toward the end of life, about seeing Rachel again in heaven. H. W. Brands writes:

> He worried as little about his salvation as he worried about most else. His conscience was as clear as it had always been. He wouldn't have said this made him a saint; on the contrary, he knew he was as sinful as the next man. But he believed that God gave credit for trying, and by his own lights he had generally done what he thought was the honest and upright thing to do. He had trouble sleeping, but it was his body, not his soul, that kept him awake.[6]

Yet Andrew Jackson had much in his life that had troubled him, scandals as a young man involving the one thing he seemed to hold most dear: his wife, Rachel.

Much mystery surrounds the courtship of Andrew Jackson and Rachel Robards, but what is known is that she was already married when the young

Jackson met her, and it is clear that they were living together as man and wife while she was likely still legally married to her first husband. By most accounts, Rachel's husband (much older than she) was abusive, and Jackson "saved" her from that life by taking her away to Natchez, Mississippi, where they apparently waited for another three years before officially solemnizing the marriage. This seemingly odd story (though probably not that odd in frontier America, where life was so difficult and where divorces and civil marriages were so hard to come by, there being an absence of government representatives) most likely would not have meant much to most men, but, of course, it would follow a man who desired to become President of the United States. When Jackson began pursuing politics, what enraged him most was when his "enemies" would bring up this long-hidden courtship and subtly (usually) accuse Rachel of adultery. Does Jackson's living with his future wife for three years before a legal marriage make him a sinner or call into question his Christianity? To some it certainly might, and there is little question that in today's political world, this would be very heavy baggage when our presidents seem to make a point of combining private morality with public virtue. But we do know that Jackson fervently defended his wife's honor, and all of his biographers, even those who did not like Jackson, agreed that he loved Rachel more than his own life—an honorable thing for any husband, president or not.

Famously, Jackson refused many times to join any church officially during his time as president, lest this would offer any ammunition to his adversaries who could accuse him of sectarianism. Here a common and powerful thread binds all the presidents during America's first century, or at least exhibits their strong attempt to keep their private religious lives separate from their public roles. They did this not necessarily to protect themselves, but to ensure the office of the president never became anything like the role of head of church and state, so familiar to Americans who clearly recalled the King of England and the abuses of established churches there and in the former colonies. Jackson did, however, eventually join the Presbyterian Church, but only when it would have nothing to do with his political career; he waited until after leaving office, in 1838, to join the church, doing so in a very small ceremony held at the Hermitage Chapel. In the account told by biographer Marquis James, the most difficult part of Jackson's profession of faith was his granting forgiveness to those who had hurt him (as might be expected, given what we know of his character), but "he made it clear that only his enemies were absolved. Those who had slandered her [Rachel] remained for God to deal with."[7] This private ceremony, whereby he joined the Presbyterian Church, takes on great significance; there was no reason for Jackson to do this unless he wanted to do it, unless he truly believed that this was an important step in his life.

Throughout the discussion of the faiths of the American Presidents, there has been little attempt to show where any given president's religious beliefs influenced his actions as president, but sometimes reviewing where faith affects policy illuminates the hidden places or shows significant contradictions between the man's professed beliefs and his actions. Jackson's actions and words toward Native Americans are particularly disturbing, though they also may show just how difficult it is to be an individual and an institution, an entire branch of government equal to Congress and the judiciary. We do not look at legislation enacted by Congress and say "that is a Christian act, so Congress must be Christian," so perhaps it is impossible to act as any one thing as president. Most memorably, when Georgia was seeking to force the Cherokee (a recognized nation, with official treaties with the United States) out of territory it considered to belong to Georgia, the Supreme Court found in favor of the Cherokee Nation, stating that Georgia must honor the treaties. But Jackson became the first president to refuse openly to carry out the rulings of the Supreme Court, thereby being complicit in the death and destruction of the Cherokee in their homeland.

Andrew Jackson's words, not just his policies, should further trouble us; Jackson went out of his way to give his unasked-for advice (after his presidency) to a military leader regarding the removal of the Seminoles, advising him to find out where the Seminole women and children were. He suggested taking them captive in order to force the warriors to submit; today any military action of this nature would likely be considered a war crime.[8] The following words of Jackson clearly communicate what was felt to be true by many Americans of the day, but this in no way should lessen their severity and should force us to wonder how a man can talk about brotherly love by Christians at one point and write this at another:

My original convictions upon this subject [Indian Removal] have been confirmed by the course of events for several years, and experience is every day adding to their strength. That those tribes cannot exist surrounded by our settlements and in continual contact with our citizens is certain. They have neither the intelligence, the industry, the moral habits, nor the desire of improvement which are essential to any favorable change in their condition. Established in the midst of another and a superior race, and without appreciating the causes of their inferiority or seeking to control them, they must necessarily yield to the force of circumstances and ere long disappear.

Ere long disappear. These are truly haunting words that make it nearly impossible to reconcile this genocidal statement with a man's profession of Christian faith, a professed "lover of the Christian religion"—both of which we have every reason to believe are sincere.

MARTIN VAN BUREN
1837-1841

★ ★ ★ ★ ★ ★ ★ ★ ★ ★ ★ ★

Martin Van Buren was an historic president. He was the first chief executive from the state of New York. He was the first president born a citizen of the United States rather than a subject of the British crown, and he was our first ethnic president, born of Dutch parents in Kinderhook, New York, on December 5, 1782.[1] About Van Buren there was, as one of his biographers puts it, a "surfeit of sobriquets."[2] He was known as Little Van, the Flying Dutchman, the Red Fox of Kinderhook, the Little Magician, and by the time his one term ended, he was referred to derisively as "Martin Van Ruin" due to the state of the economy.[3] However, Van Buren still eludes us. According to one scholar, "He's a lost president, floating in purgatory between Jackson and the Civil War."[4]

Van Buren was born into a Dutch Reformed family; both his parents were members of the Dutch Reformed Church, and his mother was considered to be especially devout. His father was an innkeeper. In 1807, Van Buren married Hannah Hoes, who also was Dutch Reformed and also considerably devout. She died twelve years into their marriage, having delivered four sons. Van Buren did not remarry and became the third widower to enter the White House.[5]

Van Buren was a lifelong churchgoer; however, there is scant evidence of his ever having formally joined a church. (The other Dutch Reformed president was Teddy Roosevelt). He was reported to have attended the Dutch Reformed Church while growing up in Kinderhook, and his funeral in 1862 was held at that particular church, with a Dutch Reformed pastor, and Van Buren's close friend, Alonzo Peter, the Episcopal Bishop of Pennsylvania, conducting the service. At Van Buren's funeral, the only music was the hymn "O God, Our Help in Ages Past."[6]

Van Buren apparently (as is the case with most presidents) never had any particular, much less keen, interest in spiritual or theological matters. There is no record of any public confession of faith or church membership or record of baptism, and he left no particular musings on religious or theological matters. At his inauguration, a Bible was opened to Proverbs 3:17: "Her ways are ways of pleasantness, and all her paths are peace." And, in his Inaugural Address of March 4, 1837, we find our eighth president hoping "for the sustaining support of an ever-watchful and beneficent Providence." He concluded his speech by saying, "I only look to the gracious protection of the Divine Being whose strengthening support I humbly solicit, and whom I fervently pray to look down upon us all. May it be among the dispensations of His providence to bless our beloved country with honors and with length of days. May her ways be ways of pleasantness and all her paths be peace."[7]

Van Buren's peroration clearly is not unusual as far as presidential rhetoric and especially inaugural addresses are concerned. There are no exclusionary sectarian or precise theological messages offered. Rather, Van Buren utters general (if not gentle) references to Providence or God or some kind of Supreme/Divine Being. Such references do not prove that Van Buren lacked a specific religious commitment. At the least they reflect the already established cultural and political expectation that the chief executive situate the country within the ambit of some kind of benevolent deity.

WILLIAM HENRY HARRISON
1841-1841

★ ★ ★ ★ ★ ★ ★ ★ ★ ★ ★ ★

The first president to be considered a Westerner, and therefore a relative outsider, was William Henry Harrison. Although Virginian by birth and education, he remained an outsider and is remembered as a President of the United States only because he died after holding the office for less than a month. Harrison supposedly became ill after being outside in the cold for a great time while delivering his famously long inaugural address. Although Harrison lived nearly seventy years before his brief presidency, we still know little about him. Unlike the other presidents who did not make much noise about their religious lives, we do not have even a record of speeches or presidential actions by which we can speculate about the man and his faith. Harrison seems to have been at least a nominal Episcopalian (though likely he was never confirmed),[1] given his likely upbringing in Virginia and as evidenced by a few noticeable choices he made at what came to be the end of his life.

While Harrison was likely reared as an Episcopalian, he attended Hampden-Sydney College in Virginia, which was a Presbyterian school, so clearly some of his religious training would have been from a Calvinist perspective. Harrison's family sent him to Hampden-Sydney probably because it was known as a more Whig-friendly institution (William's father was a signer of the Declaration of Independence), as opposed to the more accepted school among Virginia gentry, the College of William and Mary, which was known for its Tory leanings.[2] From college until the time of his marriage to a very Presbyterian Anna Symmes, little is known of Harrison's religious life. Interestingly, since there likely was no clergy readily available in the near wilderness of Ohio, Symmes and Harrison were married at her father's house by a justice of the peace (though some accounts have them eloping). So even the beginning of his married life was marked by its lack of religion.

While the large Harrison family was living near North Bend, Ohio, the future president attended the Presbyterian Church in the Village of Cleves (which Harrison founded and named for his father-in-law) with his wife and family, and he supported the new Cleves church with his time and with his money. Apparently, most of the other members of the congregation were not very well off, so the relatively wealthy Harrison (benefitting from a land deal with his father-in-law) donated the money to purchase much of the lumber for the building (1500 boards) in 1819, and he offered the use of one of his outbuildings as a home to the Reverend Horace Bushnell rent-free for as long as the pastor needed it. Rev. Bushnell told this story about Harrison's response to boys stealing grapes from his property (Harrison was intent on building a distillery and winery): "The gardener suggested the advisability of getting a watch dog to keep the bad boys of the neighborhood away. The general said he did not think much of a watchdog, but believed a Sunday school teacher would be a better remedy, 'As in that case both the grapes and the boys would be saved.'"[3] Up until at least the middle of the twentieth century, the Cleves church was the proud owner of a large pulpit Bible, used on special occasions, that was given to the church by Harrison.[4]

Despite being involved with the Presbyterian Church at least until he went to Washington for the first time as a Congressman, William Henry Harrison rented a pew at St. John's Episcopal in Washington (pew number forty-five), like most of his predecessors. Among the few purchases he made as he prepared to move into the White House were a new Bible and an Episcopalian prayer book. Further, Harrison apparently intended to become a communicant of the church during the Easter season, but his death came too soon.[5] As there was no Episcopalian Church near the Harrison home in Ohio, and also because Mrs. Harrison was a sincere Presbyterian (after her husband's death she stated that her one regret was that she had not been married by a Presbyterian minister[6]), it therefore seems plausible that Harrison never ceased being an Episcopalian, but that the larger desire was to be in a church with his family, even if that meant he would attend a Presbyterian Church for much of his life. Harrison's funeral was officiated by the rector of St. John's Episcopal, and the Bible and prayer book that Harrison had so recently ordered were placed by his coffin;[7] while his marriage had been secular, his death was marked by the religious rites of his forebears.

During his month as president, his most significant act was giving his inaugural address (two hours long—still a record), which is all we really have to understand those things he found important. Most of his address focused on a very detailed and specific account of how his administration would do away with the remnants of the Jacksonian era, but most interesting of all (and unlike the inaugural addresses of his predecessors) were the many allusions to classical history, mythology, and literature; his texts were Cicero and Homer, not Paul and Moses. Harrison's Secretary of State, Daniel Webster, had already trimmed down the speech to its two-hour form, removing the most obscure classical allusions and, perhaps, integrating the few references to religion. But Harrison's use of the classics in his writings and speeches are not there because he did not know the Bible; on the contrary, he claimed to read the Bible every day (and there were many who would confirm this) and even noted that what was "first a matter of duty . . . has now become a pleasure."[8] Maybe for Harrison, history was the appropriate well from which to draw for public discourse, not faith.

As with his inaugural address, William Henry Harrison's last words were not about God, Heaven, Hell, sin, or the state of his soul, but about the state of the nation. His reported last words, muttered to the attending physician (though thought to be meant for his vice president, John Tyler, and published in official news of the president's death) were, "Sir, I wish you to understand the true principles of the Government—I wish them carried out—I ask nothing more."[9] It is quite possible that Harrison, after listening to the 103rd Psalm read to him at his death bed at his request (a psalm thanking God for justice, for love, for mercy to these mortals whose days are like grass), felt at peace enough with his life and his faith that he only need worry about what he was leaving behind, a country in Constitutional crisis.

JOHN TYLER
1841-1845

★ ★ ★ ★ ★ ★ ★ ★ ★ ★ ★ ★

John Tyler was the first vice president in U.S. history to assume the presidency upon the death of a sitting president. On April 4, 1841, at 12:30 a.m., William Henry Harrison died of pneumonia, exactly one month into his presidency. Harrison, the nation's oldest chief executive, would be succeeded by the nation's youngest, the 51-year-old Virginian who had been active in public life since his election to the Virginia House of Burgesses at age twenty-two.

Tyler took the oath of office on April 6. Of course, he delivered no inaugural address but he did declare, "I am under Providence made the instrument of a new test which is for the first time to be applied to our institutions."[1] While others, such as John Quincy Adams, would refer to the tenth President as

"His Accidency," Tyler clearly saw himself as more than merely the acting chief executive.

Shortly after being sworn in, Tyler would declare May 14, 1841, a day of national prayer and fasting. "When a Christian people feel themselves to be overtaken by a great public calamity," stated Tyler, "it becomes them to humble themselves under the dispensation of Divine Providence."[2] One of the nation's leading ministers and evangelical voices of the early nineteenth century, Charles Finney, preached a memorable sermon in which he called on the mourning nation "to repent of its sins, which ranged from slavery and the treatment of the aborigines to desecration of the Sabbath, mercenary values, intemperance, and political corruption."

President Tyler received a letter from a Jewish American, Jacob Ezekiel of Richmond, Virginia, in which he asked Tyler for an "explanation . . . as may meet the views of those who do not profess Christianity though believers in the Supreme Being of the world." Tyler replied:

> For the people of whom you are one, I can feel none other than profound respect. The wisdom which flowed from the lips of your prophets has in time past, and will continue for all time to come, to be a refreshing fountain of moral instruction to mankind while holy records bear witness of Divine favors and protection of the God of Abraham and of Isaac and of Jacob, God of the Christian and the Israelite, to his chosen people may I then hope, sir, that this explanation will remove all difficulties, and that your voice and the voices of all your brethren will ascend to our Common Father in supplication and prayer on the day I have suggested.[3]

Of John Tyler one noted author concludes, "As presidents go, John Tyler is rarely spoken of—he was no Jefferson, no Lincoln—but he was a significant bridge figure between those two great men on the question of public religion."[4] Tyler was born into a prominent Episcopalian family in the tidewater elite of Virginia; his father had served as Governor of the Commonwealth. Following the likes of Thomas Jefferson and James Monroe, Tyler graduated from the College of William and Mary; he entered the school at the age of twelve, and graduated in 1807 at the age of seventeen. His favorite teacher there was the Reverend Bishop James Madison, the college president and second cousin of President James Madison. In his sermons and lectures, Bishop Madison consistently offered theological justifications for the expansion of the American empire—that God established the United States to spread republican values abroad.

Later in his one-term presidency, Tyler presented prescient perspectives on politics and religion in the young Republic.

The United States have adventured upon a great and noble experiment, which is believed to have been hazarded in the absence of all previous precedent—that of total separation of church and state. No religious establishment *by law* exists among us. The conscience is left free from all restraint and each is permitted to worship his Maker after his own judgment. . . . The Mohammedan, if he were to come among us, would have the privilege guaranteed to him by the constitution to worship according to the Koran; and the East Indian might erect a shrine to Brahma if it so pleased him. Such is the spirit of toleration inculcated by our political institutions. . . . The Hebrew persecuted and down trodden in other regions takes up his abode among us with none to make him afraid.[5]

In the words of Jon Meacham, "As the United States grew ever more diverse, visions like Tyler's became ever more relevant."[6]

In 1813, Tyler married a fellow Virginian and devout Episcopalian, Letitia Christian, with whom he had eight children. One of their daughters, Elizabeth, was married on January 31, 1842, in the East Room of the White House; officiating at the ceremony was the Reverend Dr. Hawley of St. John's Church of Washington, D.C. Eight months later, the President's wife died of complications from a series of strokes.

Less than three years later, Tyler married again. His new bride, Julia Gardiner, was twenty-two, and Tyler was fifty-five. The wedding took place at the Church of the Ascension in New York City. They had seven children together, one of whom, Lyon Gardiner Tyler, would later become president of the College of William and Mary. After Tyler's death in 1862, his wife became a convert to Catholicism.

Like his political hero, Thomas Jefferson, Tyler was an ardent expansionist, a strong advocate of states' rights, and, while holding to the view that slavery was a profound moral blight on the country, he also owned slaves and "like the master of Monticello, he left behind black people claiming descent from him."[7] After his presidency, Tyler was an active member of the Virginia convention that led the state's secession from the

Union, and later, he was elected to the Confederate House of Representatives but died on January 18, 1862, prior to taking office. Many at the time considered Tyler our first traitor president for his aggressive support of and involvement with Confederate policy.

Tyler once wrote his daughter, "The person who is a stranger to sickness is equally a stranger to the highest enjoyments of health. So . . . I have brought myself to believe that the variableness in the things of the world [is] designed by the Creator for the happiness of His creatures." The "person who justly contemplates the wise order of Providence can alone possess a just idea of the Deity." According to Meacham, "Like Jefferson, he was a kind of Deist who believed that reason offered rewards; like Lincoln, he was somewhat stoic."[8]

Tyler was buried with Episcopal rites in a *Book of Common Prayer* ceremony in Richmond, Virginia. We do not know, however, much about the depth or extent of his own personal religious beliefs and practices. He was said to have possessed an impressive, wide-ranging knowledge of Scripture yet we have no record of his own religious views, and there is uncertainty about his being a full communicant in the Episcopal Church.

JAMES KNOX POLK
1845-1849

★ ★ ★ ★ ★ ★ ★ ★ ★ ★ ★ ★

James K. Polk represents a very American story, especially regarding his private faith and public professions. Born to recent Scots-Irish immigrants settled in North Carolina, Polk was reared a Presbyterian (his mother was a descendant of the Scottish reformer James Knox's brother), but, because his father was an independent thinker, Polk was never baptized in the Presbyterian Church. As a young man, however, he responded to the distinctly American zeitgeist of the outdoor revival, experiencing a religious awakening from the outskirts of a Methodist camp meeting. From frontier beginnings Polk arose to occupy the highest office in the country, all the while keeping close his religious convictions, supporting religious freedom even for those groups he considered to be in error. Like some presidents before him,

Polk also echoed the growing division in American religion regarding slavery; American Methodists split due to tensions between slaveholders and abolitionists, and the African Methodist Episcopal Church was born from the ravages of slavery. Polk was a slaveholder himself, inheriting slaves from his father's estate and buying more slaves as his wealth grew, but in his will he specified that his slaves should be freed after his wife's death (though this was made moot due to the Emancipation Proclamation). He did this all while trying to balance political power between slave and free states by working to bring both the Oregon Country (free) and Texas (slave) into the United States.

Polk's paternal grandfather, Ezekiel, was a "free-thinking radical" in North Carolina who organized a debating society to discuss conflicts between reason and scripture. He contributed books to a lending library, most disturbingly books by prominent deists, such as Gibbon, Hume, and Paine. The only Presbyterian minister in the area, Parson Wallis, was greatly opposed to this deistic bent, and he spoke often from the pulpit about this evil going so far as to publish a pamphlet "to expose the errors of Paine's *Age of Reason.*"[1] So when it came time for Ezekiel's son, Sam, to have James baptized, Wallis demanded that Sam give a profession of faith, as was the Presbyterian requirement for parents of infants about to be baptized; Sam would not profess a faith that demanded belief in a providential god. Wallis therefore refused to baptize James Knox Polk— who remained unbaptized until mere days before his death.[2] Even though James' father and grandfather were unorthodox, they did believe strongly in education; so James was well-educated, attending a Presbyterian academy and eventually the University of North Carolina-Chapel Hill, where habits of daily religious devotion and instruction were inculcated into the fifty or so young men attending in those days. However, while Polk took religion very seriously, he never felt strongly enough about any church to join one.

Eventually Polk made his way to Tennessee, where he began his legal and political careers as a Jacksonian Democrat. During his days in Columbia, Tennessee, he went to a camp meeting where the preacher, John B. McFerrin, a young and forceful Methodist, had earlier helped to "convert" two Polk sisters. According to biographer Charles Sellers, "To the rigorously predestinarian Presbyterianism of his wife and mother,

Polk had never been able to respond, but McFerrin's appeal so affected him that he 'went away from the campground a convicted sinner, if not a converted man.'" Polk saw himself as a Methodist for the rest of his life ("a Wesleyan in sentiment, and believed in the doctrine and polity of the Methodist Episcopal Church"), and when his wife was away or not able to attend church, he would usually attend a Methodist Church; otherwise he would accompany her to the Presbyterian Church. Sellers also suggests that due partially to the dramatic theological differences between American Methodism and the predestinarian Presbyterianism of his wife, Sarah, Polk did not join the Methodist church or discuss his beliefs until the end of his life.[3]

As president, Polk was reserved about anything religious, at least to the public, but his diary shows that he was very thoughtful about faith and religion. A friend of Polk's had this to say regarding Polk's view on religion in the public arena: "Religion is the very best possession in the world, and the last to be spoken of. It should dwell quietly in the heart, and rule the life; not be hawked about as a commodity; nor scoured up like a rusty buckler for protection; nor be worn over the shoulders like a blanket for defence [sic]."[4] Polk's principled stance on the separation of church and state and on the privacy of one's religion certainly affected some of his decisions while President of the United States. For instance, during a time when Catholics were considered true outsiders (if not dangerous and anti-American) in much of America, Polk decided to approve several Catholic Army chaplains to serve soldiers who were fighting in Mexico, resulting in a Presbyterian minister accusing him of "fostering Catholicism." Polk responded by writing, "Thank God, under our constitution there was no connection between Church and State, and that in my action as President of the U.S. I recognized no distinction of creeds in my appointment to office."[5] Another religious controversy of Polk's day was the Mormon question, the problem of their religious freedoms and their rights to emigrate to the Utah territory and other Western areas. Polk supported the rights of Mormons to live and worship as they saw fit, despite thinking their way of life "absurd."[6] But Polk's desire to live out his religious life privately did affect some other aspects of his presidency. Famously, Polk refused to do any business on Sundays (at one point even denying a meeting to a French foreign minister on a Sunday afternoon), and Sarah refused to allow any alcohol or dancing at White House dinners or receptions.[7]

Early on during his four years as president, Polk recorded in his diary (a common act for him) his reactions to a sermon he had heard on his birthday at The Foundry Methodist Church in Washington, D.C. Reflecting on his own view of his perceived role in the world, he wrote that the sermon had:

> Awakened the reflection that I had lived fifty years and that before fifty more would expire I would be sleeping with the generations which have gone before me. I thought of the vanity of the world's honors, how little they would profit me half a century hence, and that it was time for me to be putting my house in order.[8]

It would not be until four years later that he would complete putting his house in order by asking that same preacher who had been instrumental in his spiritual awakening to come to his home and baptize him as a Methodist. Now a Methodist bishop, Rev. McFerrin baptized Polk and received him into membership in the Methodist Church, a mere week before Polk's death (likely from cholera) and only a few months after leaving the presidency and returning to Tennessee.

Polk, then, was the first United States President who was a Methodist, and he was likely the first president to have experienced a religious awakening in a camp meeting. And yet, despite the clear and strong faith Polk possessed, he was still adamant about the need to protect the rights of others to worship in their own ways and to keep his religious beliefs to himself while president; all of which were strong and consistent threads in the administrations of his presidential predecessors.

ZACHARY TAYLOR
1849-1850

★ ★ ★ ★ ★ ★ ★ ★ ★ ★ ★ ★

Zachary Taylor was President of the United States for 492 days. He won a close election over Lewis Cass in 1848, in what is considered the first modern presidential election since all votes were cast on the same day. His inauguration took place on March 5, 1849, and he died on July 9, 1850, of acute gastroenteritis after drinking tainted milk and eating raw fruit and vegetables at a Fourth of July ceremony in Washington, D.C., where he was laying the cornerstone of the Washington Monument. His funeral service was held at the White House according to Episcopalian rites. One leading figure of the day called Taylor's death "a public calamity." Yet another, Brigham Young, is reported to have said, "'Zachary Taylor is dead and gone to hell, and I am glad of it.'"[1]

Taylor was born in Virginia on November 24, 1784, but his family moved to Kentucky shortly thereafter. His family was related to both James Madison and Robert E. Lee, and his daughter would marry Jefferson Davis. Taylor was a career military man, serving in the Army from 1808 to 1848. "Old Rough and Ready," the nickname given him by his troops for his gruff demeanor and informal mode of dress, was a veteran of the War of 1812, Black Hawk's War, the Seminole War, and the Mexican War of 1846-47, where he was a hero of the Battle of Buena Vista.

Taylor was born into an Episcopalian family and married a devout Episcopalian (Margaret Smith Taylor) but never became a full communicant of the church himself. Taylor belonged to no church and we have no record of any profession of faith. The youngest Taylor daughter, Mrs. Elizabeth Bliss, offered the sole family witness about her father's faith: "He was a constant reader of the Bible and practiced all its precepts, acknowledging his responsibility to God."[2] As president and when in Washington, Taylor often worshipped where other chief executives had—at St. John's Church across Lafayette Square from the White House.

At his inauguration in 1849, Taylor delivered a brief address, concluding with reference to "the high state of prosperity to which the goodness of Divine Providence has conducted our common country. Let us invoke a continuance of the same protecting care which has led us from small beginnings to the eminence we this day occupy."[3] Perhaps the only other significant (or at least interesting) statement from Taylor concerning religion is his July 3, 1849, proclamation for "a day of fasting, humiliation and prayer" in response to the deadly cholera epidemic of 1848-49.

An earlier cholera epidemic occurred in 1832, at which time the U.S. Senate (but not the House of Representatives) requested then-President Andrew Jackson to issue a proclamation for a day of prayer and fasting. Jackson refused to do so, citing issues of separation of church and state. In Taylor's brief presidency, in response to the second outbreak, both chambers of Congress requested presidential action, and Taylor complied. "At a season when the providence of God has manifested itself in the visitation of a fearful pestilence," the proclamation urged Americans to "acknowledge past transgressions and ask a continuance of Divine mercy."[4] People in the country "should humble themselves before His throne," and should "acknowledge the Infinite Goodness which has watched over our existence as a nation and so long crowned us with manifold blessings—and to implore the Almighty in His own good time to stay the destroying hand which is now lifted up against us."[5] In this regard, Taylor's words are not unlike those often written or spoken by other occupants of the Oval Office: they combine the pastoral and the prophetic.

MILLARD FILLMORE
1850-1853

★ ★ ★ ★ ★ ★ ★ ★ ★ ★ ★ ★

John Sutherland Bonnell, the last scholar
to write a survey of the religious lives of the
United States Presidents, notes, "When we
seek to find some clue to President Fillmore's
religious views, we are baffled at every turn."[1]
This is not because we don't know where he
went to church or about his actions in this
life, but because he wrote and said so little
about religion during his long life and career.

His most significant work as president
seems to have been the Compromise of 1850
that helped to bring into law the dreaded
Fugitive Slave Act. This work alienated him
from many of those in his Whig party and
from the one church to which he actually
belonged—the Unitarian Church. Although
he had stated throughout his political career
that slavery was abominable, he also believed
that it was a fact of American life, guaran-

teed by the Constitution, as he understood it, so he would not allow the disintegration of the Union over slavery. Ultimately, this view of slavery and compromise may indicate something about Fillmore's religious life; he believed in religious causes, but there was little in the religious realm he seemed to feel strongly about.

Fillmore's father was nominally Presbyterian, and his mother was likely descended from English dissenters, but there is no indication that there was any systematic religious instruction in the log cabin, frontier home of his youth. However, Fillmore did have a passion for books and education, eventually marrying his teacher, Abigail Powers (whose Baptist-preacher father died when she was two years of age). He became an apprentice to a judge who taught him the law, and Fillmore later founded one of New York's most successful law firms. Early in his law studies, he wrote that he, "labored as hard as Jacob did for Rachel," demonstrating that at least he knew something about the Bible (there was a King James Bible in his father's home).[2] The first real record of either Abigail's or Millard's involvement in religion (other than their marriage by an Episcopalian minister at the home of Abigail's brother) was in 1831 when they moved to Buffalo, New York. They soon became members of the Unitarian Society that began building its permanent building just down the street from their home. Interestingly, they chose to join the Unitarian fellowship despite the fact that Fillmore's cousin Rev. Glezen Fillmore had started and was pastor of the first Methodist church in Buffalo (and the builder of the village's first church building), making it clear that they were having no part of Methodism, or, for that matter, with the Baptists of Abigail's family. They chose to be Unitarians.[3] Biographer Robert J. Rayback suggests that it was not only the Unitarian rejection of Trinitarian doctrine that likely attracted Fillmore, but also that the Unitarian view of humanity as virtuous and God as benevolent contrasted favorably for a man like Fillmore who had the socially dominant view that humanity is depraved and God is angry.[4]

As president, Fillmore's public record of religious discourse is similar to that of most his predecessors, that of referring to a civil religion, to a god who is in some sort of control but not a god of personal relationship. For instance, upon taking the oath of office after President Taylor's death, Fillmore stated, "I rely upon Him, who holds in His hands the destinies of nations, to endow me with the requisite strength for the task, and to avert from our country the evils apprehended from the heavy calamity which has befallen us." His other public addresses speak similarly of this Providence.[5]

But it is in Fillmore's private correspondence that we see a man who seems to understand a God that cares about personal concerns and has some involvement with individuals on a regular basis. Over the course of many years, Fillmore had a close relationship, manifested mostly in private letters, with Dorothea Dix, a leading Unitarian, educator, and philanthropist, and in these letters they both refer to God as "our Father" and to Jesus as "our Saviour," indicating something more than an abstract sense of relationship with orthodox Christianity. Furthermore, Fillmore mentions praying specifically for Dix, showing that he at least takes religion seriously and believed or hoped in a personal God's intervention.[6]

Finally, Fillmore's relationship with the Unitarian Society is not as simple as some authors have suggested. According to some, he remained a committed Unitarian all of his life, but at least one scholar contends that one particular event soured Fillmore on the Unitarian Society; Fillmore had been asked to chair the American Unitarian Association of Boston annual meeting soon after his presidency, and he had apparently been looking forward to this visible act of service (he did not leave the political arena readily, to the point of running as a third-party candidate for the presidency). However, the Boston Unitarians were overwhelmingly anti-slavery, and much of the membership regarded Fillmore as a betrayer of that significant value, especially in his signing of the Fugitive Slave Act and his seemingly sympathetic work with slavery advocates. The Association, therefore, withdrew its offer to have him chair its meeting. Bonnell says, "Fillmore was deeply hurt by this unkindly rebuff and gradually separated himself completely from the Unitarian cause." After Fillmore's second marriage, this time to Caroline C. McIntosh in 1858, he attended the Baptist church with his new wife. From time to time he was also seen in the Episcopal Church.[7] His funeral services were officiated by Baptist, Episcopalian, and Presbyterian ministers. We know, then, that Fillmore was at least a moderately religious man who was a regular church-attendee even when outside public life, and his decisions regarding which churches he attended seem to be made with some thought and concern. Furthermore, it is likely he believed in a personal God who intervened in humanity's affairs. Was he an orthodox Christian? We do not know.

FRANKLIN PIERCE
1853-1857

★ ★ ★ ★ ★ ★ ★ ★ ★ ★ ★ ★

Franklin Pierce was the darkest of dark horses. At the 1852 Democratic Party National Convention in Baltimore, after about every other legitimate, potential nominee's name was considered and rejected, this obscure lawyer-politician from New Hampshire received his party's nomination on the 49th ballot. Pierce would be elected in the fall of that year, but four years later he would become the first and only president of the nineteenth century to seek and be denied his party's re-nomination for a second term.[1]

Pierce was an experienced, popular, and, at times, magnetic politician having served in the New Hampshire legislature, the United States House of Representatives, and the United States Senate. He was an honors graduate of Bowdoin College in Maine in 1824, and in 1834 married Jane Means

Appleton, whose father once had been president of Bowdoin. Pierce was a veteran (albeit a rather undistinguished one) of the Mexican War in the mid-1840s, and has been described arguably the most handsome man ever to be elected president. However, his presidency is largely a forgettable one that suffered severely from vision deficit disorder, for Pierce either was unwilling or unable to convey a compelling vision of what he hoped to accomplish in the White House.[2]

According to Fuller and Green, Pierce was our "most pathetically unhappy" chief executive whose unhappiness "was linked with a neurotic anxiety about religious commitment."[3] At the time of his election to the presidency, Pierce had no specific denominational affiliation; he considered himself an orthodox Christian. He did not attend consistently the churches of any one particular denomination. He had been known for praying in college with his roommate but he never made any public confession of faith, or, as far as we know, never did so privately. While in the U.S. House of Representatives, he wrote to a law partner that he had been thinking "upon the truths of divine revelation" more than usual, which implies he had done so before, but just why and with what consequence, politically or theologically, is a matter of uncertain conjecture.[4] He said he believed in Christian doctrines and "perhaps have struggled somewhat harder to think and act in conformity with the precepts and commands of the New Testament than ever before—but with indifferent success as every man must who is not a humble and devoted Christian, to which character I can, I regret to say, make no pretension."[5]

His wife was the daughter of a Congregational minister, and she possessed a religious fervor and Calvinistic convictions that challenged Pierce's thoughts and actions. They were married for twenty-nine years, until her death in the early 1860s, and they had three sons, none of whom would live to adulthood. Their first son, Franklin, Jr., died after three days, and the second son died at the age of four. Their third son, Benjamin (Bennie), aged twelve, was killed in a train accident (his parents were uninjured) as they were traveling two months before Pierce's inauguration. Mrs. Pierce never recovered from the tragedy, wearing black for the duration of her husband's presidency. She also suggested that Bennie was essentially a sacrificial Isaac, taken by God so her husband would have no distractions as president. Pierce himself felt that his son's death was punishment from God for his failure to live purely, especially in the realm of politics.[6]

When Pierce was sworn in as president on March 3, 1853, he became the only president to state, "I solemnly affirm" rather than "I solemnly swear." In his inaugural address, Pierce followed the lead of more than a few of his predecessors by invoking the blessings of a rather vague and bland Providence, through references to "a manifest and beneficent Providence," God and "His overruling Providence," and that "kind Providence which smiled upon our fathers." His address ended with the words, "I can express no better hope for my country than that the kind Providence which smiled upon our fathers[7] may enable their children to preserve the blessings they have inherited."[8]

Not unlike his wife, Pierce never fully recovered from the deaths of their three sons. While in the White House, he practiced strict Sabbath observances, regularly read from the Bible each morning, and worshipped at several churches, primarily Presbyterian and Congregational. He became an Episcopalian after his wife's death, when, on December 3, 1865, he was baptized in St. Paul's Episcopal Church in Concord, New Hampshire. He was confirmed the following spring, less than four years before his death on October 8, 1869. It is believed that he became Episcopalian rather than Congregationalist because his wife's church was so strongly anti-slavery, for Pierce was essentially a Northern official with Southern sentiments.[9]

At one time, Pierce had been active in the temperance movement, in part because his wife had been so strongly against his drinking; Pierce had sworn off alcohol after the loss of their children and for roughly two decades had stayed sober. However, after his wife's death, he turned back to the bottle, declaring at one point, "After the White House what is there to do but drink?"[10]

JAMES BUCHANAN
1857-1861

★ ★ ★ ★ ★ ★ ★ ★ ★ ★ ★ ★

Disappearing in the shadow of Abraham Lincoln and obscured by the flames of the Civil War, the fifteenth President of the United States, James Buchanan, does not stand as a man of giant moral or immoral stature. Rather, he seems to have been a thoughtful politician who took Christianity seriously. His life and presidency, however, are marred by the conciliatory approach he took toward the Southern slave states, especially when compared to the example of Abraham Lincoln.

Like Jackson and Polk before him, Buchanan was of Scots-Irish descent and consequently reared as a Presbyterian. His mother wished for him to be a Presbyterian minister, and while he was unable to fulfill this particular wish, his brother did become a minister in the Presbyterian Church, which suggests that the Buchanan home was one with a defined religious structure.

Buchanan graduated from Dickinson College, which, like most American education institutions, had, at one time, a curriculum grounded in orthodox Christian thought and traditions; to this day, there is an open Bible depicted on the college seal, so Buchanan's education there was likely not radical in its religiosity or lack thereof. Buchanan talked with his family about spiritual matters, especially with his minister brother and with his niece, Harriet, who acted as hostess while Buchanan was president. While Buchanan was minister to Russia, he wrote to his brother, "I can say sincerely for myself I desire to be a Christian. My true feeling upon many occasions is: Lord, I would believe; help thou my unbelief."[1] These two sentences tell us that Buchanan knows his Bible but also that he approached his faith with thoughtfulness and seriousness, that it was something with which he intentionally wrestled. To his beloved niece he once wrote, "If I believed it necessary I would advise you to be constant in your devotions to God. He is a friend who will never desert you."[2]

Most significantly, despite his religious upbringing and his clear religious beliefs, he did not officially join the Presbyterian Church until after his presidency. Part of the issue was that he wanted to make certain he was actually a Christian, and neither did he wish to have his membership become a political issue. While he was still president, Buchanan met with the Rev. Dr. William M. Paxton, pastor of the First Presbyterian Church of New York City. Afterward, Buchanan wrote, "I hope that I am a Christian. I think that I have much of the experience that you describe. As soon as I retire from my office as President, I will unite with the Presbyterian Church." (Buchanan did join the Presbyterian Church in 1865.)[3] Here Buchanan appears to be dealing with the particularly Calvinistic dilemma that one can only be a Christian if indeed God had chosen him. Being a Christian was not only a matter of belief or even of behavior; it was a state of being, partly determined by circumstances outside the individual's control and as established by the omnipotent God.

The second significant aspect of Buchanan's statement to Paxton dealt with the role of religion in political life. As we have seen already with previous presidents, these presidents during the nation's first 100 years were deeply concerned with not politicizing religion, mostly because it could be explosive for a president to seem to favor one sect over another. Further, some sects were considered to be affiliated with various political causes more than others—most obvious, of course, would be the two New England sects, Congregationalists and Unitarians, which were overwhelmingly abolitionist groups. So for a president in 1858 to say he was a Presbyterian might very well have been taken as an overt statement that he was not anti-slavery and that he favored the thinking of Andrew Jackson (pro-slavery), rather than John Adams (abolitionist).

But Buchanan could not escape the moral mire of slavery and its stain on the nation (and on one's faith). Even while he was Polk's Secretary of State, Buchanan was embroiled in the slavery controversy. The Polk administration tried to purchase the island territory of Cuba from Spain, partly due to its physical proximity to the United States, but mostly because it was already a territory that practiced American-style slavery. In a document known as the "Ostend Manifesto," Buchanan and two U.S. ambassadors (to Spain and France) advocated the purchase of Cuba or, if necessary, its acquirement by force stressing, "The danger that the Spanish might abolish slavery in Cuba, they [the ambassadors and Buchanan] insisted that this must be prevented because of its danger to slavery in the United States."[4] As president, Buchanan sought to bring Kansas into the Union as a slave state, so as to end the Free Soiler movement and to calm some of the growing turmoil, but Buchanan did not have enough political capital, thus alienating himself from the ever-distancing Southern Democrats and the increasingly strident Republicans. Ultimately, we remember Buchanan's presidency as a failure in many regards: it is the presidency that ended in the secession of seven southern states, with Buchanan failing to take a strong, moral, Christian stand against slavery or to hold the Union together. Despite his desire to be a Christian, Buchanan's legacy is defined by the national sin of slavery.

ABRAHAM LINCOLN
1861-1865

★ ★ ★ ★ ★ ★ ★ ★ ★ ★ ★ ★

Abraham Lincoln, according to one leading
American historian of religion, "Stands at
the center of American history and increasingly is seen as the theological thinker whose
reflections are most apt and profound."[1]
More words have been written, indeed, more
books have been published on Abraham
Lincoln than any other person in U.S. history, and yet, when it comes to making sense
of Lincoln's religious beliefs, Lincoln seems
like Churchill's Russia: a riddle wrapped in
a mystery inside an enigma. Raised by strict
Calvinist Baptist parents, Lincoln, early in
his life, was labeled a religious skeptic. But
after tragedies struck his family including
the deaths of two of his sons, Lincoln appeared to take God and religion more seriously. And, in his White House years, given
the daunting demands and duties during the

Civil War, Lincoln clearly pondered the efforts of human behavior in a mysterious, if not perceived-to-be malevolent, universe. "He was," according to Reinhold Niebuhr, "that rare and unique human being who could be responsible in executing historic tasks without equating his interpretation of the task with the divine wisdom."[2]

Making sense of Lincoln is not easy. Unlike John Adams and his son John Quincy, Lincoln kept no diary; neither was he a "church-going animal" as Adams father and son were. He left behind no library as did Jefferson. Nor did he attend church consistently, converse with ministers intimately, or support churches in any denominational or creedal capacity. He was a politician, and an ambitious one; as his one-time law partner William "Billy" Herndon famously put it: Lincoln's ambition "was a little engine that knew no rest." And, Lincoln's "moral understanding of the demands of power was not founded on a conventional Christian faith. But the evolution of his religious thought, his quest to understand divine purposes during the war, his Calvinistic frame of reference, and the ease with which he rooted his arguments in Scripture make it essential to take his religion seriously."[3]

Lincoln was never baptized in nor ever joined any church. His parents, Thomas and Nancy Hanks Lincoln, belonged to the Little Mount Separatist Baptist Church in Kentucky. Nancy Lincoln died when her son was only nine; Thomas remarried (Sarah Bush Lincoln), and in Indiana they belonged to the Little Pigeon Creek Baptist Church. The churches were "Hard-shell" Baptists, strict Calvinists and strong believers in predestination, opposing international missions and other such endeavors. Lincoln's father died in 1851, and reflecting their long-standing estrangement, Lincoln neither attended his father's funeral nor ever arranged for a tombstone for the gravesite. Lincoln was much closer to Sarah; Sarah always praised her stepson with fondness, and often remarked that she thought he did take religion particularly seriously.

Lincoln enjoyed less than two years' worth of formal education. He once filled out a questionnaire for a Congressional directory, simply writing "Defective" in the space for his public education. He described his life once as simply consisting of "the annals of the poor." Yet he read anything he could get his hands on, including the King James Bible and especially Shakespeare. He favored *Macbeth* and often quoted Hamlet, "There's a

divinity that shapes our ends, Rough-hew them how we will."[4] As Allen
Guelzo has written, especially of Lincoln in his pre-White House years,
"The young Lincoln, like [Herman] Melville and [Nathaniel] Hawthorne,
found the all-powerful and all-controlling God of his parents simultaneously unbelievable and mesmerizing, and the combination made Lincoln
both a fatalist in philosophy and a skeptic in matters of religion, a kind of
secularized Calvinist."[5] Another scholar of Lincoln's religious life, William E. Barton, once wrote that before Lincoln reached the age of twenty-
eight he may not have encountered a single Baptist preacher who would
admit that the earth was round.[6]

After Lincoln and Mary Todd married in 1842 and for most of their
years in Illinois, they either belonged to no church or were irregular in attendance. Mary Lincoln was raised Episcopalian in Kentucky, and they
were married by an Episcopalian minister in a sister's home. Following the
death of their young son, Edward Baker Lincoln, who died in 1850 at the
age of three following a 50-day illness, Mary joined the First Presbyterian
Church of Springfield because its minister presided at Eddie's funeral. She
would retain her membership there until her own death; their son Thomas
or "Tad" was baptized there, and Lincoln rented a pew there and at times
attended services there until he left for the White House in February, 1861.
But he never joined the church or made any kind of profession of faith.

According to the noted American historian, Mark Noll, "Warfare—
and the more cataclysmic the better—has sometimes been the mother of
theological profundity."[7] The Civil War, and especially the raging national
conflict surrounding slavery, challenged and crystallized Lincoln's thinking. There was a pronounced, sometimes public, often private sense of
the workings of Providence in Lincoln's spoken and written comments
but without the idolatrous triumphalism or evangelical self-righteousness
encountered in others, both North and South. This serious seeking after
the meaning of the war, albeit an elusive, mysterious meaning, is perhaps
best seen in the one vital document that did not become public until after
Lincoln's death. Written most likely in early September 1862, and discov-
ered by one of Lincoln's secretaries in a desk drawer after Lincoln's assassination, the "Meditation on the Divine Will" is as theologically profound
a statement as any American president ever has spoken or written.[8] In
essence, it offers a foretaste of what Lincoln would provide in what one

scholar has called "America's Sermon on the Mount,"[9] Lincoln's unparalleled Second Inaugural Address, and it deserves quoting in its entirety:

> The will of God prevails. In great contests each party claims to act in accordance with the will of God. Both **may** be, and one **must** be wrong. God cannot be **for**, and **against** the same thing at the same time. In the present civil war it is quite possible that God's purpose is something different from the purpose of either party—and yet the human instrumentalities, working just as they do, are of the best adaptation to effect His purpose. I am almost ready to say this is probably true—that God wills this contest, and wills that it shall not end yet. By his mere quiet power, on the minds of the now contestants, He could have either **saved** or **destroyed** the Union without a human contest. Yet the contest began. And having begun He could give the final victory to either side any day. Yet the contest proceeds.[10]

These words reflect, in part, what Lincoln already had expressed in October 1858 when he sought to debunk the theological pro-slavery thesis. Lincoln had said, "Certainly there is no contending against the will of God; but still there is some difficulty in ascertaining, and applying it, to particular cases."[11] During this time period in the war, ministers from the North who were there to communicate to the President what they believed God had revealed to them, often visited Lincoln at the White House. Patiently, and often with an interesting mix of candor and humor (and not a little bit of theological sophistication), Lincoln would welcome them, thank them for their comments, and then ruminate over the fact that miracles appeared to be in short supply and that God had not revealed His will to Lincoln yet. Lincoln, noted historian Mark Noll, "a layman with no standing in a church and no formal training as a theologian, propounded a thick, complex view of God's rule over the world and a morally nuanced picture of America's destiny."[12]

In his magisterial Second Inaugural Address, which is only 703 words and took him less than ten minutes to deliver, Lincoln delivers what Frederick Douglass would describe as more "sermon than state paper."[13] Noll describes the address of March 4, 1865, as "a theological statement of rare insight."[14] The ideas were rare for theologians of his day, rarer still for any occupant of the Oval Office at any time. Lincoln neither offered the North unalloyed praise nor the South damning denunciation. Rather, he offered, for the United States and the rest of the world, a vision of peace. Mixing scriptural passages with carefully drawn insights about American destiny, Lincoln said, "Neither party expected for the war, the magnitude, or the duration, which it has already attained . . . Each looked for an easier triumph, and a result less fundamental and astounding. Both read the same Bible, and pray to the same God; and each invokes His aid against the other. It may seem strange that any men should dare to ask a just God's assistance in wringing their bread from the sweat of other men's faces; but let us judge not that we be not judged. The prayers of both could not be answered; that of neither has been answered fully. The Almighty has His own purposes."[15]

Lincoln thought this speech was his finest. On March 15, 1865, he wrote to a political ally about "the recent Inaugural Address. I expect the latter to wear as well as—perhaps better than—any thing I have produced; but I believe it is not immediately popular. Men are not flattered," Lincoln continued, "by being shown that there has been a difference of purpose between the Almighty and them. To deny it, however, in this case, is to deny that there is a God governing the world."[16]

Less than a month later Lincoln is dead, and virtually overnight becomes a sacred saint, in part because of his murder on Good Friday but also because of his image as the Great Emancipator. Overnight, in the words of the influential Lincolnian Harold Holzer, "The once-controversial politician became a second Washington, a latter-day Moses, an American Christ."[17] Count Leo Tolstoy would later refer to the slain president as "a Christ in miniature, a saint of humanity,"[18] and H. L. Mencken, in the early twentieth century, worried that we had turned Lincoln "into a plaster saint. Worse, there is an obvious effort to pump all his human weakness out of him, and so leave him a mere moral apparition, a sort of amalgam of John Wesley and the Holy Ghost."[19]

Lincoln sought to know and do the will of God while conceding the difficulty in doing so. He did not see himself as God's messenger, and he saw us as God's "almost chosen" people, and as we all know from his First Inaugural Address, he urged us to heed "the better angels of our nature."[20] Scholars, theologians, politicians and pastors have been contesting Lincoln for not quite two centuries, and the quest for his soul (and ours?) probably won't stop any time soon. In the words of Ted Widmer, "[T]he point is not that he followed this or that doctrine; it is that he wrestled honestly with his beliefs throughout his life."[21]

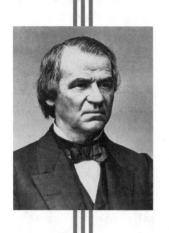

ANDREW JOHNSON
1865-1869

★ ★ ★ ★ ★ ★ ★ ★ ★ ★ ★ ★

Andrew Johnson is the first President of the United States who was not affiliated at all with any sort of church, although it would seem he was, indeed, a Christian. Throughout his life he was very clear that he believed in Christian tenets but also that he was not religious at all. Apparently this meant that he was not evangelical and seemed to care nothing for the things of church or for religious rites. His wife, Elisabeth, however, was a Methodist, and he had many friends who were Methodists; he also attended the Methodist church with his wife and family.[1] Also, it is clear that Johnson had no qualms with rites or belonging; he was a Mason of very high degree and proud of this affiliation. Perhaps his Masonic relationships and works provided him with the same sort of fraternity that churches provide for many others.

One fascinating aspect of these nineteenth century presidents is how their backgrounds varied, and yet, so many of them had a strong desire for religious freedom, Johnson not the least of them. While it seems most other presidents had opposing views regarding freedom for African Americans, religious freedom was a central tenet of American political life. There were many religious men who attempted to gain political power and who wished to "save" the country from secularism or from the "evils" of Catholicism, but at least until Grant, none of these ascended to anywhere near the presidency. As a congressman and military governor, Johnson worked against the Know-Nothing Party (anti-immigrant, anti-Catholic), and as often as it came up, he opposed the states' or federal government's taking any actions that appeared as if they were establishing religion in any form. As a U.S. Congressman Johnson was instrumental in helping to kill a resolution that would allow ministers to open legislative meetings with prayer. He was forced to justify this to some of his constituents who believed that since he fought this resolution he must not be a Christian, or even worse, he must be anti-Christian. One minister, who also was running against Johnson for his House seat, accused Johnson of being an infidel. Johnson responded with an open letter to the "Freemen of the First Congressional District of Tennessee":

> That the charge of infidelity, as preferred against me in the late canvass, is utterly and absolutely false from beginning to end; and that, so far as the doctrines of the Bible are concerned, or the great scheme of salvation, as founded, taught, and practised[sic] by Jesus Christ himself, I never did entertain a solitary doubt . . . A belief in the pure and unadulterated principles of Democracy, is a belief in the religion of our Saviour, as laid down while here upon earth himself—rewarding the virtuous and meritorious without regard to station, to wealth, or distinction of birth. One of the principal tenets laid down in the great scheme of regeneration of man, is Democracy in its purity—that is to say, the just and pure are to be rewarded in heaven with crowns of glory; the unjust and vile sinner is to be punished in a hell "where worm dieth not and the fire is never quenched," each rewarded unto their merits or demerits, upon their own irresponsibility. My religious

creed first, my Democracy next; they are one and inseparably connected. God and my country first—God and my country last.[2]

While this passionate statement may have been motivated only by politics, we nevertheless find here an interesting man who states clearly a belief in some sort of Christianity, but at the same time is willing, for the sake of the Nation, to prevent even those of that same faith from using the United States government to make religious statements or to take dramatic religious stances.

Johnson—who had climbed from being a run away and nearly illiterate tailor's apprentice, to congressman, senator, governor, and finally president—saw that American democracy was a parallel to Christianity and that neither was concerned with where a politician or penitent came from, only with what one's individual merits were. This is a quintessentially American view of both these institutions, and in this, Johnson represents some of the best that these institutions can offer to America. This is not to say that Johnson was some sort of saint: he could be a racist, and, to radical Republicans, he was too soft on the South after the Civil War.

One notable story told by Johnson biographer Hans L. Trefousse recounts a time when Johnson, serving as military governor of Tennessee during the Civil War, called a Methodist minister (Granville Moody) to the capital to pray for the safety of the city and state from encroaching rebels. After a supposedly fervent prayer session between the two men, which even included Johnson's placing his arm around Moody, Johnson stood and said, "Moody, I feel better!" After exchanging some sentences about supporting each other through this difficult and frightening time, Johnson passionately added:

> Oh! Moody, I don't want you to think I have become a religious man because I asked you to pray. I am sorry to say it, but I am not, and have never pretended to be, religious. No one knows this better than you; but, Moody, there is one thing about it—I DO believe in AL-MIGHTY GOD! And I believe also in the Bible, and I say "'d—n'" me, if Nashville shall be surrendered![3]

Rough around the edges, bigoted and flawed, Andrew Johnson was nevertheless extremely loyal to the idea of the Union, endangering all that he had by being the only Southern senator to remain in his seat after secession and by accepting Lincoln's appointment to be military governor of Tennessee. The Republican house rewarded President Johnson with impeachment (though not convicted by the Senate), but the people of Tennessee justified him by voting him back into his own Senate seat. He seemed never to have joined a church, but he also seemed to be at peace at life's end—at peace with his political decisions and with his unreligious faith. Soon after his death, this statement was found in his papers: "I have performed my duty to my God, my country and my family. I have nothing to fear. Approaching death to me is the mere shadow of God's protecting wing."[4]

ULYSSES SIMPSON GRANT 1869-1877

★ ★ ★ ★ ★ ★ ★ ★ ★ ★ ★ ★

On September 30, 1875, President Ulysses S. Grant spoke in Des Moines, Iowa, to a reunion of the Army of the Tennessee. Part of the political climate of the time was the national movement for a religious separation amendment to the U.S. Constitution. As one scholar has written, "Following the Civil War, when the crisis over slavery no longer eclipsed anti-Catholicism, many theological liberals and native Protestants feared that the nation stood on the brink of another great constitutional struggle—this time with the Catholic Church over the principle of separation."[1]

Throughout his life Grant maintained a consistent near-silence on religious matters. In the preface to his *Personal Memoirs*, written at the encouragement of his friend Mark Twain as Grant was dying from cancer and meant to provide some financial comfort for his family, Grant included the words from St. Thomas à Kempis, "Man proposes and God disposes." Grant would not turn to religion again in his *Memoirs*.

Yet, in the political arena, and responding to the anti-Catholic sentiment of the time, in Des Moines, and later the same year in his Annual Message to Congress in December, Grant proposed a constitutional amendment to prevent aid to parochial schools, i.e., Catholic schools. "If we are to have another contest in the near future of our national existence," Grant argued, "I predict that the dividing line will not be Mason and Dixon's, but it will be between patriotism and intelligence on one side, and superstition, ambition and ignorance on the other. Encourage free schools, and resolve that not one dollar appropriated to them shall be applied to the support of any sectarian school . . . Leave the matter of religion to the family altar, the church, and the private school, supported entirely by private contributions. Keep the Church and State forever separate."[2] At least, that is, separate from any undue, unacceptable Catholic influence.

Ulysses S. Grant (born Hiram Ulysses Grant, but when he was appointed to West Point his congressman wrote in "Ulysses S." and that's how it remained) was born on April 27, 1822, in Point Pleasant, Ohio. His parents were nominal Methodists. His mother, Hannah Simpson Grant, was "quietly devout in her Methodism." (She was also a dyed-in-the-wool Democrat—during Grant's eight years as president, she never visited the White House). His parents observed the Sabbath carefully, but did not especially embrace the revivalism of their day as presented primarily by preachers riding circuit in the Western Reserve of Ohio.[3]

Grant's father secured an appointment for his son to West Point, which Grant was reluctant to attend but finally did so since it was his only means to attend college. By no means was Grant a studious cadet, and once received demerits for not attending services at the Episcopal chapel with his company. Grant thought that such forced attendance was anti-republican in spirit.

Grant married Julia Dent on August 22, 1848. She was a lifelong Methodist, and he attended church regularly with her but never joined it or any other church. He never received baptism or made any public confession of faith. They attended church while Grant was president at what was then Metropolitan Methodist Church in Washington, D.C., and after the presidency Grant's wife was a member of Metropolitan Methodist Church of New York City.

Grant thought of God as an impersonal, somewhat removed Providence. At his first inauguration on March 4, 1869, he asked the nation to pray "to Almighty God" for his administration's efforts following the conclusion of the Civil War, and in his Second Inaugural Address of March 4, 1873, he referred again simply to "Providence." He also declared, "I believe that our Great Maker is preparing this world in His own good time to become one nation, speaking one language, and when armies and navies will no longer be required."[4]

Historians and political scientists always rank Grant's presidency near the bottom of effective and ethical administrations. Yet Grant was the only president between Abraham Lincoln and Woodrow Wilson to be elected to two consecutive terms of office. One noted historian has described Grant as the most underrated American in history. As Jean Edward Smith argues, "Grant was condemned because of what he stood for. As president, he fought for black equality long after his countrymen had tired of 'the Negro question.'"[5] In his First Inaugural Address, for example, Grant called for the adoption of the Fifteenth Amendment. He "hated vindictiveness," according to Smith, and no other president "carried on such a determined struggle, against such hopeless odds, to protect the freedmen in the exercise of their constitutional rights."[6]

In his Second Inaugural Address, Grant also addressed the plight of American Indians. "Wars of extermination," he said, "are expensive even against the weakest people, and are demoralizing and wicked. Our superiority of strength and advantages of civilization should make us lenient toward the Indian. The moral view of the question should be considered and the question asked, 'Can not the Indian be made a useful and productive member of society by proper teaching and treatment?' If the effort is made in good faith, we will stand better before the civilized nations of the earth and in our own consciences for having made it."[7]

Grant died on July 23, 1885, and his funeral in New York City "was a testament to national reconciliation."[8] In his dying days in the spring and summer of 1885, a Methodist minister and Bishop, the Reverend J. P. Newman, spent time (uninvited as he was) with Grant, trying to secure some kind of confession of faith from Grant, but without any success.

Shortly after his death, in one of his pockets Julia Grant found a note he had written to her, which read in part, "Look after our children and direct them in the paths of rectitude. It would distress me far more to hear that one of them could depart from an honorable, upright and virtuous life than it would to know that they were prostrated on a bed of sickness from which they were never to arise alive . . . I bid you a final farewell, until we meet in another and, I trust, better world."[9]

RUTHERFORD BIRCHARD HAYES
1877-1881

★ ★ ★ ★ ★ ★ ★ ★ ★ ★ ★ ★

For a time in United States' history, Republicanism and Methodism seemed to go hand in hand. This was certainly the case for the compromise president, Rutherford B. Hayes (who lost the popular vote, but won the presidency by a single electoral college vote and much Republican maneuvering). Perhaps it was because many northern Methodists were abolitionists and the Republican party of the nineteenth century was heavily equated with abolition that the two were so often found together in electoral life. Perhaps there was something about traditional Methodist frugality that resonated with Republican ideals of pro-business fiscal conservatism. Regardless, Hayes attended the Methodist church all of his married life, though unlike his wife, Lucy, he never became a member of the church. Interestingly, and even surprisingly, only about 35 percent of Americans were "communicants" in churches in 1870 compared to 45 percent in 1890, so Hayes was in the majority of those not joining a church.[1] From this we could speculate one of three scenarios: Americans as a whole were not very "religious"; there were not many opportunities to join churches (though some data suggests that even in highly populated areas membership was only 35 percent of the population); or one's lack of a church affiliation did not necessarily dictate one's religious faith, which seems to be the case for Hayes in particular.

Based on Hayes's diary entries, it is clear that not only was he concerned with his personal behavior and contribution to the world, but he also was thoughtful about what he believed. He continually parsed through creeds and verses to try to understand faith and the eternal. In an 1853 diary entry, Hayes writes that he had "been reading Genesis several Sundays, not as a Christian reads for 'spiritual consolation,' 'instruction,' etc., not as an infidel reads to carp and quarrel and criticize, but as one who wishes to be informed and furnished in the earliest and most wonderful of all literary productions."[2] He struggled with the doctrine of God's omnipotence and omniscience, writing in 1845:

> Now it seems to me that Providence interferes no more in the greatest affairs of men than in the smallest, and that neither individuals nor nations are any more the objects of a special interposition of the Divine Ruler than the inanimate things of the world. The Creator gave to every creature of his hand its laws at the time of its creation; and whatever can happen in accordance with those laws He doubtless foresaw, and it cannot be supposed that his laws are so imperfect that special interpositions are necessary to render them capable of fulfilling their design nor that it is possible for them to be violated.[3]

In these last sentences, especially, we see how Hayes's view of Providence varied from many other Christians, but it was certainly not out of the pale for presidents during America's first hundred years of existence. Democratic values also flow through these words suggesting that God cares no more for him, the President of the United States, than for any other human.

Hayes's Christianity, then, is not a complex one, in that the fineries of theology and dogma do not seem to play much of a role. He read the Bible, he went to church, he tried to act like Christ. Hayes wrote to his future wife in

1851 about the way he understood his Christianity (it appears he is addressing some concern she may have had, since she seemed to be fairly orthodox):

> The test of Christianity is the state of the heart and its affections, not the state of a man's intellectual belief. If a man feels the humility becoming one prone to sinfulness, looks above for assistance, repents of what he does that is wrong, aspires to purity of intention and correctness of conduct in all the relations of life, such a man is a Christian, for he adopts the spirit of Christ's teaching and imitates his example—this, too, in spite of his faith—whether it be Calvinistic, Unitarian, Universalist, or Papist. That I can comprehend. The half of the orthodox creeds I don't understand and can't fully believe.[4]

Certainly there are many who would say that Hayes could not have been a Christian because he did not subscribe to a creed. But we also have seen that the definitions of "Christian" vary greatly during that time in our nation's history and today.

While president, Hayes instituted, for the first time, a Sunday-evening hymn sing at the White House, at which guests would be given hymnals and all would sing hymns like "Majestic Sweetness Sits Enthroned" and "Tell Me the Old, Old Story."[5] This may, of course, have been due to Mrs. Hayes's influence, for it is well known that she was responsible for banning alcohol from White House events (earning her the nickname "Lemonade Lucy"), but neither of these White House actions were against the President's will. Hayes's choice not to join a church was probably not for any political concern, but instead, a matter of conscience, (since he was willing for all to know that he participated in hymn-singing outside the church).

A few months before his death, Hayes wrote to his cousin Mary Fitch, a missionary to Shanghai, saying, "The teachings of Christ, meaning his words as interpreted by Himself in his life and deeds, are in truth the way of salvation. Wishing and striving to do this I know I am safe."[6] He was writing in response, perhaps, to her concern for his eternal state. In an 1893 diary entry (just days before his death), Hayes summed up the state of his spirit both for himself, and possibly to those he knew would one day read his private words: "I am a Christian, according to my conscience, in belief, not, of course, in character and conduct, but in purpose and wish; not, of course, by the orthodox standard. But I am content and have a feeling of trust and safety. Let me be pure and wise and kind and true in all things."[7]

JAMES ABRAM GARFIELD
1881

★ ★ ★ ★ ★ ★ ★ ★ ★ ★ ★ ★

James Abram Garfield is the only American president who was also a minister. Upon being elected to the presidency in 1880, Garfield left the ministry, declaring, "I resign the highest office in the land to become president of the United States."[1]

Garfield's presidency is one of our least remembered ones, in large measure simply because it was one of our briefest ones. Garfield was shot roughly four months into his term in office, on July 2, 1881, at Union Station as he was traveling to Williams College for a class reunion. He died several months later, on September 19, 1881.

Garfield was born November 19, 1831, in Orange, Ohio. His parents joined the Disciples of Christ denomination when Garfield was less than one year old, and when Garfield was two his father died. His mother, Eliza, would daily read the Bible and sing hymns to her young son. At one point early in life Garfield attended a Baptist church, where he liked to argue with congregants about their theology, particularly, as he saw things, their strongly held, Calvinistic doctrine of damnation. On March 4, 1850, at the age of eighteen, as an Ohio schoolteacher, he wrote, "Today I was buried with Christ in baptism and arose to walk in newness of life."[2] That day he was baptized into the Disciples of Christ or Church of Christ. Throughout his twenties and into his thirties, he would preach and hold revivals until he went to Congress in 1863, where he would serve for eighteen years before entering the White House in 1881.

In 1857, Garfield delivered a sermon, "The Material and the Spiritual," in which he urged his listeners "to follow Him, not as the Nazarene, the Man of Galilee, the carpenter's son, but as the ever living spiritual person, full of love and compassion, who will stand by you in life and death and eternity."[3] As a Campbellite (after Thomas and Alexander Campell, the founders of Disciples of Christ), especially until the time of the Civil War, when he began to move away from some of the tenets of the church, Garfield considered himself an orthodox Christian. He believed in the divinity of Christ and traditional Protestant Christianity, with an emphasis on adult baptism, reason over mere emotion, and a central focus on the Bible rather than detailed creedal affirmations. Garfield was considered a zealous believer, often engaging in theological disputes with Baptists, Methodists, and Presbyterians. At one point he argued in favor of the proposition, "Christians should not participate in political or governmental affairs."[4]

In 1880, he was nominated for president by the Republican Party on the thirty-ninth ballot; he was elected over Winfield Hancock by less than 1 percent of the popular vote. At his inauguration on March 4, 1881, Garfield's Bible was opened to Proverbs 21:1: "The king's heart is in the hand of the Lord, as the rivers of water: he turneth it whithersoever he will." Among other subjects, his inaugural address focused on the nature of the Union following the Civil War, which Garfield had seen as a holy crusade, given his strong anti-slavery views; it also focused on the need for education. As he said, in referencing Isaiah 11:6, "Let our people find a new meaning in the divine oracle which declares that 'a little child shall lead them,' for our own little children will soon control the destinies of the Republic."[5]

Most interesting of all the subjects he spoke to in his inaugural address, however, was the issue of religious freedom, and in particular, how it was defined in the late nineteenth century with respect to the free exercise of religion and the Church of Jesus Christ of Latter-Day Saints (Mormons). According to Garfield, "The Constitution guarantees absolute religious freedom."[6] However, in Garfield's eyes, "The Mormon Church not only offends the moral sense of manhood by sanctioning polygamy, but prevents the administration of justice through ordinary instrumentalities of the law. In my judgment, it is the duty of Congress, while respecting to the uttermost the conscientious convictions and religious scruples of every citizen, to prohibit within its jurisdiction all criminal practices, especially of that class which destroy the family relations and endanger social order. Nor can any ecclesiastical organization be safely permitted to usurp in the smallest degree the functions and powers of the National Government."[7]

Clearly Garfield's opinion echoed that of most Americans, and reflected the Free Exercise Clause that had become federal law in the ruling in 1879 of *Reynolds v. United States*. Garfield ended his inaugural by invoking "the support and blessings of Almighty God."[8] Such blessings, however, did not extend equally to all Americans.

CHESTER ALAN ARTHUR 1881-1885

Chester A. Arthur came to Washington as a result of political maneuvering and compromise resulting from a power battle between New York's Senator Roscoe Conkling and President Rutherford B. Hayes. When Conkling's Republican machine could not get Ulysses S. Grant (a friend of Conkling's political machine and spoils system) nominated for the presidency again, the Conkling faction settled on having Arthur nominated as the vice president. By July of 1881 (the very year of President Garfield's inauguration), the compromise vice president, Chester Arthur, became President of the United States after the assassination of President Garfield. For the following four years President Chester Arthur worked to reform the American civil service (though it still had many problems), and apparently Arthur left office fairly well respected. Arthur did allow his name to be considered for the Republican nomination in 1884, but he was not nominated (the last sitting president not to be nominated by his party), partly due to his poor campaigning (which, in turn, may have been partially a result of his quickly failing health). More than anything, Arthur will probably be remembered for his connections with the presidential spoils system that was in place at least since the presidency of Andrew Jackson.

Chester Arthur grew up in a very religious home—his father was an anti-slavery, Irish Baptist preacher who "clung to his pulpit and preached the doctrines of Christianity, but was ever ready to extend the right hand of fellowship to . . . any other anti-slavery lecturer in the country."[1] Like so many pastors and missionaries serving early evangelical Christian churches, Arthur's parents moved from parish to parish and were always one step from total economic disaster. Especially in their later years, there was little monetary support for the aging Arthurs, yet both Chester and his brother, William, seemed to feel as though the church not only gave their parents little, but that their parents gave everything they had in service to the church, leaving little time and energy for the family. Perhaps that is why, according to biographer Thomas C. Reeves, the two sons were estranged from their parents and hostile to their parents' faith.[2] While Chester Arthur went to church fairly regularly with his wife, it was the church of the establishment, the Episcopal Church, that he attended—a far cry from the Baptist faith of his parents. This never stopped Arthur's mother, Malvina Arthur, from pleading in long letters to her sons that they once again "accept the Truth" of the faith of their childhood.[3]

Like many Washington presidents before him, President Arthur attended St. John's Episcopal Church. Also like many other presidents, he never joined any church, but he did pay for a stained-glass window to be placed in St. John's Episcopal in remembrance of his wife who had died before he took office. He asked that it be installed on the south side of the church so that he could see it from the White House.[4] During his swearing in as president by the Chief Justice of the Supreme Court, Arthur had the Bible opened to the thirty-first Psalm and "reverently kissed the page," choosing that psalm because it "reminded him of the Te Deum, which his wife . . . frequently sang in the Episcopal choir."[5]

Another interesting and nearly private religious moment in Arthur's life may provide a deeper look into his heart; the event occurred near the end of his presidency, indeed the end of his life. Arthur was on a recreational trip to Florida, spending a great deal of time by himself, mostly fishing. In St. Augustine on one particular Sunday, Arthur attended, apparently without fanfare, three different churches: Episcopal, Catholic, and African-American Methodist.[6] His wife was gone, his children and aides elsewhere, yet Chester Arthur went to church three times, and at the African-American church there wasn't a single person who could be considered a constituent, so Arthur seems to have sought the spiritual, not the material. It also appears that he had a deep reverence for Christianity, even if not for the Christianity of his parents. Perhaps since all of America knew about Arthur's darker political machinations in New York, he did not want to appear to be using religion as a means of dressing up himself or his legacy as president. But when alone, whether in the White House and looking at the window reminding him of Ellen or in the farthest southern tip of America, Chester Arthur sought something of value (peace, comfort, grace) in church and faith. Ironically, it was on this trip to Florida that Arthur contracted malaria, further weakening him and advancing the mortal kidney disease he had been nursing for so long.

GROVER CLEVELAND
1885-1889, 1893-1897

★ ★ ★ ★ ★ ★ ★ ★ ★ ★ ★ ★

"Grover Cleveland" is the answer to an easily missed presidential trivia question: "Who is the only president to serve two non-consecutive terms?" Stephen Grover Cleveland (he was named after a close family friend who was a minister) was elected in 1884 in a very tight contest with James G. Blaine. Four years later voters ousted Cleveland in favor of the Civil War hero Benjamin Harrison, even though Harrison received fewer popular votes, and in an 1892 rematch with Harrison, Cleveland prevailed and returned to the White House. His timing was less than impressive, however, for in the same year that Cleveland began his second term, the country would face The Panic of 1893, an economic depression, and Cleveland would battle his own personal crisis with cancer. He would undergo a serious, secretive surgery for a cancerous growth in his mouth, a surgery the public would not discover for over two decades.[1]

When Cleveland was elected in 1884 he was the first Democrat elected since James Buchanan in 1856, and his presidency stands out, in part, because in the period between Abraham Lincoln and Theodore Roosevelt, noteworthy presidents were rare. Cleveland, although not really a national figure at the time of his first presidential race, was a highly experienced politician, whose offices ranged from county sheriff and assistant district attorney of Erie County, New York, to mayor of Buffalo and then Governor of New York State. He argued that the presidency was invested with powers meant to be used, not surrendered or kept in reserve. Upon entering the White House in 1885, he also lamented, "I look upon the four years to come as a dreadful self-inflicted penance for the good of my country."[2]

Cleveland's father, Richard Cleveland, was a Presbyterian minister, as was his brother, William. His father was a graduate of Yale and Princeton Theological Seminary. (He himself had next to no formal education, yet read for the law, apprenticed in a law office, and then started a legal career in New York.) The second president after Chester Arthur to have a minister father, Cleveland once said, "I have always felt that my training as a minister's son has been more valuable to me than any other incident of my life."[3] Unfortunately, he did not elaborate to any length about the principles or lessons derived from this fact and how they applied to his political ascendancy.

Cleveland was a lifelong Presbyterian; he joined the church during his father's pastorate in Fayetteville, New York, and while in the White House he attended First Presbyterian Church (later National Presbyterian) in Washington, D.C. When he was elected in 1884, he was a 47-year old-bachelor, but in a June 2, 1886, ceremony in the Blue Room of the White House, Cleveland married Francis Folsom, 28 years his junior. The wedding was performed by the minister of First Presbyterian. Grover and Francis would have five children, yet one daughter, Ruth, died in 1904 of diphtheria. In his diary on January 15, 1904, Cleveland wrote, "God has come to my help and I am able to adjust my thought to dear Ruth's death with as much comfort as selfish humanity will permit."[4]

Cleveland's opponents in the 1884 presidential race attempted to discredit him with charges of immoral behavior on his part. Specifically, allegations in newspapers stated he had fathered an illegitimate child in the 1870s. He refused to either admit or deny paternity. Some alleged he was covering up for a married friend who may have fathered the child with the woman who was "known" to more than a few men in Buffalo. To his friends and campaign aides, he simply advised, if they were asked about the charges, "Just tell the truth." Cleveland did help out with financial contributions to the child who later was adopted and enjoyed a successful life. The whole sordid mess and campaign allegations would, in part, lead to a rather memorable campaign ditty: "Ma, ma, where's my Pa? Gone to the White House, ha, ha, ha."[5]

At each of his inaugurals Cleveland used the family Bible, one inscribed to him by his mother. His religious rhetoric in each inaugural address was typical of the time period. On March 4, 1885, Cleveland concluded his relatively brief remarks with this sentence, "And let us not trust to human effort alone, but humbly acknowledging the power and goodness of Almighty God, who presides over the destiny of nations, and who has at all times been revealed in our country's history, let us invoke His aid and His blessing upon on labours."[6]

On March 4, 1893, Cleveland delivered his inaugural address for his second term, in which he declared, "Above all, I know there is a Supreme Being who rules the affairs of men and whose goodness and mercy have always followed the American people, and I know He will not turn from us now if we humbly and reverently seek His powerful aid."[7] In this same address, Cleveland warned the public about an "exaggerated confidence in our country's greatness," about "the unwholesome progeny of paternalism," and "the waste of public money" should people "regard frugality and economy as virtues which we may safely outgrow." And, perhaps most insightful (even controversial for the day, given that *Plessy v. Ferguson* is only three years away) is Cleveland's counsel, "Loyalty to the principles upon which our Government rests positively demands that the equality before the law which it guarantees to every citizen should be justly and in good faith conceded in all parts of the land. The enjoyment of this right follows the badge of citizenship wherever found, and, unimpaired by race or color, it appeals for recognition to American manliness and fairness."[8]

During his presidency, Cleveland issued the standard, expected proclamations for Thanksgiving and other public occasions. What is perhaps most interesting about his political faith and religious convictions is what we find in his annual messages to Congress. Cleveland subscribed fully to the established consensus concerning the duty to "civilize" American Indians, and also to protect the country from the then-widely pronounced (and prosecuted) protests against the Mormon Church. It was his hope that he could protect the public from the violence threatening both Mormons and public order, as he saw it and especially to protect Americans from the practice of polygamy. For instance, in his December 8, 1885, annual message to Congress, Cleveland went to some length to describe "the Mormon question" as a grave threat to the American experiment. According to Cleveland, whether one believed in or practiced polygamy, the threat was the same, "Thus is the strange spectacle presented of a community protected by a republican form of government, to which they owe allegiance, sustaining by their suffrages a principle and a belief which set at naught that obligation of absolute obedience to the law of the land which lies at the foundation of republican institutions."[9]

With respect to members of the Church of Jesus Christ of Latter-Day Saints, Cleveland was much less tolerant or understanding than he was toward those who practiced or counseled discrimination against Asian or African Americans. Cleveland tried to distinguish between what he called "race prejudice" with respect to hostility and violence against Chinese and Japanese in the United States, and what he considered legitimate prosecution of those in Utah and elsewhere who threatened, as Cleveland saw it, the very existence of the country itself. Cleveland pictured the peril as so menacing that he argued, "There should be no relaxation in the firm but just execution of the law now in operation, and I should be glad to approve such further discreet legislation as will rid the country of this blot upon its fair name. Since the people upholding polygamy in our Territories are reinforced [sic] by immigration from other lands, I recommend that a law be passed to prevent the importation of Mormons into the country."[10]

Cleveland was both responding to and trying to develop public opinion with such comments and recommendations. The Supreme Court of the United States, for example, in its decision in 1879 of *Reynolds v. United States* already had concluded that the federal government had vast powers to attack polygamy and in effect turn Mormons into second-class citizens, at the least. And the Court, Congress, and overwhelming public opinion viewed polygamy if not the Church itself as a dire and direct threat to the progress of American civilization. Cleveland clearly reflected that political and religious consensus of his time. At least on this issue, Cleveland's presidency is an instructive case study for how an occupant of the Oval Office attempts to construct public policy (and his presidency) around his political and religious faiths.

BENJAMIN HARRISON
1889-1893

★ ★ ★ ★ ★ ★ ★ ★ ★ ★ ★

There is little doubt about Benjamin Harrison's religious beliefs, about his religious education, or about his religious practices. He was reared in a very religious Presbyterian home in which religion was a critical part of life—especially on Sundays, when his family strictly honored the Sabbath by prohibiting secular and rambunctious activities (such as the playing of games; even letter-writing was forbidden). According to Harry Joseph Seivers, author of *Benjamin Harrison: Hoosier Warrior* and *Benjamin Harrison: Hoosier Statesman,* the Harrison children looked forward to the day, especially to the family hymn-singing that lasted from four until bed time.[1] In fact, later on, Harrison's faculty and peers at the then-struggling tiny school, Miami University, considered Harrison to be very religious. And, according to

115

Seivers, the faculty even thought that destiny would call Harrison into the Presbyterian clergy. This desire for service in the church was not merely something that came from his upbringing, however. Apparently Harrison experienced a significant religious conversion experience at a revival while he was a student; it was there he made a decision to be an active Christian.[2]

During his time at Miami, Harrison fell in love with Caroline Scott, the daughter of a Presbyterian minister (and founder of a college for women), and married her after his graduation. Just prior to his admittance to the Indiana bar (at the age of twenty), Harrison was still struggling with the desire to become a Presbyterian clergyman, but the familial push toward the law and, eventually, toward civil service won his time. Nevertheless, throughout his entire adult life Harrison was dedicated to serving the Presbyterian Church and those outside the church, especially frontier children, young men, and settlers. By the age of twenty-eight, Harrison was elected elder (a position he held until his death), and, according to the minutes of his local presbytery, "he became a teacher in the Sabbath School, he was constant in his attendance on church services; his voice was heard in prayer meetings; he labored for and with young men, especially in the Y.M.C.A. And, in whatever way opened, whether public or private, he gave testimony for his faith and the lordship of his Master."[3]

Like many of his predecessors, Harrison (the great-grandson of William Henry Harrison) worked to bring more of North America into the United States, and he worked diligently to open western lands to American settlers. It was during his presidency that the U.S. Army horribly slaughtered Sioux women, children, and elderly at Wounded Knee. Furthermore, Oklahoma Indian Territory opened, through violence and coercion, to white settlers while Harrison was in office.

We cannot say for certain how much or how little Harrison's religious life and beliefs affected his presidency, but the powerful belief in unwavering, undeniable destiny that is a central aspect of traditional Presbyterianism would allow for and inform Harrison's pursuit of manifest destiny and belief in American exceptionalism. In his inaugural address, Harrison echoed the ideas of his political forebears concerning God's dealings with America by saying,

> God has placed upon our head a diadem and has laid at our feet power
> and wealth beyond definition or calculation. But we must not forget

that we take these gifts upon the condition that justice and mercy shall hold the reins of power and that the upward avenues of hope shall be free to all the people.

However, "all the people" did not have access to justice and mercy, to "avenues of hope." While Harrison was a man of clear religious conviction and practice, he was also, like so many of us, a pragmatic actor in a political world.

WILLIAM McKINLEY
1897-1901

★ ★ ★ ★ ★ ★ ★ ★ ★ ★ ★

"My belief embraces the Divinity of Christ and a recognition of Christianity as the mightiest factor in the world's civilization."[1] These words of William McKinley from May 26, 1899, express clearly and succinctly his foundational and fundamental religious faith. Born into a Methodist family in Ohio, raised a Methodist, baptized a Methodist, and buried a Methodist, McKinley has long and widely been considered one of our most religiously devout presidents.

McKinley was born January 29, 1843, in Niles, Ohio, the seventh of nine children. His parents were Methodists; his father was a strong abolitionist, and his mother, Nancy Alison McKinley, had a profound impact on her son. She had high hopes he would become a Methodist bishop. While McKinley did not help his mother realize this particu-

119

lar ambition, he did remain in the Methodist church his entire life, and was an active, influential member, engaging in practices including Sunday school teacher, member of the Epworth League, trustee of the First Methodist Church of Canton, Ohio, and strongly endorsing Methodist missionary efforts abroad.

In Ohio, McKinley attended a revival at the age of ten and became a probationary member of the Methodist church, and about five years later, before he left to attend Allegheny College in Pennsylvania, he joined the Poland, Ohio, Methodist Church. In his youth he regularly attended church and Sunday school and midweek prayer meetings, and he and his family conducted daily prayer and Bible readings. After he married Ida Saxton in 1871, they joined the First Methodist Episcopal Church of Canton, Ohio, where he was active in various church activities, including Sunday school superintendent. He and his wife had two daughters, neither of whom survived to adulthood: the oldest died when she was five, and the youngest lived less than five months. At one point, the American Protective Association, a Know-Nothing-like group of the mid to late nineteenth century, claimed that McKinley and his wife actually had two children in a Roman Catholic convent, that his father was buried in a Roman Catholic cemetery, and that McKinley himself was a closet Catholic taking orders from a Catholic bishop. McKinley simply ignored the outlandish and clearly false accusations. (If anything, in his 1896 presidential campaign against William Jennings Bryan, a rather godly man himself, such obnoxious, anti-Catholic allegations against McKinley rallied Catholic support to his candidacy.)

In his first Inaugural Address on March 4, 1897 (having defeated Bryan in a relatively close election), McKinley stated, "Our faith teaches that there is no safer reliance than upon the God of our fathers who has so singularly favored the American people in every national trial, and who will not forsake us so long as we obey His commandments and walk humbly in His footsteps."[2] Near the end of his speech, after repeating the presidential oath, McKinley declared, "This is the obligation I have reverently taken before the Lord Most High. To keep it will be my single purpose, my common prayer."[3] McKinley's language here clearly is both similar to and different from other inaugural addresses, in that he invoked a God who primarily blesses the American experiment, although McKinley does insert the conditional "so long as we obey." He also offered the rarely used, somewhat exclusionary "Lord Most High" language, reflecting his orthodox Christianity and his apparent assumption, not unfounded at that point in the late nineteenth century, that others held to similar beliefs in a largely Protestant, culturally Christian America.

At his first inaugural, McKinley's Bible was open to 2 Chronicles 1:10, and Solomon's prayer, "Give me now wisdom and knowledge, that I may go out and come in before this people: for who can judge this thy people, that is so great?" At his second inaugural, on March 4, 1901, after defeating Bryan a second time in a contest not nearly as close as the first, McKinley's Bible was open to Proverbs 16:21-22, "The preparations of the heart in man, and the answer of the tongue, is from the Lord . . . A man's heart deviseth his way: but the Lord directeth his steps." In his Second Inaugural Address, he reverted to the more tradition-laden references to "Almighty God" and "the fear of God" as the country sought its way in a largely new environment of internationalism, interventionism, war, and yet still hoping for what McKinley called "the reign of peace to be made permanent by a government of liberty under law."[4]

In other speeches and private remarks, McKinley conveyed his apparently deep and sincere conviction that God destined America for great and lasting accomplishments, and that central to the American mission was assisting others in the acquisition of peace and prosperity. For example, during his presidency, the United States would engage in war with Spain over Cuba and the Philippines, and would acquire those lands and their inhabitants, along with Puerto Rico. McKinley was not an early advocate of war or what he saw as intervention abroad on humanitarian grounds. He was our last president to serve in the Civil War, having survived the battle at Antietam. As he told one military figure, "I shall never get into a war until I am sure that God and man approve. I have been through one war; I have seen the dead piled up; and I do not want to see another."[5] Nonetheless, war with Spain did come in 1898, in part precipitated by McKinley's sending the battleship *Maine* to the Havana harbor early in 1898. In his address to Congress on December 6, 1897, McKinley argued that *if* the U.S. were ever to "intervene with force, it shall be without fault on our part and only because the necessity for such action will be so clear as to command the support and approval of the civilized world."[6]

After the Spanish-American war ended with the signing of the Treaty of Paris (whereby we purchased the Philippines for $20 million), McKinley stated that the U.S. would work "in every way in our power to make these people whom Providence has brought within our jurisdiction feel that it is their liberty and not our power, their welfare, and not our gain, we are seeking to enhance. Our flag has never waved over any community but in blessing."[7]

McKinley's words lack the awareness of and appreciation for the historically, theologically contingent we find in the words of Lincoln; they reflect the all-too-commonly expressed belief that somehow, to borrow from Reinhold Niebuhr, America is "the darling of divine Providence."[8]

McKinley, as did almost all of his predecessors in the presidency, issued annual Thanksgiving Day Proclamations. What made his a bit unusual was his use of more restrictive religious rhetoric. In 1897, he called on Americans "to praise the Lord in a spirit of humility and gratitude,"[9] and in 1898 he asked the country to extend "praise to the Lord of Hosts."[10] In October of 1900, after the devastation of Galveston, Texas, by a horrific hurricane, McKinley argued that even that "tragic visitation" clearly demonstrated "the sentiments of sympathy and Christian charity by virtue of which was our one united people."[11] As a result, he concluded, the people should offer "praise to Him who holds the nations in the hollow of His hand."[12]

It has been argued that the process "by which McKinley decided what the United States should do with the Philippines is one of the most explicit examples of how a president's faith influenced a major policy decision."[13] It is said that on November 21, 1899, five Methodists from the denomination's General Missionary Committee met at the White House with the President. As the meeting was about to adjourn, McKinley is said to have conceded to his fellow believers that he had struggled greatly over what to do with the islands. "The truth is I didn't want them, and when they came to us as a gift from the gods, I did not know what to do with them." So, McKinley continued, after asking for counsel from others with no great success, "I walked the floor of the White House night after night until midnight; and I am not ashamed to tell you, gentlemen, that I went on my knees and prayed to Almighty God for light and guidance more than one night." He told them it was revealed to him that the U.S. had to purchase the archipelago in order to "educate the Filipinos, and uplift and civilize and Christianize them, and by God's grace do the very best we could by them, as our fellow-men for whom Christ also died."[14] Some scholars generally accept this account on its face; others are dubious at best. Two scholars argue that the five Methodists there that day never refuted the account published after McKinley's assassination. And, of course, McKinley did not survive to confirm or deny the veracity of the event. Perhaps about the most that can be said is that the remarks do bear similarity to McKinley's evangelical religious and political beliefs and motivations, and to remarks offered in other contexts, as in a speech in South Dakota on October 14, 1899, where he stated that the Philippines fell "into our lap," due to the "Providence of God, who works in mysterious ways."[15]

On Friday, September 6, 1901, McKinley spoke at the Pan-American Exposition in Buffalo, New York. While greeting people following his speech, he was shot twice by an anarchist, Leon Czolgosz. McKinley, fearing for the assassin's life, raised his hand and pleaded, "Let no one hurt him; may God forgive him." McKinley seemed to get better, then began to fail, and before he died on September 14, 1901, he prayed the Lord's Prayer, and uttered some of the words of his favorite hymn "Nearer, My God, to Thee." Reporters present wrote that his last words were, "Good-bye all, good-bye. It is God's way. His will, not ours, be done."[16] One member of Congress predicted that McKinley's death would be remembered as the most Christ-like death since Calvary.

THEODORE ROOSEVELT
1901-1909

★ ★ ★ ★ ★ ★ ★ ★ ★ ★ ★ ★

No doubt Theodore Roosevelt is one of the most iconic American Presidents, a man who has reached virtually mythical proportions (given his face is engraved on Mt. Rushmore). He is credited with almost single-handedly crafting the American identity of rugged individualism, supporting a robust international political role for the United States, and invigorating the movement to see America's historical and natural legacies protected for posterity, so integral to shaping a national character and sense of history. In so many ways Theodore Roosevelt has come to embody (in his own life and in the popular imagination) so much that we see as "American," yet there is one aspect of his personality that rarely enters into the discussion of this youngest president—his religious life and faith. This absence of a sense of Roosevelt's religion is interesting because it may say something more about us as Americans, what we find to be truly important in a president, than it says about Theodore Roosevelt's life or personality. In other words, there were other issues that were important to Americans during the first part of the twentieth century that took precedence over presidential religious affiliation or orthodoxy. Simply put, Roosevelt's religion was part of his life and helped define how he understood the world. The way in which his religious faith shaped his actions was that he saw Christianity as a faith for the strong, and he believed that Providence shaped the world—a Providence that was just, harsh, and deterministic. Some of the ways Roosevelt understood God were shaped by his religious affiliation, naturally (Dutch Reformed), but it seems that much of the way he understood religion was shaped more by the way he understood the world, rather than the other way around.

From his youngest childhood days, Theodore Roosevelt seemed to understand that God was on his side and, therefore, on the side of the United States. His sister Corinne recounts a tale told to her by their caretaker/aunt about Roosevelt as a child during the Civil War (when he was about four years old). This aunt said she once overheard the boy praying to his God, "and feeling that she would not dare interrupt his petition to the Almighty, [Roosevelt] would call down in baby tones and with bent head the wrath of the Almighty upon the rebel troops." She said that she "could never forget the fury in the childish voice when he would plead with Divine Providence to 'grind the Southern troops to powder.'"[1] In his voluminous autobiography, Roosevelt writes much about his influences, about his depth and breadth of reading, but he does not recount devotional, theological, or religious texts as being among those interests; this does not suggest that they did not enter his life or mind, but they were not in the forefront of how he defined himself. Yet Roosevelt is perfectly willing in his nearly 600 pages of self-description to prescribe reading, exercise, and diet regimens for his young readers—none of which include devotional texts or spiritual practices. His sister does recount, however, that the young Roosevelt enjoyed hearing Unitarian preaching while he was a student at Harvard.

Theodore Roosevelt's religion seems to echo his understanding of the way the world works, that God helps those who work to be strong, that God is an arbiter of justice, and that God has chosen America to be a grand actor in the world. His faith, according to one author, was in a "muscular Christianity," a religion of confidence and of action,[2] not a religion of "young Christians with shoulders that slope like a champagne bottle."[3] This is not to say that Roosevelt's religion was incorrect, was in some way unorthodox. Rather, there is a practical nature to the ways he understands religion—that it has no place in his world if it is only preparing one for the next world. Spiritual battles were about right actions, about weakness and strength, not about only the intangible. To the poet E. A. Robinson, Roosevelt wrote quite thoughtfully about battles with temptation, about battles against the self:

> There is not one among us, in whom a devil does not dwell; at some time, on some point, that devil masters each of us; he who has never failed has not been tempted; but the man who does in the end conquer, who does painfully retrace the steps of his slipping, why he shows that he has been tried in the fire and not found wanting. It is not having been in the Dark House, but having left it, that counts.[4]

Salvation is what one works out, as God demands of us, in Roosevelt's view.

Accordingly, Theodore Roosevelt did see a formative role for religion to play in the national life, not necessarily a role leading to national or individual salvation, but religion (and Christianity in particular) that makes for a better world. To another poet, Frederic Mistral, Roosevelt outlines his beliefs in the nation's soul:

> Factories and railways are good up to a certain point, but courage and endurance, love of wife and child, love of home and country, love of lover for sweetheart, love of beauty in man's work and in nature, love and emulation of daring and of lofty endeavour [sic], the homely work-a-day virtues and the heroic virtues—these are better still, and if they are lacking, no piled-up riches, no roaring, clanging industrialism, no feverish and many-sided activity shall avail either the individual or the nation. I do not undervalue these things of a nation's body; I only desire that they shall not make us forget that beside the nation's body there is also the nation's soul.[5]

Furthermore, religion served as a means by which one became American, became a joiner in the traditions of Washington, Adams, Jefferson. To *The Ladies' Home Journal* in 1917, Roosevelt wrote:

> Therefore, on Sunday go to church. Yes, I know all the excuses; I know that one can worship the Creator and dedicate oneself to good living in a grove of trees or by a running brook or in one's own house just as well as in a church, but I also know that as a matter of cold fact, the average man does not thus worship or thus dedicate himself. If he stays away from church he does not spend his time in good works or in lofty meditation.
>
> ... Besides, even if he does not hear a good sermon, the probabilities are that he will listen to and take part in reading some beautiful passages from the Bible, and if he is not familiar with the Bible, he has suffered a loss which he had better make all possible haste to correct. ... I advocate a man's joining in church work for the sake of showing his faith by his works; I leave to professional theologians the settlement of this question, whether he is to achieve his salvation by his works or by faith which is only genuine if it expresses itself in works. Micah's insistence upon love and mercy, and doing justice and walking humbly with the Lord's will, should suffice if lived up to. ... Let the man not think overmuch of saving his own soul. That will come of itself, if he tries in good earnest to look after his neighbor both in soul and in body—remembering always that he had better leave his neighbor alone rather than show arrogance and lack of tactfulness in the effort to help him. The church on the other hand must fit itself for the practical betterment of mankind if it is to attract and retain the fealty of the men best worth holding and using.[6]

Roosevelt seemed to understand religion's role as a societal institution, as a shaper of character, conscience, and polity. In his public pronouncements, then, Roosevelt seemed comfortable discussing religion in American life, as it directly affected American life in a measurable way. However, in keeping with most of his presidential predecessors, we hear or read little from Roosevelt about Jesus, about spirituality or prayer, about individual devotion to God. Roosevelt's religion seems to be a civil religion, drawing from the language and imagery of Christianity.

Theodore Roosevelt's understanding of Christianity, particularly as it intersected with political life and international affairs, seemed to focus more on how one fails or succeeds on one's own merits, as opposed to trying to draw on God's grace and mercy, or on God's desire that we be merciful and gracious to one another. For instance, when referring to the horrifying Turkish genocide of Armenians, Roosevelt blamed the Armenians for their own suffering and blamed the world's powers for their focus on peace through disarmament rather than punishing unrighteous nations, writing, "It is almost useless to attempt to argue with these well-intentioned persons, because they are suffering under an obsession and are not open to reason. They go wrong at the outset, for they lay all the emphasis on peace and none at all on righteousness."[7]

Once again we come to a president about whom we know a great deal, but we have no way of really understanding his relationship with Jesus Christ, or his individual faith. Roosevelt went to church regularly (to the Episcopal church of his second wife while away from Washington, to the Dutch Reformed Church while at the capital); read the Bible; preached the doctrine of God's working through the self-determined; was more concerned about Marxism's effects on individual autonomy and ambition than about its atheism;[8] believed in protecting the truly powerless from the powerful. But his religion seemed to be one of works, rather than faith. Yet as Roosevelt suggested, perhaps we should leave these distinctions between "true" Christians and "cultural" Christians to the theologians, assuming they are better judges than we. When Theodore Roosevelt was first inaugurated as president, the Bible on which he laid his hand while taking the oath of office was opened to Micah 6:8, "He hath shewed thee, O man, what is good; and what doth the LORD require of thee, but to do justly, and to love mercy, and to walk humbly with God?"[9]

WILLIAM HOWARD TAFT
1909-1913

★ ★ ★ ★ ★ ★ ★ ★ ★ ★ ★ ★

William Howard Taft's presidency suffers by comparison, in that his administration is sandwiched between Theodore Roosevelt and Woodrow Wilson. It is not completely surprising that Taft's presidency is not particularly remarkable, for Taft's motivating ambition was not to occupy the White House. Rather, his overarching desire was to be a member of the United States Supreme Court, which he once said was his idea of what heaven must be like. Of course, Taft eventually would not only join the Court, he would be its chief justice from 1921 to 1930, nominated for the High Court by President Harding. Taft is the only person in U.S. history to have served as president and chief justice.

Taft was the last president who was a Unitarian, and his church affiliation often caused controversy and no small amount of duress for Taft. At various times his life in and outside the political arena was buffeted by allegations of atheism or at least lack of sufficient religious orthodoxy. In the presidential campaign of 1908, when William Jennings Bryan was his opponent, one fundamentalist religious newspaper opined, "Think of the United States with a President who does not believe that Jesus Christ was the Son of God but looks upon our immaculate Savior as a common bastard and low, cunning imposter."[1] Taft's reply was a measured and most thoughtful one: "Of course I am interested in the spread of Christian civilization, but to go into a dogmatic discussion of creed I will not do whether I am defeated or not . . . If the American electorate is so narrow as not to elect a Unitarian, well and good, I can stand it."[2]

On June 17, 1908, an article in the *New York Times* was titled, "Taft as a Churchman: Belongs to Unitarian Church of Cincinnati, and Has a Pew in Washington."

Taft was born in Cincinnati on September 15, 1857, and his parents were active Unitarians there in the Western Unitarian Conference Church, where young Will or "Big Lub" as he known by his friends, attended the church Sunday school. In 1886 Taft married Helen "Nellie" Herron, whose mother was Unitarian, yet Nellie was Episcopalian. She and Taft would have four children, each of whom was raised in the Episcopalian church of their mother, while Taft remained a lifelong, faithful and active Unitarian. While president, Taft would attend and become a member of All Souls Unitarian Church in Washington, D.C. This is the church where his funeral was held after his death on March 8, 1930.

Taft's resume before becoming president was an enviable one. After graduating second in his class at Yale, he attended and graduated from the University of Cincinnati Law School, and then launched a lengthy career in public service, ranging from assistant prosecutor of Hamilton County to solicitor general under President Benjamin Harrison, then federal appellate judge on the newly created Sixth District of the United States Court of Appeals, to professor of law and dean of the University of Cincinnati Law School, to civil governor of the Philippines, and then secretary of war under President Roosevelt beginning in 1904. In this latter post, Taft essentially was a foreign policy ambassador-at-large for Roosevelt, handling issues from Russia to Cuba to the supervision of initial work on the Panama Canal.

In addition to these offices, in 1889, while he was a judge of the Superior Court of Ohio in Cincinnati, Taft's name surfaced as a candidate for the presidency of Yale University, which was still affiliated with the Congregational Church. In a letter to his brother, in which Taft decided not to let his name go forward for Yale's presidency, he wrote, "I am a Unitarian. I believe in God. I do not believe in the Divinity of Christ, and there are many other of the postulates of the orthodox creed to which I cannot subscribe. I am not, however, a scoffer at religion."[3]

Before, during, and after his presidency, including his tenure as chief justice, Taft was engaged in Unitarian governance at the national and international levels. He took part in church affairs in Cincinnati and at All Souls in the nation's capital. In 1909 he was a primary founder of the National League of Unitarian Laymen. He belonged to the American Unitarian Association, and from 1916 to 1922 was its vice president. In 1915 he was chosen president of the National Conference of Unitarian and Other Liberal Christian Churches, chairing their biennial conferences until 1925, and also served on the Executive Committee of the Unitarian Laymen's League in the early 1920s. In 1927, Taft was elected president by acclamation of the International Congress of Religious Liberals in Prague, a post he held until his death in 1930.

Taft delivered a major address in Montreal in 1917 at the annual meeting of the National Conference of Unitarian and Other Liberal Christian Churches in his capacity as presiding officer. The speech, "The Religious Convictions of an American Citizen," was Taft's most comprehensive public statement of what it meant to be Unitarian. "A Unitarian believes that Jesus Christ founded a new religion and a new religious philosophy on the love of God for man, and of men for one another, and for God, and taught it by his life and practice, with such Heaven-given sincerity, sweetness, simplicity, and all-compelling force that it lived after Him in the souls of men, and became the basis for a civilization struggling toward the highest ideals. . . . Unitarianism offers a broad Christian religious faith that can be reconciled with scientific freedom of thought and inquiry into the truth."[4]

WOODROW WILSON
1913-1921

★ ★ ★ ★ ★ ★ ★ ★ ★ ★ ★ ★

What do we pray for in the second petition of the Lord's Prayer?

> In the second petition, which is, Thy kingdom come, we pray that Satan's kingdom may be destroyed; and that the kingdom of grace may be advanced, ourselves and others brought into it, and kept in it; and that the kingdom of glory may be hastened.

At a relatively young age, Theodore Woodrow Wilson memorized these words from the Shorter Westminster Catechism (along with the rest of the catechism) and in many ways they seem to have been the guide for much of Wilson's public life. This is especially true as he sought to bring the world into the League of Nations and to have the United States sign the Treaty of Versailles—neither of which were to happen, and Wilson would die soon after his failed attempts to lead the world into a more peaceful community. While we cannot say that Wilson's two terms as President of the United States were marked as being those of a "Christian" president, we do know that the words, sounds, and culture of the Presbyterian Church marked all of Wilson's life, and it would be a grave mistake not to realize these influences in at least some of his policies. Interestingly, Wilson's main opponent in the 1912 election, Theodore Roosevelt, saw America's involvement in European war as Armageddon, the battle to end the world (and though these were his words, he probably did not mean them literally). But in the horrifying European conflagration Wilson saw the actual possibility that in the war's aftermath, there might be a way to bring an end to major wars, to create a peaceable kingdom, or at least to lay the kingdom's foundations.

From the beginning of his life to its end, Woodrow Wilson had before him the image of his Presbyterian minister father, and the words and faith of his father reached out to Wilson while he sat in the fourth pew every Sunday until he went to college. Wilson later wrote of his father's preaching, "I wish that I could believe that I inherited that rarest gift of making great truths attractive in the telling and of inspiring with great purposes by sheer force of eloquence or by gentle stress of persuasion." In the words of biographer George C. Osborn, "The acceptance by Tommy [a family nickname for the young Woodrow] of his father's faith was complete, and the striving for his father's eloquence was never relinquished. . . . Anyone who would understand Woodrow Wilson must know well the cardinal virtues, as well as the grave deficiencies, of the Presbyterian society that nourished him."[1] None of this is to say that Wilson was a dogmatic or sectarian Presbyterian; one of the central concepts of Reformed theology is that God is truly Provident, but not in the sense that every act is ordered, that there is no human culpability. Rather, God has given the world to be governed by humanity, according to God's known will. Therefore, Wilson had little concern for converting others to his religion (since personal conversion was not religion's proper role), or for "moral uplift," or for personal evangelism. In fact, though Wilson believed that Christians should work against injustice, work toward improving the world, this work should be accomplished through dismantling systemic institutional injustices, not through ridding individuals of distasteful or vice-ridden behaviors through moral crusades; those who sought to change the world through those means and in their images he saw as being "priggish."[2] Religion to Wilson was a deeply, profoundly private matter, so much so that he disdained the Evangelical movement's reliance on emotionalism and personal conversion. However, Wilson believed God was indeed interested in human salvation—particularly communal salvation, as opposed to individual salvation. Shortly after the outbreak of war in Europe, for example, Wilson told a Y.M.C.A. audience, "For one, I am not fond of thinking about Christianity as a means of saving individual souls."[3] It is important to remember that all the stress of the Westminster Catechism is on the centrality of God and of humanity's proper responses to the known will of God. In the eyes of Wilson and many others, Evangelicalism seems dangerously human-centered, especially when humans purport to know God's will whether that be in politics, or in anything that God has not explicitly stated through scripture.

During most of Wilson's academic career at Princeton University (then known as the College of New Jersey), the school was overtly Presbyterian, with incredibly strong ties to the church. As its president, Wilson attended chapels and closed each chapel with prayer. It was during his college presidency, however, that Princeton profoundly shook off some of its sectarianism—and this came with Wilson's direct influence. It was Wilson who hired the school's first Jewish and Catholic faculty members.[4] But it was because of his Presbyterianism that Wilson was appointed to be president of the institution. The depth of Wilson's commitment to and identity with Presbyterianism ironically made him a rather secular president (especially compared to those who succeeded him). Wilson believed that because Christianity is an identity, "bred in the bone," there is no need to convert others or to be worried about any individual's salvation, or to prove one's religiosity. Further, religion is intensely private, allowing a man like Wilson to kneel in prayer every day, to attend church faithfully, to ask forgiveness for sins,[5] and then to go about the work of government without trying to assert one's private religion on the office or on the nation.

Not long after taking office, Woodrow Wilson's first wife, Ellen, died, and as one might imagine, this was a difficult time for the president; for according to many sources, he functioned best when there was a central woman in his life. About that loss he wrote, "My life would not be worth living if it were not for the driving power of religion, for faith, pure and simple. I have seen all my life the arguments against it without ever having been moved by them."[6] Within a few short years, during the Great War, Wilson received a birthday letter from British Methodist and Baptist leaders, supporting him, and he responded by writing "I think one would go crazy if he did not believe in Providence. It would be a maze without a clue. Unless there were some supreme guidance we would despair of the results of human counsel."[7] While Wilson seemed to count on a faith in Providence to deal with loneliness and doubt, he also was clear that he was at least skeptical of humans who claimed to know the will of God, to give political advice based on what God would want that might not be explicitly set down in the Bible. Wilson's stenographer wrote in his diary that Wilson's response to a telegram calling for his declaring war on Germany in God's name was a scoffing. "War isn't declared in the name of god; it is a human affair entirely."[8] At another time Wilson proclaimed, "We do not pour our blood out to vindicate philosophies and politics."[9]

Due at least in some part to his strong private faith built of tradition, education, and discipline, Wilson continued to draw clear lines between religion and public life, without the fear that somehow he would be weakening his faith in God or falling short in his position as president. Jon Milton Cooper, Jr., writes, "Wilson drew a sharp distinction between the 'two great empires of human feeling'—religion and politics. Whereas religion embodied spirit and thought, politics found expression 'in institutions . . . Not in our own souls merely, but in the world of action outside as well,' and it required order, adjustment, and adaptation."[10] For Wilson, his religion served as guiding principle, not a series of explicit religious dictates governing politics: "Wilson's principles, derived from his religious faith, were his North Star, which pointed him in a general direction. Expediency, the actual sailing on the sea, required dealing with winds, tides, currents, obstacles, crew, and other vessels in following the course set by principle."[11]

President Wilson may have seen his religious faith as having pointed him in general directions, but it is important to understand that expediency seemed often to be the brighter beacon, especially when refusing to deal with the racial struggles in his own country while he was trying to guide the ships of many states toward his League of Nations. In 1915 (before the war), the Wilson administration began enforcing segregation in government work places, lunchrooms, and restrooms. As African-American veterans of the European war returned to the South after the war, they faced the preposterous threat of lynching, which increased dramatically for a number of years (partly due to the Red Scare), but Wilson stayed out of the issue, and his anger about lynching was directed at the perpetrators not because of the horror or injustice but because of "the passion, disorder, and sullied international image of white Americans."[12] According to Cooper,[13] the star of Wilson's religious beliefs seems to have been obscured, at least when concerning racial relations, by his truly Southern upbringing. During the League of Nations conferences, Wilson and his representatives even worked behind the scenes to dispel quietly an amendment from the Japanese delegation that called for racial equality among the world's citizens.[14] As is true for so many of us (maybe all of humanity), Wilson's religious convictions and practices fell short in significant ways—his blind spot seemed to obscure the injustice perpetrated on the persons of color in the world.

It is strangely fitting that a president who so earnestly sought to separate the two realms of private faith and public policy should be the only United States President to be entombed at the young Washington National Cathedral; and in fact, the only president buried in a church or in Washington. One of his grandsons would one day serve as dean of this very cathedral (Wilson's second wife was Episcopalian, and Wilson's service was officiated by both Presbyterian and Episcopalian ministers). To many Americans, Woodrow Wilson looked and spoke like a preacher (and he was sometimes referred to as "the parson"), but he conscientiously kept his devout religious life relatively private and spoke humbly about God's role in shaping the nations. Like presidents before and after, Wilson publicly gave thanks to the god of all nations in his inauguration and in Thanksgiving Proclamations, but outside of the claims made in the Westminster Shorter Catechism, Wilson seemed careful not to claim any special knowledge of God's will or ways.

WARREN GAMALIEL HARDING
1921-1923

★ ★ ★ ★ ★ ★ ★ ★ ★ ★ ★ ★

The presidency of Warren G. Harding of Ohio invariably is considered near or at the bottom of the rankings of American presidents. Scandal and corruption enveloped his administration, up to and including his death in San Francisco on August 2, 1923. One American historian once wrote that Harding's sin, similar to that of President Grant, "was excessive loyalty to crooked friends."[1] In the acerbic language of Theodore Roosevelt's daughter, Alice Roosevelt Longworth, "Harding was not a bad man. He was just a slob."[2]

Harding's life began as the Civil War ended; he was born in what is now Blooming Grove, Ohio, on November 2, 1865. When he was in college his parents moved to Marion, Ohio, where Harding later would start his professional and political careers, and where he would meet and marry Florence Kling De Wolfe, who was a member of one of the most prominent families in Marion, and whose father once threatened to kill Harding if he married his daughter. Supposedly, the father was opposed to his daughter Florence or "Flossie" marrying Harding because some of his ancestors were alleged to be African-American. Nonetheless, they were married in 1891; she brought a child into the marriage from a previous one, yet Harding and Florence never had any children between them.

Harding's father was not especially religious, and his mother, Phoebe, who taught Harding to read at the age of four using Sunday school material, later would become a Seventh Day Adventist, and his sister, Victoria, was a missionary in India and Burma. One of Harding's friends and political appointees wrote of his mother, "She was an extremely religious soul, and the strong religious and ethical feeling which is so evident in all that President Harding wrote was inherited from her."[3] She also insisted repeatedly that her son would become president someday. In his adult years, and throughout his mother's life, Harding gave or sent her flowers every Sunday.

Harding was an American Baptist, attending and supporting several Baptist congregations in his life, beginning with Marion's Trinity Baptist Church, founded in 1912. He was a trustee at Trinity Baptist and other churches from the age of seventeen until the time of his death. Of Harding it has been written, by Edmund Fuller and David E. Green, "He was a Baptist. He had genuine religious belief, but translated it into his life perhaps less effectively than any other President."[4] Harding was not, according to one of his biographers, Samuel Hopkins Adams, "innately nor profoundly religious. He supported and attended the church of his faith . . . That he was a believer is as plain as that his life and conduct were not patterned upon the code inspired by his creed. Facing duties too onerous for fearless contemplation, he turned naturally to a compassionate Deity for support," as if American presidents "were, *ex officio*, so to speak, taken under divine guidance."[5]

Harding made his early mark in Marion by buying a newspaper about to be auctioned at sale, and he thus entered the publishing business until his election to the United States Senate in 1914, when the first election of senators was decided by popular vote under the Seventeenth Amendment adopted in 1913. Six years later Harding was elected president with 61 percent of the vote in a massive landslide over a Democratic Party ticket whose vice presidential nominee was Franklin Roosevelt. After Harding declared his candidacy for the White House in 1919, he wrote to a friend, "The only thing I really worry about is that I am sometimes very much afraid I am going to be nominated and elected. That's an awful thing to contemplate."[6]

Harding's presidency lasted only 882 days and one of his biographers contends, "Few presidents have fallen from adulation to excoriation as fast as Harding did after his death in office on August 2, 1923."[7] Harding trusted his appointees too blindly, and seemed to be much more concerned with being liked and having fun playing poker and partying with friends and cronies than he did with being an effective chief executive. Harding was a kindly man, yet in his own words once remarked, "I don't seem to grasp that I am president." Two years into his presidency, he said to Nicholas Murray Butler, president of Columbia University, "I am not fit for this office and should never have been here."[8]

In his Inaugural Address of March 4, 1921, Harding declared, "I must utter my belief in the divine inspiration of the founding fathers. Surely there must have been God's intent in the making of this new-world Republic." At his swearing in, Harding's Bible was opened to Micah 6:8, "He hath showed thee, O man, what is good; and what doth the Lord require of thee, but to do justly; and to love mercy, and to walk humbly with thy God?"[9] In the aftermath of World War I, Harding famously sought a return to "normalcy" by stating, "Our supreme task is the resumption of our onward, normal way." Harding clearly saw America's role to be "a high place in the moral leadership of civilization," and he praised "the unselfishness and the righteousness of representative democracy." He ended his address by invoking "the favor and guidance of God in His Heaven," and in seeking "reassurance in belief in the God-given destiny of our Republic."[10]

Harding's administration, and his presidential legacy, weren't the only signs of the rampant corruption that occurred on his watch. "Handsome Harding" also attracted the ladies; his father is reported to have told him once that it was a good thing he was not a woman for he could never say no. Allegations of womanizing surfaced early, and lingered throughout his career, and appear to have been based, at least in part, on fact. One of his mistresses, who also was a German sympathizer during World War I, tried to blackmail Harding; she was given hush money by the Republican Party, and another mistress, thirty years younger than the president, was given a job in Washington, D.C., so she could be close to Harding. Their affair lasted until his death (after which his wife would allow no autopsy), and this mistress, Nan Britton, of Marion, Ohio, claimed to have had a child with Harding, and wrote a book about it entitled *The President's Daughter*.

In his Inaugural Address, Harding argued, "Service is the supreme commitment of life. I would rejoice to acclaim the era of the Golden Rule and crown it with the autocracy of service." Harding did try to pursue what in one of his Thanksgiving Proclamations he called "the privilege of service."[11] Nonetheless, his presidency is one we should not seek to see emulated.

CALVIN COOLIDGE
1923-1929

★ ★ ★ ★ ★ ★ ★ ★ ★ ★ ★ ★

Writing a sort of spiritual biography about a man who was infamously evasive and quiet is, perhaps, an act of either hubris or futility. But there are some things we do know about Calvin Coolidge's religious life, and a few more things that are reasonably speculative. For instance, we know that Coolidge attended the Congregational Church through his youth, but that neither his father nor his grandfather (both attendees of the Congregational Church in Massachusetts) became communicants. We should not, however, conclude that Coolidge's forebears were unreligious or un-Christian; rather, it was common for individuals to join the Congregational Church when they had experienced some sort of spiritual awakening or significant spiritual change. Therefore, we could just as easily speculate that Coolidge (who had not joined the church as a young man) and his ancestors would not join a church just for appearances. Further, in the nineteenth-century United States, church membership was nearing a two-hundred-year low, so likely there was less pressure on individuals to join the church during that time. Even though Coolidge had not joined a church until relatively late in life, this was not anomalous, nor does it prove that he was not a Christian. However, he was not able to partake in the most central of Christian sacraments at his church, the Lord's Supper, which to many meant he had not partaken of a meaningful means of God's grace until after he became president.

One popular pastime in presidential studies is to exchange Coolidge quips that so wittily communicated Coolidge's quiet, New England reserve, and there are, of course, quips related to religion. According to his wife, Grace, once they had a Baptist minister to their house for dinner before he was to speak (there is no reference as to when this took place or why they had entertained the man), but the preacher would not eat very much, saying, "temperance in eating improved his ability to preach." After attending the service and listening to the sermon, Coolidge reportedly told his wife that the preacher "Might as well have eaten."[1] An apocryphal story that is often recounted (because it seemed to those who knew him to reveal the sense of the man) tells of a time when Grace asked her husband to tell her what a preacher had said in his sermon about sin; Coolidge replied "He was against it."[2]

Likely there would not be a chapter about Coolidge in this book had President Harding not died while in office, and one anecdote about Coolidge and his faith is recounted in many sources that deals with the death of Harding and the weight of the office laid on Coolidge. Upon receiving the telegraph with news that Harding had died, supposedly the vice president and his wife knelt in their room to pray before going downstairs. One source states that they prayed for "God's blessing on the nation's people and for the strength to serve them, a prayer he [Coolidge] was frequently to repeat during his years in the White House."[3] After Coolidge took the oath of office, administered by his father (a notary public), he went by train to Washington, where he was met by the pastor of Washington's First Congregational Church (at the new president's request), perhaps for prayer, leadership, or comfort. The following Sunday

Coolidge publicly professed his faith by taking communion at the First Congregational Church. There were many critics at the time, and since, who suggested that Coolidge joined the church simply because that was what a president should do. Just as easily, however, we could speculate that this unsought weight of the presidency sparked a change in Coolidge and inaugurated a religious experience. Politically it was probably advantageous for Coolidge to show the country a president who was grounded in faith and tradition in this time of political, social, and economic turmoil. One piece of evidence that Coolidge's religious experience was sincere is that even after he left the White House and returned to Northampton, he and Grace continued to attend Edwards Congregational Church regularly, where the rumor was Coolidge spent more time determining who was absent from church than in thinking about the sermon[4]—perhaps the sermons were not difficult to understand.

It would perhaps be unfair not to mention some of the dramatic claims that were made about Coolidge's religious faith in what seems to be a propagandistic campaign biography published in 1924 (a presidential election year—Coolidge's first and last presidential election). In *The Preparation of Calvin Coolidge: An Interpretation*, author Robert A. Woods writes in his understated manner that

> Any attempt to understand President Coolidge will go far amiss which does not take the fullest account of the great power of religious faith which has been continuous and increasing in his life. Beginning with his early nurture, greatly strengthened and broadened at Amherst, rising steadily as the responsibilities of life so steadily and so broadly increased—his faith in God with its correlative of faith in men, his sense of sustaining and lifting spiritual realities, is, in modern terms, not less real to him and not less definite in its command and its re-enforcement to righteousness that it was to the Puritans of old.[5]

Earlier in the same book Woods states that Coolidge was "deeply versed in the philosophy and the loyalty that made and maintain the American political system, he is the present-day exponent, in thought and life, of that faith in a righteous civic order which is at the heart of the Puritan conception of a divine commonwealth."[6] Perhaps Woods felt the need to make up for all the words the generally silent Coolidge refused to say. Woods even goes on to suggest that perhaps the reason Coolidge had not joined a church before

Harding's death was because he was too shy and did not want to express his religion publicly. As odd as this may seem considering the ways in which we know everything about our presidents in today's endless media circus, there may be truth to Woods's assertion. Another admiring biographer, Charles McCoy, claimed that Coolidge was so concerned with privacy and with appearing stable and in control, that he was careful not to pray when anyone outside his family could hear him.[7] In thinking of Jesus' advice for his followers to pray in their closets rather than be like the Pharisees who pray so that everyone can hear them, one must admit that a president who has a silent faith and refuses to make his religion part of his political identity is, perhaps, a distinctly Christian choice.

Calvin Coolidge's own choice, select words are probably the most fitting way to summarize his faith: "I have found that when a man does right, he is increasingly supported. I believe in God."[8]

HERBERT CLARK HOOVER
1929-1933

★ ★ ★ ★ ★ ★ ★ ★ ★ ★ ★ ★

On August 11, 1928, speaking at Stanford University on his fifty-fourth birthday and accepting his party's nomination for the presidency, Herbert Hoover stated simply, "I come of Quaker stock."[1] These five words tell us a great deal about Hoover, his extraordinary career of public service, his one-term presidency and his failure to receive a second term in 1932 against Franklin Roosevelt. His public career, which in essence began when he helped organize the effort to get over 120,000 Americans out of Europe after World War I started in 1914, and continued into the 1960s, one of the more extraordinary careers of the twentieth century.

Herbert Clark Hoover was born on August 10, 1874, in West Branch, Iowa, a town founded by members of the Society of Friends. His father, Jesse, and his mother,

Huldah Minthorn Hoover, were from long-standing, devout Quaker families in the United States and Canada. His mother, like two of her sisters and one of her brothers, was a recorded Quaker minister, and after Hoover's father died when Bert, as he was known by family and close friends, was six, his mother often left him and his siblings with other family members as she went about the state ministering to other Quakers, or Friends, for she was a prominent preacher in the lay Quaker tradition.

Hoover's mother died when he was nine. Although he, his brother and sister all would eventually settle near each other in Oregon, immediately after their mother's death they were separated from each other, with Hoover sent to live with his uncle, Henry John Minthorn, a physician, in Newberg, Oregon. Prior to his parents' deaths, Hoover was raised in a loving but strict traditional Quaker home with family prayers, daily Bible reading, and simple living—living that prohibited musical instruments, playing cards, other forms of amusement, tobacco, and alcohol. Such a life would continue in Oregon. As a biographer of Hoover has written, "Of most indelible influence on Hoover, as on all young Friends, was the Quaker silent worship at Fifth Day (Thursday) and First Day (Sunday) meetings."[2] Hoover himself would later write that before he left Iowa, "I had read the Bible in daily stints from cover to cover."[3]

Later in life, Hoover, who would become more a secular Quaker than remain an orthodox, practicing Quaker, would criticize some of the customs of the church. In his *Memoirs*, for instance, remembering the Quaker meeting house and the silent meeting, Hoover wrote about "the intense repression upon a ten-year-old boy who might not even count his toes."[4] In thinking of his Quaker heritage, he also stated, "Their protest against religious rote up to the recent times expressed itself in their peculiar garb of 'plain clothes' and adherence to the 'plain language.' But as times went on, these very customs, the uniform architecture meeting houses, the method of conducting meetings, became a sort of formalism itself."[5]

One of Hoover's favorite tales from his early Quaker years describes one particular meeting in some detail. "The men and women," he wrote, "sat divided by a low partition. The elders of the women who sat upon the high 'facing bench' were the only ones of that sex that I could see. 'Aunt' Hannah occupied the first place on this bench. At one point, Hannah, 'moved' by the meeting, rose to denounce a proposal of the youngsters that they should have singing in Sabbath school . . . She was bitter in her warnings of the wrath to come, and as a peroration made the prophecy that if these things came to pass," the church "might even become a 'the-a-ter.'"[6] Hoover then concluded, and you can see him writing with a bit of a mischievous grin on his face, the story by revealing that "Aunt" Hannah was in fact prophetic, for later a new, more modern meeting house was erected, and the old one became a movie theater![7]

In Oregon, after attending Friends Pacific Academy, which would become what is today George Fox University, Hoover almost went East to attend Earlham College, a Quaker institution, until he found out it did not offer the engineering program he strongly desired. He found out about a new school opening in Palo Alto, California, started by Senator Leland Stanford. One of Stanford's math professors, Dr. Joseph Swain, who also happened to be Quaker, was in Portland, Oregon, conducting entrance exams. Hoover decided to attend Stanford, and became a student in Stanford University's first class of around 500 students when its doors opened on October 1, 1891. Of Dr. Swain Hoover would write, "Dr. Swain was a well-known Quaker, so that his association with the otherwise suspiciously godless institution served to overcome the family hurdle."[8]

While at Stanford, Hoover would meet Lou Henry, another undergraduate, three years behind Hoover, also studying geology (the only female at Stanford doing so at the time). She would become Quaker herself, and wanted a Quaker wedding, but when they decided to marry, the town in California not only was lacking a Quaker meeting house, it had no Protestant minister. One of her family friends was a Catholic priest, and he was able to receive special dispensation to perform their wedding ceremony.

When Hoover came to the White House in 1929, after defeating Alfred Smith, Democrat of New York in a race highlighted by Smith's Catholicism, he arguably had more international experience than any other president save John Quincy Adams. He also had not a small amount of prior public service, including secretary of commerce in the Harding and Coolidge Administrations. (Hoover, in fact, is our last president to go to the White House from a full Cabinet post). For instance, he helped organize the effort to get 120,000 Americans out of Europe after World War I started; he led the relief program with respect to Belgium as chair of the Commission for Relief in Belgium; and headed the United States

Food Administration, to which he was appointed by President Wilson when the United States entered the war in 1917. As he would write later, "I was on the slippery road of public life."[9] And, at the end of World War I, the *New York Times* named Hoover one of the "Ten Most Important Living Americans."

One of Hoover's biographers offers a most insightful observation of Hoover's "Pauline strategy of being in the world but not of it."[10] According to Burner, "We cannot be sure that he consistently thought of himself as a Friend, yet all kinds of similarities between the Quaker mentality and Hoover's suggest themselves: a blunt plainness; a belief that people will work well together and that in rational discussion minds can be persuaded to meet; a dedication to peace; and in these things a shrewd involvement in worldly matters and a conviction that good common reason and strategy accord well with the conscience and its affairs."[11]

Central to Hoover's political thinking was his conception of the Quaker notion of "ordered freedom," which Hoover referred to in his March 4, 1929, Inaugural Address as, "ordered liberty, the vital force of progress."[12] As he argued there, "Our whole system of self-government will crumble either if officials elect what laws they will enforce or citizens elect what laws they will support."[13] He was addressing specifically the Eighteenth Amendment and our national experiment with Prohibition, which, by the way, Hoover endorsed in public but did not necessarily faithfully adhere to in private.

Perhaps the greatest evidence of the impact of Quakerism on Hoover is in the area of world peace, militarism, and international intervention. His 1929 inaugural in essence hinges on his succinct statement, "The whole world is at peace." He argued, "Surely civilization is old enough, surely mankind is mature enough so that we ought in our own lifetime to find a way to permanent peace."[14] He clearly had a peace-oriented approach to international affairs. He rejected Theodore Roosevelt's Monroe Corollary, Taft's Dollar Diplomacy, pulled troops out of Nicaragua and attempted to do the same in Haiti, and was opposed to territorial imperialism and aggressive intervention abroad. As he wrote in the second volume of his *Memoirs*, "My ambition in our foreign policies was to lead the United States in full cooperation with world moral forces to preserve peace."[15]

Hoover was no pacifist, at least not in an absolute sense of the word, but he did possess pacifistic proclivities. According to one Hoover scholar, he was "the President closest to being a pacifist. He passed up more opportunities for intervention abroad than any other twentieth-century American chief of state, notably in Manchuria, Panama, Honduras, and Cuba. Moreover, he consistently sought sensible, moral ways to avoid war. Hoover maintained that Quakers were not ostriches, but rather active workers against war."[16] In 1937, when Japan attacked China Hoover wrote to a friend, "There are plenty of ways that we can establish our honor and our dignity without going to war . . . I am not particularly a pacifist, but I have felt that war should be resolved as the answer to assaults upon our national freedom and this alone."[17] According to Wilson, Hoover "was particularly appalled by militarism, which he defined as 'the direct or indirect fostering of the belief that war is ennobling to a nation, that war is the moment of a nation's greatness, that a martial spirit is a beneficent catalyzer of the blood and spirit of the nation, that nations even in peace gain in power and add to their prestige and prosperity by dominating armament.'"[18]

In his 1928 acceptance speech quoted earlier, Hoover revealed another aspect of his Quakerism. He declared, "I stand for religious tolerance both in act and spirit."[19] He instructed his campaign aides neither to engage in nor encourage any form of anti-Catholic bigotry or electioneering against Smith. As he wrote in his *Memoirs*, "I reprimanded many of those who agitated this question." And in 1960, when a Catholic again led the Democratic ticket, Hoover stated publicly, "I abhor bigotry."[20] As a Quaker, he knew and believed that God is immanent in all persons; that all possess the Inner Light.

During his presidency, a visitor at the White House asked Hoover what tenet of Quakerism meant the most to him. He replied, "Individual faithfulness."[21] A necessary and proper response to the "Inner Light" was pivotal for Hoover. He once was described as "a Quaker in a quagmire."[22] In many respects, such as in education, children's affairs, Indian policy, and women's issues, Hoover's policies reflected real reformist tendencies. Hoover's religious faith was more than narrowly or privately pietistic, yet his Quakerism prevented public posing. While President, Hoover and his wife attended the Friends Meeting House on Florida Avenue, which they had helped organize and establish.

President Hoover died at the age of 90 on October 21, 1964, of colon cancer. Among presidents, only John Adams had lived longer. His funeral service was held in New York City at St. Bartholomew's Episcopal Church, according to the rather simple Order for the Burial of the Dead, with readings from Psalms 23 and 121. He and his wife are buried at West Branch.

FRANKLIN DELANO ROOSEVELT
1933-1945

★ ★ ★ ★ ★ ★ ★ ★ ★ ★ ★

Franklin D. Roosevelt, the eighth cousin of President Theodore Roosevelt, was reared in a family that possessed authority, wealth, and a mighty sense of responsibility to the nation. The Episcopal Church was a part of every turn in FDR's life, and he willingly made religion a part of his public life, concluding many of his radio broadcast "fireside chats" with prayers for the nation. At the same time Roosevelt could be crass, commanding, vain, elitist, bigoted, devious, ambitious, and likely unfaithful; surely he was a New York politician and a complicated Christian, though the way he saw religion and theology was, perhaps, simplistic.

Shaped by Dr. Endicott Peabody, the rector and headmaster of the elite Episcopalian Groton School in Massachusetts, Roosevelt's early private-school education

155

stressed "manliness" and integrity. Religion and ethics in the Anglican tradition were a core part of the curriculum at Groton, and Roosevelt called his former headmaster and spiritual mentor to his side throughout his public life and until Peabody's death before Roosevelt began his fourth term as president. Dr. Peabody officiated at the wedding of Franklin and Eleanor, and Peabody led three of the private inauguration-day prayer services initiated by Roosevelt. These private services with Peabody, family, and some members of the administration were an important aspect of Roosevelt's faith and religious life, and they, along with so much else of his spiritual life were shaped by Episcopal liturgy and forms. Like many presidents before him, Roosevelt was a vestryman for his home Episcopal Church. But unlike the majority of those presidents, Roosevelt was very active in his role as vestryman and warden of St. James' Church in Hyde Park, continuing an active hand in church affairs even while he was in Washington, D.C.[1]

In his home life with Eleanor and their children, Roosevelt was fairly uninvolved; he may have stated that the children would go to church every Sunday (just as he had to do when he was a child), but it would usually be Eleanor who was to take them and not Roosevelt, since he would often be playing golf.[2] Likely Roosevelt thought himself secure enough in his faith that he no longer needed to attend church very often, but as he moved deeper into public life, he gave another excuse for not attending church regularly, according to his secretary of labor, Francis Perkins:

> I can do almost everything in the "Gold-Fish-Bowl" of the President's life, but I'll be hanged if I can say my prayers in it. It bothers me to feel like something in the zoo being looked at by all the tourists in Washington when I go to church. . . . Do you know what they rigged up in that church? I know it was meant in good part, but they put red plush cushions in a couple of pews way down front in the middle aisle. They also put a red silk cord and tassels around those pews to reserve them for the President of the United States. Can you beat that? No privacy in that kind of going to church, and by the time I have gotten into that pew and settled down with everybody looking at me, I don't feel like saying my prayers at all.[3]

Others who knew Roosevelt well also suggested that since experiencing the crippling effects of polio he also did not like to venture into public, especially when his arrivals and departures could not be orchestrated in such a way as to diminish any appearance of his being unable to walk on his own. While he did not go to church much as an adult, and he did not often attend church with his children, the children did testify to what they saw as his true religiosity. According to his son James, "Father never preached much to us—or to anyone—about piety and virtue, but, to him, religion was a real and personal thing from which he drew much strength and comfort."[4] And comfort was needed in the family, for the father and for the rest, especially at the death of the president's son, Franklin, at eight months old. Biographer Kenneth S. Davis wrote about this period when Roosevelt "remained an optimistic fatalist whose fatalism had a simple Christian definition. Whatever happened that was against his wish or will, yet beyond his power to change—whatever present he saw as irrevocable, whatever future he saw as inevitable—was accepted by him without protest or complaint as the will of God."[5] But not many things in the world fell into the category of what Roosevelt would think of as beyond his power to change, whether those things be polio, worldwide depression, world war, or harnessing the power of the atom for military use.

While Eleanor Roosevelt's often-quoted statement that her husband's faith was simple, that Roosevelt himself was a "very simple Christian,"[6] can easily be taken as a slightly derogatory description. The person who seems to have first recorded this statement by the First Lady, Secretary of Labor Francis Perkins, however, suggests this was a positive statement, that "[Roosevelt's] Christian faith was absolutely simple. As far as I can make out, he had no doubts. He just believed with a certainty and simplicity that gave him no pangs or struggles."[7] Kenneth S. Davis enlarges this aspect of Roosevelt's faith by writing that "an effect of his faith was a profoundly optimistic attitude toward the world and its challenges. . . . Indeed, there were times when he seemed perfectly assured that he himself was a special favorite of the Lord's."[8]

For the most part Roosevelt was orthodox in his Christianity, but he definitely leaned more to the New Testament teaching of Jesus than to the Old Testament, eschewing controversies about God's judgment, the role of Israel as God's chosen race, and the fear of a retributive God. Instead Roosevelt was drawn more to what was known in the early twentieth century as the "new scientific" Christianity which tended to combine the teachings of the Apostles and Jesus with modern concepts of positive thinking and scientific advancement; Roosevelt wrote in an early book that he saw this newer way of understanding Christianity as "opening the way for a simpler faith, a deeper faith, a happier faith, than ever our forefathers had."[9] Those closest to Roosevelt throughout his adult life consistently suggest that he was more interested in the moral-uplift aspects of Christianity than in miracles, judgment, or sectarian and theological lines. Roosevelt believed that service to God was best expressed through service to other humans, not in any particular set of beliefs or practices.[10] While Roosevelt did apparently struggle with the doctrinal concept of original sin (disregarding it earlier in his life but finding in it a way to try to comprehend the evil of the Nazis),[11] he mostly tended to see the evil in the world as a result of broken institutions that could be redeemed, not as a result of human depravity.[12] In his basic beliefs, therefore, Roosevelt was squarely a main-line American Protestant, and he would probably not have been at home in a twenty-first century Evangelical, non-denominational Christian church; and parishioners of those churches may have been skeptical of Roosevelt's claims to Christianity.

Among the chroniclers of Roosevelt's life who knew him best (spouse, secretaries, cabinet members), there is a clear consensus that Roosevelt's policies were often directly derived from how he understood God's will was to be done on Earth, and he arrived at that understanding from his continual reading of the Sermon on the Mount. Perkins, who had been working closely with Roosevelt since he had been governor of New York, writes that Roosevelt was "willing to do experimentally whatever was necessary to promote the Golden Rule and other ideals he considered to be Christian, and whatever could be done under the Constitution of the United States and under the principles which have guided the Democratic Party."[13] Presidential scholar Gary Scott Smith asserts that Roosevelt, "perhaps more than any other president, his faith in the Sermon on the Mount influenced his policies."[14]

One aspect of Roosevelt's time in office that is particularly interesting regarding religion was his choice to meet privately for prayer services beginning with his first inauguration and continuing on the inauguration's anniversary each year until his death. Unlike the Presidential Prayer Breakfasts that Eisenhower would later initiate, or the Presidential

Thanksgiving Proclamations that were all so openly religious (even to the point that the religious aspects became subsumed to the political, or lost meaning until they became part of a civil religion), most Americans did not know about these meetings; there were no announcements, no journalists, no reports. Secretary of Labor Perkins recounts that first service in 1933:

> Late on the eve of the Inauguration, we had had a telephone message from one of the secretaries that Roosevelt would like members of the cabinet and their families to meet him for worship and intercession at St. John's at ten o'clock on the morning of Inauguration Day. . . . It was a simple but memorable service, following the outline of the book of Common Prayer, with the hymns and Psalms chosen by Roosevelt after conference with Dr. Endicott Peabody. . . . We were in a terrible situation [the nation as a whole, at the beginning of the Great Depression]. . . . If ever a man wanted to pray, that was the day. [Roosevelt] did want to pray, and he wanted everyone to pray for him. It was a closely-kept secret, and it was days before the world knew that the President had gone to church before his Inauguration. . . . It was impressive. Everybody prayed, it seemed. . . . We were Catholics, Protestants, Jews, but I doubt that anyone remembered the difference. On succeeding Inauguration Day anniversaries each year [Roosevelt] went to St. John's to repeat the prayers and service of the first Inaugural. The President grew to have great faith in this particular service and to feel rewarded and strengthened by it.[15]

As much love as Roosevelt had for Episcopalian services, he also appreciated the lively, spirited services (at least in those days) of Methodists and Baptists. After one memorable Christmas during World War II, someone reproached Roosevelt for not taking Prime Minister Winston Churchill to St. John's Episcopal for the Christmas service, to which Roosevelt responded "It is good for Winston to sing hymns with the Methodys[sic]."[16]

Franklin Delano Roosevelt was no saint, and the horrifying power unleashed by the atomic bombs on Hiroshima and Nagasaki (the Manhattan Project was begun during the Roosevelt administration) cannot be reconciled with "Just War" theory, much less the Sermon on the Mount. Likely Roosevelt had a long-term affair with his wife's social secretary Lucy Mercer, and all of his economic and social programs could be seen as merely political tactics to maintain power. Roosevelt was no idealist when it came to the political world, either; as with other presidents, one's faith seems only to take one so far until one has to deal with subterfuge, machinations, and violence. At the beginning of the twenty-first century, many of the social/economic reforms enacted under the Roosevelt administration are being questioned by fiscal conservatives, often those who call Roosevelt's reforms "socialist" and therefore incompatible with Christian, American ideals. Yet we know as well as we can ever know about anyone that Roosevelt believed he was a Christian, prayed regularly, worshipped in Episcopalian community, and led those who knew him to believe he was a Christian. When asked once by a reporter what was his [Roosevelt's] political philosophy, Roosevelt responded "Philosophy? I am a Christian and a Democrat—that's all."[17] Eleanor Roosevelt stated about her husband years after his death that

> I am quite sure that Franklin accepted the thought of death as he accepted life. He had a strong religious feeling and his religion was a very personal one. I think he actually felt he could ask God for guidance and receive it. That is why he loved the Twenty-third Psalm, the Beatitudes and the Thirteenth Chapter of First Corinthians. He never talked about his religion or his beliefs and never seemed to have any intellectual difficulties about what he believed. . . . He still held to the fundamental feeling that religion was an anchor and a source of strength and guidance, so I am sure that he died looking into the future as calmly as he had looked at all the events of his life.[18]

HARRY S. TRUMAN
1945-1953

★ ★ ★ ★ ★ ★ ★ ★ ★ ★ ★ ★

"The American people stand firm in the faith which has inspired this Nation from the beginning. We believe that all men have a right to equal justice under law and equal opportunity to share in the common good. We believe that all men have the right to freedom of thought and expression. We believe that all men are created equal because they are created in the image of God. From this faith we will not be moved."[1] President Harry S. Truman made this proclamation in his Inaugural Address of January 20, 1949, following the electric election of 1948 when so many observers and pundits expected Truman to lose to Thomas Dewey of New York.

Truman was the second Baptist (Harding the other) to be president. Born in Lamar, Missouri, on May 8, 1884, he was raised a Baptist, as ancestors on both sides, the Trumans and the Youngs, were members of the church. His mother, Martha Young Truman, "was a fun-loving woman who called herself a lightfoot Baptist because she ignored condemnations of social dancing and enjoyed a good party."[2] According to one Truman biographer, "She handled a 16-gauge shotgun as well as most men. Independent, opinionated, and assertive, she was as tough as a barrel of roofing nails."[3] She taught Harry to read from the large-print family Bible, and she had very high hopes for his education and advancement in life. Truman joined the local Baptist church at the age of eighteen, and was baptized in 1903. After his family moved to Independence, Missouri, Truman attended a Presbyterian Sunday school, where he met Elizabeth (Bess) Wallace, an Episcopalian, whom he would marry on June 28, 1919, at the Trinity Episcopal Church in Independence. Truman would remain a Baptist all his life, as his wife would remain Episcopalian. They had one daughter, Margaret, born on February 17, 1924. In 1918 Truman wrote a letter to Bess saying, "I had a Presbyterian bringing up, a Baptist education, and Episcopal leanings, so I reckon I ought to get to heaven somehow, don't you think so?"[4] We have no record of her answer.

Truman is reported to have read the Bible through twice before turning twelve, with his favorite passages contained in the Sermon on the Mount. At his inauguration in 1949, Truman was sworn in using two Bibles—one was opened to the Beatitudes in Matthew 5:3-11, and the other was opened to the Ten Commandments in Exodus 20:3-17. While in the White House, he often attended the First Baptist Church in the District of Columbia, in part because the pastor, Edward H. Pruden, made no show of Truman's attendance. In his diary of February 8, 1948, Truman wrote, "I go for a walk and go to church. The preacher always treats me as a church member and not as the head of a circus. That's the reason I go to the 1st Baptist Church. . . . I don't go to church for show."[5] He also often attended St. John's Church near the White House. In one of the more interesting stories about Truman, it is said that when he would go out for walks on Sunday mornings, he hated to stop at traffic lights; he'd approach an intersection, and he'd continue along the street until he was obstructed by a red light, and that's how he'd come upon a church to attend. If the minister made any kind of fuss about the president being in the sanctuary, Truman was likely not to return. He truly despised stuffed shirts! One can easily get an idea of Truman's mind on these matters with this passage from his diary dated June 1, 1952:

> A couple of golden crowns with all kinds of expensive jewels have been stolen from a Roman Catholic shrine in Brooklyn. The crowns were on images of Jesus Christ and Mary his mother. I've an idea if Jesus were here his sympathies would be with the thieves and not with the Pharisees who crowned him with gold and jewels. . . . He came to help the lowly and the down trodden. But since Constantine the Great he has been taken over by the Despots of both Church and State. . . . If Jesus Christ were to return he'd be on the side of the persecuted all around the world. He would not be wearing a golden crown and fine raiment, he'd most likely be wearing a ready made sack suit and be standing on a street corner preaching tolerance, brother love and truth. He'd be stoned and persecuted by the most liberal of our modern day followers of the man with the golden crown. He'd probably be placed in a sanitarium in the free countries. He'd be shot, hanged or sent to a slave labor camp behind the iron curtain. . . . He taught that every man is the creation of a merciful God, that men are sinners and that he had come into the world to teach sinners how to approach his Father. . . . The way is direct and straight. Any man can tell the Almighty and Most Merciful God his troubles and directly ask for guidance. *He will get it.*[6] (Emphasis in original.)

Perhaps virtually everyone knows the story that occurred in early April 1945 when Presidential Press Secretary Stephen Early summoned then Vice President Truman to the White House where he was informed of the death of Franklin Roosevelt at Warm Springs, Georgia. Truman had been vice president for less than three months, and when he delivered his first speech to Congress on April 16, 1945, he stated humbly, "I ask only to be a good and faithful servant of my Lord and my people."[7] Approximately one month later, on May 13, 1945, Truman would write in a private letter, "It is a very, very hard position to fall into as I did. If there ever was a man who was forced to be President, I'm that man. . . . But I must face the music and try to the best of my ability. You just keep on praying and hope for the best."[8]

There is a fascinating entry in Truman's diary for August 15, 1950, where Truman reveals a prayer that he has said, "over & and over, all my life, from eighteen years old and younger." The prayer reads:

Oh! Almighty and Everlasting God, Creator of Heaven, Earth and the Universe: Help me to be, to think, to act what is right, because it is right; make me truthful, honest and honorable in all things; make me intellectually honest for the sake of right and honor and without thought of reward to me. Give me the ability to be charitable, forgiving and patient with my fellowmen—help me to understand their motives and their shortcomings—even as Thou understandest mine! Amen, Amen, Amen.[9]

Following the recitation of this prayer, Truman continued, "The prayer on the other side of this page has been said by me—by Harry S. Truman—from high school days: as window washer, bottle duster, floor scrubber in an Independence, Mo., drug store, as a time-keeper on a railroad contract gang, as an employee of an untruthful and character assassinating newspaper, as a bank clerk, as a farmer riding a gang plow behind four horses and mules, as a fraternity official learning to say nothing at all if good could not be said of a man, as a public official judging the weaknesses and shortcomings of constituents, and as President of the U.S.A."[10]

A few months later, Truman wrote a letter to a cousin, telling of meeting a young man in San Francisco, as Truman was there to give a major address. While the president studied for the speech, this young man visited briefly. "I autographed his Bible for him," Truman wrote, "and marked some passages for him to read. Then I asked him what Church he belonged to. He said, 'I'm a Christian Science reader.' He gave me his blessing and his prayers. So everything turned out all right—in spite of the passages I marked. 149th Psalm, Isaiah 40, Ecclesiastes 12, Matthew 5, 6, 7 and Luke 6, v. 26. Hope he doesn't look at Ecc. 12."[11]

Truman seemed to see religion, especially Christianity, as a highly instructive moral code, one that could, if but consulted closely, influence for the better the behavior of individuals and nations. In numerous speeches throughout his presidency, and especially after the advent of the Cold War, Truman would make statements such as, "Men can build a good society, if they follow the will of the Lord."[12] This sentence from a speech given at Gonzaga University in Spokane, Washington, on May 11, 1950, is a bit unusual, given the more sectarian reference to "the Lord," for normally Truman would talk in terms of people being "the children of God" or being directed by the Almighty or even having within them "the Divine spark that can lead them to truth, and unselfishness, and courage to do the right." In the Gonzaga speech, Truman also exhorted his audience to remember, "Those of us who believe in God, and who are fortunate enough to live under conditions where we can practice our faith, cannot be content to live for ourselves alone, in selfish isolation. We must work constantly to wipe out injustice and inequality, and to create a world order consistent with the faith that governs us."[13]

When one looks at Truman's presidency, if not his entire public career, "What emerges," according to historian Elizabeth Edwards Spalding, "is a man of deep, if simple, faith, who depended only a little on formal religion but prayed daily."[14] In the words of one scholar, Truman believed that "all Christians, even every revealed religion, could agree on the meaning as well as the value of the biblical precepts of the Ten Commandments and the Sermon on the Mount."[15] As Truman himself once said, "I've always believed that religion is something to live by and not to talk about." Yet, talk about it Truman often did, perhaps most revealingly so in his private diary. After his presidency, in the mid-1950s, Truman spoke at the Scottish Rite Temple in St. Louis on behalf of a fellow Mason. Later, in recounting the ceremony, Truman wrote, "I've never thought that God gives a damn about pomp and circumstance, gold crowns, jeweled breast plates, and ancestral background. When the Gates of Heaven are reached by the shades of the earth bound, the rank and riches enjoyed on this planet won't be of value. Some of our grandees will have to do a lot of explaining on how they got that way. Wish I could hear their alibis! I can't for the probabilities are I'll be thinking up some for myself."[16]

Perhaps the greatest decision of Truman's presidency, clearly the one with the longest-lasting legacy, was one of his earliest ones: deciding to use nuclear weapons against Japan to end World War II. After those two bombs were dropped on August 6 and August 9, 1945, Truman declared August 19 as a Day of Prayer. In his *Memoirs: 1945, Year of Decisions*, he wrote, "We were not unmindful of the divine Providence that had enabled us to prevail." Truman pretty much saw the atomic weaponry and the victory of Japan as gifts from God. For him victory "has come with the help of God, who was with us in the early days of adversity and disaster, and who has now brought us to this glorious day of triumph."[17]

Truman believed that God challenged the United States to try to fulfill its destiny at home and abroad, to seek peace and prosperity for itself and allies around the world, and to combat the forces of tyranny that revealed themselves in the forms of fascism and communism. As he spoke on April 3, 1951, when laying the cornerstone of the New York Avenue Presbyterian Church, where Lincoln once had worshipped, he said,

> Religion is not an easy thing. It is not simply a comfort to those in trouble or a means of escaping from present difficulties, as some people today would have us believe. Religion is not a negative thing. It is not merely a series of prohibitions against certain actions because they are wicked. Our religion includes these elements. But it also includes much more. It is a positive force that impels us to affirmative action. We are under divine orders—not only to refrain from doing evil, but also to do good and to make this world a better place in which to live.[18]

In addition, according to Truman, "Our religious faith gives us the answer to the false beliefs of communism. Our faith shows us the way to create a society where man can find his greatest happiness under God. Surely, we can follow that faith with the same devotion and determination the Communists give to their godless creed. . . . If we truly believe in God, we ought to ask ourselves what He may be thinking of our present attitude and our present conduct. Considering all the advantages that God has given us as a nation and all the mercies that He has shown to us from our beginnings, we ought to ask ourselves whether we today are worthy of all that He has done for us."[19]

Harry S. Truman entered the White House, what he once called that "Great White Prison," accompanied by low expectations from folks who believed he just was not ready for political prime time. He left the presidency in 1953 with an approval rating that no one envied. After all, as many people at the time heard or said, "To err is Truman." At one time he was considered, as two scholars of the presidency have pointed out, "the patron saint of unpopular presidents."[20] However, by the time of his death on December 12, 1972, he would be more of a patron saint of those wishing for straight talk and simple faith from the occupant of the Oval Office.

DWIGHT DAVID EISENHOWER 1953-1961

★ ★ ★ ★ ★ ★ ★ ★ ★ ★ ★ ★

Dwight D. Eisenhower is often considered to be one of the more successful and popular presidents in American history. After all, who has not heard the campaign slogan "I like Ike"? Not only is Eisenhower often viewed through the rosy light of post-war prosperity and American supremacy, he also left us with three nearly canonical texts of American civil religion: he was instrumental in having "under God" placed in the Pledge of Allegiance; "In God We Trust" adopted as the national motto; and "In God We Trust" was placed for the first time on U.S. paper currency during his presidency. In the American popular imagination, the 1950s reign as the very image of America at its zenith: large-finned cars, rock and roll, sock hops, and American military dominance. (Of course we should also remember the Korean War, racial segregation, race riots, McCarthyism, nuclear weapons, and the Cold War.) Surely this man who helped place God in the pockets and on the tongues of every American and presided over what many see as America's hey day must have been a deeply religious and Christian man. And perhaps he was those very things.

One thing is certain: Eisenhower was reared in an intentionally religious home. His childhood church-going and religious experiences were not casual appointments on Easter or Christmas—or of prayers only when things were going terribly wrong. His paternal grandfather was active as a minister in the River Brethren Church (a Mennonite sect) until his death,[1] and Eisenhower is often listed as having been River Brethren and Presbyterian. Indeed, Eisenhower's immediate family was River Brethren until he was six years old, but that was not the dominant religious influence in his early life. In 1896 young Dwight's parents (he was named after the evangelist Dwight L. Moody) became "Russellites," or "Bible Students," common names for what would become Jehovah's Witnesses. His mother (a Witness until her death) was the guiding religious force in Eisenhower's early life, ". . . a deeply religious woman who knew the Bible almost by heart," according to the historian Stephen Ambrose.[2] Until he left for West Point, Dwight Eisenhower lived in a home in which fifteen Bible Students met for lessons and services, so it is reasonable to imagine that the Jehovah's Witness church influenced his life at least as much as did the River Brethren.

Most Eisenhower biographers, however, neglect to mention Eisenhower's Jehovah's Witness upbringing, preferring instead to focus on his joining the Presbyterian Church after becoming president. We know from Eisenhower's own words, though, that he believed in the efficacy of his mother's prayers, and there is no sense that he thought his mother's religion to be false. (His father eventually rejected the Jehovah's Witnesses when, among other things, all of their eschatological prophecies failed to come true.) For when he was twelve years old Eisenhower scratched his leg in normal boyhood activities, but the wound became septic, threatening his leg and even his life. Even though the doctors and his own parents agreed that the leg should be amputated, the boy refused. During this time, a brother stayed by his side to protect him from those who believed the operation was necessary to save his life. Eventually the leg turned swollen and black, but still Eisenhower's mother respected her son's convictions, and she and her church prayed diligently for his healing, which, amazingly, came to fruition. Eisenhower always attributed this healing to his parents' prayers.[3] The Jehovah's Witness faith of his mother seemed to save Eisenhower's life. Eisenhower also stated clearly that it was due to his mother's teaching and encouragement that he worked steadfastly to avoid hatred of anyone. So with these clear evidences of Eisenhower's faith in his mother, why have so many historians avoided the specifics of the Eisenhower family's religion? It seems likely that for Eisenhower and his political contemporaries the subject of his Jehovah's Witness background should be avoided, for many orthodox Christians see the Watchtower movement as being a cult, or at least not following Christian orthodoxy. The central doctrine that separates Jehovah's Witnesses from orthodox Christianity is that the church teaches there is only God the Father, and that believing in the Trinitarian nature of God (the Father, the Son, the Spirit) is a form of idolatry. Also, in a political climate that stressed God, Country and overall "Americanism," (in opposition to the Communist Soviet Union), it may have been politically dangerous to Eisenhower if voters knew he came from a background that did not allow military service, did not allow oaths of office, did not celebrate religious holidays, and did not allow Witnesses to say the Pledge of Allegiance—as these were all considered forms of idolatry. There is a certain irony that the president who is credited with doing so much to place "God" overtly in our national identities came from a background which saw "In God We Trust" on the dollar as being idolatrous.

To be entirely fair to Eisenhower, it should be noted that as a young adult he intentionally rejected the teaching of his mother's church—not vocally, not by a different profession of faith—but by joining the military and eventually going to war, by taking many oaths, and by joining another church, albeit long after his mother's death. Assuming that Eisenhower had some level of integrity, which seems consistent from what those who knew him said of him, we should believe that his religious choices were sincere and not merely political machinations. At the same time, we should not dismiss his religious upbringing. As president, Eisenhower was clear about his connection to orthodox Christianity, having a service at the National Presbyterian Church on the day of his inauguration. According to John Sutherland Bonnell, author of *Presidential Profiles: Religion in the Life of American Presidents*, Eisenhower was so inspired by this service that he wrote a prayer in response, which he read during the inaugural ceremonies:

> Almighty God, give us, we pray thee, power to discern right from wrong, and allow our words and actions to be governed thereby and by the laws of this land. Especially we pray that our concern shall be for all the people, regardless of station, race, or calling, so that all may work for the good of our beloved country and thy glory. Amen.[4]

We should note, though, that while Bonnell works to establish Eisenhower's orthodoxy, he mentions nothing about Eisenhower's significant religious upbringing as a Jehovah's Witness. In fact, Bonnell states unequivocally that Eisenhower was reared as a River Brethren. Again, this does not negate Eisenhower's sincerity, but it is one more interesting way in which Eisenhower's religious roots have been obscured, whether intentionally or not.

During his presidency, Eisenhower also initiated the presidential prayer breakfasts, which were led by the Reverend Billy Graham, who usually "gave a religious invitation."[5] Within fifteen days of becoming president, Eisenhower joined the Presbyterian Church through baptism and profession of faith; his wife, Mamie, was a lifelong Presbyterian. His interior secretary, Fred Seaton, recounts that once he "walked unannounced into the President's White House office, Eisenhower was on his knees in prayer beside his desk. . . . Making a crucial decision that could mean war or peace in the Far East and was praying for guidance in selecting the best course."[6] Many sources recount that Eisenhower tried to require that all his cabinet members go to church, and he apparently chose to open cabinet meetings with silent prayer. One administration official claimed that, as president, "Eisenhower was convinced that the government of the United States was based on religious belief," so his requirements for his cabinet were perfectly consistent with his simple beliefs.[7]

The relationship between African Americans and whites was problematic for many Christians during the 1950s (before and since, too). This was also true for Eisenhower during his presidency. In his book *Eisenhower: The President Nobody Knew*, Eisenhower's undersecretary of labor and speech writer, Arthur Larson, was particularly troubled by his president's views on the growing civil rights movement. Recalling the world-changing Supreme Court Case *Brown v. The Board of Education,* Larson remembers Eisenhower's response this way: ". . . he was determined not to take sides on the merits of the Supreme Court decision. . . , that had held in 1954 that school segregation was a violation of the Constitution. But then he dropped a bombshell. 'As a matter of fact,' he said, 'I personally think the decision was wrong.'"[8] Larson also noted that Eisenhower, on a separate occasion, expressed a distaste for the word "discrimination," adding that "as one who had lived in the South, he wanted to be sure to make it clear that social equality of political and economic opportunity did not mean necessarily that everyone has to mingle socially—'or that a Negro should court my daughter.'"[9] Perhaps most Americans felt this way in the 1950s, but who would be so bold as to say that they were not Christians? Clearly, however, there was and is a contradiction between the life of Christ and racial bigotry.

We know from his own accounts and the accounts of those who knew him that Eisenhower prayed and believed that prayer made a difference in the world. We know that Eisenhower sought to know God's will, and he believed that God did not owe America anything, but that "the nation's success was tied to the Grace of God."[10] Eisenhower publicly proclaimed belief in the tenets of the Presbyterian Church, and he faithfully attended church and prayed often. He may have been bigoted, but he eventually chose to support the Supreme Court's decision in Brown vs. The Board of Education by sending troops to support integration. When given a similar choice, whether or not to support the rights of a minority group by upholding a Supreme Court decision, one of Eisenhower's Presbyterian and presidential predecessors, Andrew Jackson, chose to reject the Supreme Court's decision, dooming the Cherokee to a life outside their ancestral lands. In a critical national moment, Eisenhower supported the Constitutional separation of powers and human rights.

While it is certain that Eisenhower had bigoted tendencies, he was an orthodox Christian with an interesting and heterodox religious upbringing who weakened the separation between church and state, perhaps in response to what many saw as the growing power of international atheism.

JOHN FITZGERALD KENNEDY
1961-1963

★ ★ ★ ★ ★ ★ ★ ★ ★ ★ ★

John F. Kennedy is and remains our only Chief Executive who was Roman Catholic. Looking back on that pivotal election of 1960, it still seems a bit of a wonder that Kennedy actually was elected. As his speechwriter and special counsel, the late Ted Sorensen once said, "The single biggest obstacle to his election was his religion. You should have seen the hate mail that came in, both from rednecks and from liberal intellectuals who should have known better."[1] Kennedy barely was able to overcome the widespread, deep-rooted doubts about his fitness to be president on account of his Catholicism; at forty-three, he was the youngest man ever elected to the presidency. And, as one scholar contends, Kennedy "is central to any examination of religion and the presidency."[2]

The author Richard Reeves, one of Kennedy's many biographers, argues, "I think the most important thing in John Kennedy's life, in forming his character and his view of life, was the fact that he was a man who received the last rites of the Roman Catholic Church at least four times."[3] As a result, according to Reeves, Kennedy's approach to life was fatalistic; he believed that what would happen, would happen, and life was meant to be experienced as fully as possible.

On May 29, 1917, Kennedy was born in Brookline, Massachusetts, into a devout Catholic family, whose story has been closely chronicled and often critically examined. His father, Joseph Kennedy, was a wealthy businessman who also had been chairman of the Securities and Exchange Commission, and United States Ambassador to England. His mother, Rose Fitzgerald Kennedy, was the daughter of a former Boston mayor; she worshipped daily at Mass and led the family in devotions and prayers. Kennedy, like his brothers, primarily attended private, non-sectarian schools; he spent less than one full academic year at an exclusive Catholic academy, the Canterbury School in New Milford, Connecticut. He graduated from Harvard College, where, among other things, he wrote for the Harvard *Crimson* and was a member of St. Paul's Catholic Club.[4]

Not since Warren Harding in 1920 had a president gone directly to the White House from the United States Senate. And while Kennedy defeated Vice President Richard Nixon rather handily in the Electoral College, his margin of victory in the popular vote was roughly the equivalent of one vote per precinct nationwide. Kennedy's January 20, 1961, Inaugural Address, while one of the briefer ones in presidential history, is one of the most memorable inaugural speeches, in which Kennedy, who was the first president born in the twentieth century, declared "that the torch has been passed to a new generation of Americans."[5] One author has noted that on the inaugural podium that cold, windy January, one of every seven people was a Kennedy.[6]

Prior to his inauguration ceremony, Kennedy attended Mass alone at Holy Trinity Catholic Church in Georgetown. His breakfast Friday morning included several strips of bacon, for Catholics in the D.C. area were given a special dispensation in recognition of the historic occasion.[7] Kennedy's speech that day was replete with theocentric religious imagery. After an early reference to Almighty God, Kennedy declared, in recognition of the work of previous generations of Americans, our foundation in "the belief that the rights of man come not from the generosity of the state but from the hand of God."[8] And he concluded his address, one that contained quotes from Isaiah 58: 6 ("To undo the heavy burdens, and to let the oppressed go free"), and Romans 12:12 ("Rejoicing in hope; patient in tribulation"), with this challenge: "With a good conscience our only sure reward, with history the final judge of our deeds, let us go forth to lead the land we love, asking His blessing and His help, but knowing that here on earth God's work must truly be our own."[9]

As effective as his inaugural speech was, perhaps the most important one Kennedy gave was on September 12, 1960, at the Crystal Ballroom in the Rice Hotel in Houston, Texas. The audience was several hundred ministers (estimates range from 600 to 1,000 in attendance that night); the Greater Houston Ministerial Association sponsored the event.[10] Kennedy was addressing what he called "the so-called religious issue."[11] According to Ted Sorensen, the speech would make or break Kennedy's candidacy,[12] and one Kennedy biographer has written that the setting for the speech had the "earmarks of an inquisition."[13] As Sorensen later would argue, "It was the best speech of the campaign and one of the most important in his life. Only his Inaugural Address could be said to surpass it in power and eloquence."[14]

The speech lasted just a little over ten minutes, and was televised across the state of Texas. Texas was a critical state for the Kennedy-Johnson ticket, and one, as with others in the South, where "the religion issue" was prominent. Kennedy's Catholicism, and legitimate concerns and paranoid conclusions about it, had put religion front and center in the election. One recently formed group, the National Conference of Citizens for Religious Freedom, which included such national religious figures as Norman Vincent Peale and Billy Graham, had concluded that Kennedy was unacceptable as president on account of his religion. Large numbers of individuals and groups feared that Kennedy would be a vassal of the Vatican, a White House Pontiff-in-Chief.[15] His strong desire, according to Sorensen, "was to state his position so clearly and comprehensively that no reasonable man could doubt his adherence to the Constitution."[16]

Kennedy stated, "Contrary to common newspaper usage, I am not the Catholic candidate for president. I am the Democratic Party's candidate for president, who happens also to be a Catholic. I do not speak for my church on public matters, and the church does not speak for me."[17] (As Kennedy remarked years before in a congressional hearing, "We have an old saying in Boston that we get our religion from Rome and our politics at home.")[18] What Kennedy stressed was his commitment to the separation of church and state, the free exercise of religion, and his independence from any kind of clerical cabal that would control his presidency. He viewed the presidency as "a great office that must neither be humbled by making it the instrument of any one religious group, nor tarnished by arbitrarily withholding its occupancy from the members of any one religious group. I believe in a president," Kennedy argued, "whose religious views are his own private affair, neither imposed by him upon the nation, or imposed by the nation upon him as a condition to holding that office."[19]

In what Sorensen has called "the most controversial paragraph of the speech,"[20] Kennedy stated that "if the time should ever come—and I do not concede any conflict to be even remotely possible—when my office would require me to either violate my conscience or violate the national interest, then I would resign the office; and I hope any conscientious public servant would do the same."[21]

More than a few observers found it interesting if not ironic that Kennedy was forced to show he was such an acceptable Catholic, for they viewed him, as one remarked, as one who took his religion "lightly."[22] He clearly did not wear his religion on his sleeve. His wife, Jacqueline Bouvier Kennedy, whom he married at St. Mary's Catholic Church in Newport, Rhode Island, on September 12, 1953, protested, "I think it is unfair for Jack to be opposed because he is a Catholic. After all, he's such a poor Catholic. Now if it were Bobby: he never misses Mass and prays all the time."[23] Sorensen has written that Kennedy, who faithfully attended Mass each Sunday, "cared not a whit for theology," and "not once in eleven years—despite all our discussions of church-state affairs—did he ever disclose his personal views on man's relation to God."[24] When one of Kennedy's sisters was approached by a writer who mentioned he'd like to write a book on President Kennedy's religion, she remarked, "That will be a very short book."[25] Sorensen noted, "He [Kennedy] did not believe that all virtue rested in the Catholic Church, nor did he believe that all non-Catholics would (or should) go to hell. He felt neither self-conscious nor superior about his religion but simply accepted it as a part of his life."[26]

As presidents before and following Kennedy have done, Kennedy regularly used Biblical quotations and religious imagery in his speeches. As one author noted recently, "There was, naturally, a political and cultural calculus to Kennedy's rhetoric."[27] Two critical speeches reflecting such efforts are from June of 1963: Kennedy's televised address on civil rights, in which he called for new (and long overdue) federal legislation on civil rights, and his commencement address at American University on June 10, 1963, delivered the day before the civil rights speech. In each address, Kennedy clearly linked the American political experiment and experience to the pursuit of justice and peace. In his evening June 11 speech on civil rights, Kennedy argued, "We are confronted primarily with a moral issue. It is as old as the scriptures and is as clear as the American Constitution."[28] Kennedy challenged each American to examine her conscience with respect to racial equality. And, in his American University speech, Kennedy argued that Americans should reexamine their attitudes about the Soviet Union, the Cold War, and especially "the possibilities of peace," for, as he put it, "in the final analysis, our most basic common link is that we all inhabit this small planet. We all breathe the same air. We all cherish our children's futures. And we are all mortal."[29] This speech has been characterized by one JFK biographer as "the greatest speech he ever made, one of the greatest speeches ever made by any American."[30] In this speech at American University, and again the next night on television, Kennedy demonstrated his commitment to peace and justice, associating our pursuit of the two with a national mission commissioned by divine Providence to defend freedom and spread liberty at home and abroad.

The year before these two major speeches the United States Supreme Court handed down its controversial, precedent-setting ruling concerning government-mandated school prayer, the *Engel v. Vitale* case from New York State. In response to the outcry, usually expressed in terms of the Warren Court "kicking God out of the classroom," Kennedy offered some sage counsel of his own: "I think that it is important . . . that we support the Supreme Court decisions even when we may not agree with them. In addition, we have in this case a very easy remedy and that is to pray ourselves . . . We can pray a good deal more at home, we can attend our churches with a good deal more fidelity, and we can make the true meaning of prayer much more important in the lives of all of our children. That power is very much open to us."[31] Lawrence Fuchs argues that Kennedy "revealed a simple trust in a benign God whose hand moves in a shadowy but benevolent way in the affairs of men."[32] As Kennedy himself said in February, 1961, "No man who enters upon the office to which I have succeeded can fail to recognize how every President of the United States has placed special reliance upon his faith in God. Every President has taken comfort and courage when told, as we are told today, that the Lord 'will be with thee. He will not fail thee nor forsake thee. Fear not—neither be thou dismayed.'"[33]

LYNDON BAINES JOHNSON
1963-1969

★ ★ ★ ★ ★ ★ ★ ★ ★ ★ ★

Lyndon Baines Johnson came from a long line of Baptists (one writer calls it an "awesome" line of Baptists), but he is one of only two Presidents to be affiliated with the Disciples of Christ, or Christian Church. Technically, according to church tradition, anyone who is a follower of Jesus Christ is a member of the Christian Church, the church universal. The two nineteenth-century movements of Disciples of Christ and the Christian Church rose up in response to what its founders saw as an unbiblical and growingly divisive sectarianism in American Christianity, so they attempted to re-create what they understood to be the atmosphere of the first century Christian movement. Without going into the whole story of these two simultaneous movements and their relationship through the twentieth century, suffice it to say that

179

there were splits, disagreements, fundamentalists, liberals, and the whole assorted cast of those who come to play a role in religious movements. To the young Johnson there would have been nothing he heard in those early revival meetings that would have sounded so different from what he had heard in the Baptist church growing up—emphasis on full-immersion baptism, no catechism nor creed, and a strong emphasis on independence. However, the central distinguishing feature of this movement (especially of the Disciples of Christ) from other American-grown denominations is the centrality of Communion, which was to be taken every Sunday.

The stories of how Johnson came to be a member of the Christian Church have one thing in common: he was a young, brash man. The official story is that the young Johnson accompanied two female cousins to several Christian Church revival meetings, and at the end of one particularly emotional service he professed faith in Jesus as the Son of God—forthwith being baptized. The even better story, however, recounted by a family friend, was that LBJ was very enamored of a young woman who was part of the Christian Church, so he went with her to several of the revival meetings, and on the last night he joined the church.[1] His home church remained the Christian Church in Johnson City, Texas, throughout Johnson's life. We know little about Johnson's church attendance during his early years, but we do know that he attended churches of many denominations during his long tenure in Washington and that, while Lady Bird would join him almost wherever he went, she always maintained her membership with the Episcopal church.[2]

Who of us can possibly know which influences are more important or are truly seminal in our lives or in the lives of those around us? This brings up a fascinating question regarding Johnson's life: which events influenced him most profoundly, his religious experiences, or his time spent with the poor of Texas? Perhaps that is a false dichotomy, since, if one believes the Gospels, one first must understand poverty and its suffering before working to carry out the Gospel by alleviating them. Joseph A. Califano, Jr., (Johnson's domestic adviser) argues that the seminal period for shaping Johnson's view of poverty was when he was a first-year teacher in a poor, rural, immigrant school in Cotulla, Texas, where Johnson states he saw "what poverty and hatred can do when you see its scars on the hopeful face of a young child."[3] In fact, Califano defines the entirety of Johnson's presidency through the rubric of Johnson's experience with southern poverty and racism:

> His commitment to racial justice and to eliminating poverty was genuine and consuming. It stemmed in part from a Texas youth in which he witnessed the effects of poverty and bigotry and in part his southern populist's gut. Equal opportunity became, for him, a constitutional obligation, and he pursued it with messianic conviction. . . . I believe that his dark moments after he left office were spent less in self-pity than in self-examination, wondering what he could have done differently to get the American people to understand his conduct of the war and to achieve greater racial equality.[4]

Califano's explanations of Johnson's actions in and out of office might well be the long-time aide's attempt to recast the shadowed leader's legacy, but throughout his six years as president, Johnson seemed to be moving toward a deeper faith in Providence and a shakier reliance on his own decision making.

To a gathering of 150 Democratic candidates in 1966, Johnson talked about the center of his domestic policy, attempting to both encourage the candidates and to gain support for his domestic agenda. In the center of this speech he argued that what he (and those listening to him) must care about were persons, individuals, those with names—not corporations, but "the folks" (interesting given our recent Supreme Court ruling that corporations have the rights of individuals). And he claimed that all of his domestic goals were built on this simple ideal: "to put food in peoples' stomachs and clothes on their backs . . . all the education their minds can take . . . and all the health their bodies can get from modern knowledge. Food for your stomach, clothes for your back, education and training and skill for your mind, and health for your body. . . . Is anything more fundamental?"[5] We can always disagree about the best ways to accomplish those goals—whether through government, church, or both—but the goals themselves must be desirable for Christians. One aspect of Johnson's war on poverty that was significant to him but that many Christians disagreed with profoundly was ensuring the availability of birth control to the poor. President Lyndon Johnson said that promotion of family planning in the U.S. and in the rest of the world was "a positive duty of government." Since the 1960s the phrase "family planning" seems to have become a red herring for "abortion," but that is not necessarily the case. However, many conservative Christians, particularly Catholics, were upset when Johnson and his administration accepted the Margaret Sanger Award in World Leadership (Sanger was the founder of Planned Parenthood)—Johnson has been the only U.S. President to receive and accept the award.[6]

As with so many presidents before him, Johnson would remark that knowing Americans prayed for him was a powerful and uplifting assurance: "No man could live in the house where I live and work at the desk where I work without needing and seeking the support of earnest and frequent prayer. Prayer has helped me to bear the burdens of the first office, which are too great to be borne by anyone alone."[7] And yet according to others who knew him quite well, like his speechwriter and now respected journalist Bill Moyers, Johnson was still concerned for his constituents, particularly those who were often ignored. Moyers says that during a 1964 campaign stop in Denver, Johnson had been talking with some Latino Americans after a speech there, and Lady Bird essentially scolded him, worried that too much time spent like this would wear him out. Moyers wrote:

> He made me [Moyers] go get the Gideon Bible out of the hotel drawer and turn to that passage in the New Testament where it talks about: there may be ninety and nine and all safely protected for the night, but the Lord worries about the one. He said, with that familiar twinkle in his eye, 'Now, Bird, if God worries about the one, you don't expect the president of the United States to forget him, do you?'[8]

At the same time Johnson seemed to be genuinely concerned about the nation's poor and disenfranchised. There was a much darker struggle going on that clouds and obscures our understanding of Johnson and his faith: the escalation of the Vietnam War.

From personal accounts and recordings made in the Oval Office, we know that President Lyndon Johnson was painfully aware very early in his time in office that the war in Vietnam was likely un-winnable, yet he continued to escalate the war, sending more and more young Americans to potential death. And, of course, those young Americans were to kill young persons in Vietnam for a war the outcome of which was probably predetermined. This populist, Christian Texan was guilty of what many would consider to be murder, and this may be one of the many difficulties and conundrums of the presidency—the man and the role.

Ironically, it was this moral mire that led Johnson on a spiritual quest in search, perhaps, of both solace and redemption. "I just know," Johnson told adviser Califano during a 1966 Vietnam bombing campaign, "that one of our Texas Boys, probably from Johnson City, will drop one of those bombs down the smokestack of some hospital or on some school and kill a thousand civilians or children."[9] That night Johnson's daughter Luci (by that time a Catholic), after talking to her father about this weight on his shoulders, suggested they go together to St. Dominic's Cathedral Church in Washington to see her "little monks." The two of them went to the Cathedral (opened just for them that night) and prayed silently in the third pew. As his presidency passed and the strains of Vietnam and the growing racial violence at home weighed on him, Johnson began celebrating Mass at Catholic churches (fourteen times in 1967). Califano states,

> In the last year in office, he [Johnson] went to mass more frequently, almost every other week, to the point where I wondered at times whether he would follow Luci into the church. Johnson especially enjoyed services at St. Dominic's in Washington and St. Francis Xavier Catholic Church in Stonewall, Texas, where he formed a close friendship with the pastor, Father Wunibald Schneider, who became a spiritual adviser. Over time, the President talked more often about seeking guidance from the Almighty and praying. I had a sense that he found comfort in his relationship with God, particularly during his final year in office.[10]

Regarding Johnson's record with the Vietnam War, at least, none of us knows if faith can wash away the blood of innocents. This spiritual and moral dilemma may be necessary for the President, but it is still a monumental burden, at least for someone like Lyndon Johnson. On Johnson's last full day in office (a Sunday), he celebrated the Catholic Mass with Luci, offered by a priest just for the two of them in the White House solarium. On the same day, Johnson also went to services with Billy Graham at the National City Christian Church, thus bringing together two of the important religious threads in his life.[11]

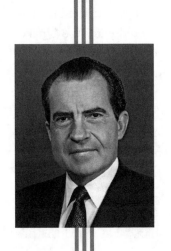

RICHARD MILHOUS NIXON
1969-1974

★ ★ ★ ★ ★ ★ ★ ★ ★ ★ ★ ★

On March 31, 1968, Dr. Martin Luther King, Jr., delivered a Passion Sunday sermon, "Remaining Awake Through a Great Revolution," at the National Cathedral in Washington, D.C.; it was his last Sunday morning sermon. That evening, President Lyndon Baines Johnson spoke to the nation from the Oval Office, beginning his speech addressing "peace in Vietnam and Southeast Asia" and concluding with the surprising announcement, "I shall not seek, and I will not accept, the nomination of my party for another term as your President." Almost immediately, Richard Nixon would return from the political wilderness and resurrect his political career by seeking and acquiring the office that eluded him less than a decade before.[1]

Richard Milhous Nixon was raised a Quaker. His mother, Hannah Milhous,

185

came from a long line of Quakers; she was extraordinarily devout, and Nixon often referred to her simply as "a saint." She often expressed, as have a fair number of other presidents' mothers, a strong desire that Nixon would enter the ministry.[2] At one time, several of his classmates at Whittier College, the Quaker institution from which Nixon graduated in 1934 with a B.A. in History, were convinced Nixon would enter the Quaker ministry, given not only his apparent religious commitments but also his impressive oratorical skills. However, he had a different pulpit in mind. As Nixon himself would write in *Six Crises*, which appeared the same year he lost the California gubernatorial race, "The last thing my mother, a devout Quaker, wanted me to do was go into the warfare of politics. I recall she once expressed the hope that I might become a missionary to our Quaker mission fields in Central America. But true to the Quaker tradition, she never tried to force me in the direction she herself might have preferred."[3]

After entering the White House in 1969, Nixon described himself as "a life-long Quaker and church-going Christian."[4] He stated that his "Quaker upbringing and my religious experience in the Society of Friends strengthen me today as they have in the past. My Christian creed includes the noble insight of Quaker Founder George Fox: 'There is that of God in every man'; and therefore every man the world around—regardless of his race or religion or color or culture—merits my respect."[5] Echoing these sentiments, in his 1969 Inaugural Address Nixon declared, "The greatest honor history can bestow is the title of peacemaker. This honor now beckons America—the chance to help lead the world at last out of the valley of turmoil, and onto that high ground of peace that man has dreamed of since the dawn of civilization."[6]

Nixon's 1969 inaugural was replete with religious imagery and even biblical cadences. (At each of his inaugurations, Nixon's Bible was opened to Isaiah 2:4: "And he shall judge among the nations, and shall rebuke many people: and they shall beat their swords into plowshares, and their spears into pruning hooks: nation shall not lift up sword against nation, neither shall they learn war any more.") He argued, "We are caught in war, wanting peace. We are torn by division, wanting unity. We see around us empty lives, wanting fulfillment . . . To a crisis of the spirit, we need an answer of the spirit."[7] He challenged the country to "build a cathedral of the spirit—each of us raising it one stone at a time, as he reaches out to his neighbor, helping, caring, doing."[8] In a refrain echoing St. Francis, Nixon offered what he called "a summons to greatness," in which we "take as our goal: where peace is unknown, make it welcome; where peace is fragile, make it strong; where peace is temporary, make it permanent." And, in his peroration, he would then "add this sacred commitment: I shall consecrate my office, my energies, and all the wisdom I can summon, to the cause of peace among nations."[9] According to Nixon, "The peace we seek to win is not victory over any other people, but the peace that comes 'with healing in its wings,'"[10] a quote from Malachi 4:2 of the Hebrew Scriptures. Nixon clearly saw the United States poised at a pivot point in history, and he believed he was to help the nation realize its (and his) historical calling.

However, and in spite of being reelected in the largest presidential landslide in history, fewer than six years later Nixon would become the first (and to this day *only*) president to resign the presidency, leaving the White House on August 9, 1974. His presidency, in spite of outstanding achievements, especially in the realm of international relations, seemed to follow more closely the maxims of Machiavelli than the Quakerisms of George Fox.

Coming to peace with Richard Nixon and trying to make sense of Nixon are imperative for understanding the American presidency and the role of religion in its institutional history and in the lives of our presidents. In the case of Nixon, for instance, we have the paradox "of the Quaker president who ordered more bombs dropped than any man in history."[11] For example, between March 1969 and May 1970, during the "secret" bombing of Cambodia (secret perhaps only to Congress and the American electorate), over 4,000 sorties dropped over 100,000 tons of bombs in an intensive campaign that caused untold destruction and massive civilian deaths especially of Cambodian farmers.[12] Nonetheless, during his first term in office, Nixon would state, "I rate myself as a deeply committed pacifist, perhaps because of the Quaker heritage of my mother. But I must deal with how peace can be achieved and how it must be preserved. . . . The kind of relative peace I envision is not the dream of my Quaker youth. But it is realistic."[13] He spoke these words in the same year (1971) that he was named "Churchman of the Year" by Religious Heritage of America.

Both of Nixon's parents, Hannah Milhous and Frank Nixon, were Quakers; his mother by birth, his father by choice. Each was deeply religious, with prayer and devotions and Bible reading at home daily. Nixon and his brothers, along with their father and mother, attended East Whittier Friends Church usually four times on Sunday and once during the week on Wednesday nights. As did his father before him, Nixon would teach Sunday school at East Whittier Friends, even after he returned to Whittier following graduation from Duke Law School and became assistant city attorney of Whittier.[14] He also was active in Quaker youth groups, played the piano in church, and spoke in church and church-sponsored activities on a regular basis. In addition to these activities in Nixon's youth, his father would drive him and his brothers to various revivals in the Los Angeles area, hearing such preachers as Billy Sunday and Aimee Semple McPherson. At one of these revivals, in 1926, as Nixon later wrote, "We joined hundreds of others that night in making our personal commitments to Christ and Christian service."[15] During this time Nixon read daily from the Bible Hannah had given him for his eighth-grade graduation.

Nixon's maternal grandmother, Almira Burdg Milhous, and his mother were pacifists. Of her he would write, "She had strong feelings about pacifism and very strong feelings on civil liberties. She probably affected me in that respect."[16] And in 1968, in his acceptance speech at the Republican National Convention Nixon would say of his mother (and himself), "A gentle Quaker mother with a passionate concern for peace quietly wept when he went to war, but she understood why he had to go."[17] During World War II, when he served for the most part in the Navy in the Pacific theater, Nixon would acquire two nicknames, one he loathed and the other he embraced: "Tricky Dick" (for his poker-playing prowess), and "Fighting Quaker."[18] (*Time* magazine used the latter sobriquet for its cover story on Nixon in 1952.)

While at Whittier College, as Nixon later would concede, he began to repudiate his family's Quakerism. In one paper he wrote his senior year in the fall of 1933, Nixon revealed, "My parents, 'fundamental Quakers,' had ground into me, with the aid of the church, all the fundamental ideas in their strictest interpretation. The infallibility and literal correctness of the Bible, the miracles, even the whale story, all these I accepted as facts when I entered college four years ago. Even then I could not forget the admonition to not be misled by college professors who might be a little too liberal in their views! Many of those childhood ideas have been destroyed but there are some which I cannot bring myself to drop. To me, the greatness of the universe is too much for man to explain. I still believe that God is the creator, the first cause of all that exists. I still believe that He lives today, in some form, directing the destinies of the cosmos."[19] In the words of Nixon biographer Stephen Ambrose, "He had found a balance between what he had learned in his church and what he learned in school that satisfied him. Thereafter, there was nothing approaching a crisis of conscience or belief for Richard Nixon."[20]

Nixon's political, and especially his presidential aspiration, was quite straight forward: he wanted to be, in the words of Elliot Richardson, "The Architect of his Times."[21] He cared next to nothing about domestic policy, about what he once called "building outhouses in Peoria."[22] His key arena of ambition was world affairs, international diplomacy, and relations among nations. And yet it was domestic behavior, with more than a small boost from Nixon's own dark moods and political character that proved to be his undoing. He saw himself as a man of peace, but several times after his resignation he argued his greatest blunder as president was not Watergate but rather his delay in bombing North Vietnam more vigorously in a war he had promised to end upon entering the White House.[23]

In his Second Inaugural Address on January 20, 1973, Nixon stated, "As we meet here today, we stand on the threshold of a new era of peace in the world. The central question before us is: How shall we use that peace?" He would conclude his speech by declaring, "We shall answer to God, to history, and to our conscience for the way in which we use these years."[24] The Nixon years, what one scholar has not without reason called The Era of Nixon, are likely always to be rated as consequential (China, U.S.-Soviet relations, Vietnam, the Middle East, and Latin America) and controversial (Watergate, The Plumbers, Dirty Tricksters, The Enemies List). Nixon may go down, as one of his aides opined, as "the permanent unknown of American politics."[25]

Throughout his presidency Nixon wrote self-improvement notes to himself; notes that at the least border on secularized versions of guides to better Quaker faith and action. One he wrote in November, 1970, reads, "I have learned about myself and the Presidency. From this experience I conclude: The primary contribution a President can make is on Spiritual lift—not material solutions." He explored other lessons learned, and then wrote of the need "for spiritual lift—each Sunday."[26] Nixon would pursue such a lift not by venturing out of the White House to worship with a local congregation or take part in a local Quaker meetinghouse, as Herbert Hoover often did. Rather, Nixon brought the church inside the White House, beginning on January 26, 1969, with Sunday services held in the East Room, with Nixon approving the program and actually acting as master of ceremonies as Billy Graham preached and George Beverly Shea sang.[27]

GERALD RUDOLPH FORD
1974-1977

★ ★ ★ ★ ★ ★ ★ ★ ★ ★ ★ ★

In many ways President Gerald R. Ford was a transitional president, coming to office when his two predecessors (Vice-President Agnew and President Nixon) had both resigned from office, at least one of them for intentionally breaking the law. Ford came to the presidency when the default for Americans had been to trust their elected leaders. Therefore, Ford may have been the last president who did not feel the need to prove to the country how religious a man he was, the last president for whom religion was not to be an overt aspect of the electoral process. As we have already discussed in this book, though, religion has often played a significant part of the political process in the United States, at least at the presidential level. But Ford noticed religion was becoming a litmus test of office, and he was not actually ready for that change, did not think that he needed to address religion in any significant manner while he was running against Ronald Reagan in the 1976 Republican primaries or against Jimmy Carter in the general election. Ford, who grew up in an Episcopalian Michigan family with his mother and stepfather (Ford did not know that his stepfather was not his birth father until Ford was a teenager), had learned from Mr. Ford that being a Christian and a joiner were significant roles for citizens to play, and Ford remained a committed Episcopalian and active citizen his entire life. Mr. Ford was a vestryman in the Episcopal church, a Shriner, a Mason, an Elk, and a supporter of the Boy Scouts.[1] That commitment to the oaths and groups one joins appears to have been always with Ford; the same Episcopal church that he and his parents had joined in the early 1940s was also the site of the future president's marriage and the former president's funeral.

As with several other presidential changes during time of tumult, fear, and relative chaos, the transition from Nixon to Ford following Nixon's resignation pressed Ford to turn to his faith, God, and religion for solace and guidance. According to Ford in his autobiography (suitably titled *A Time to Heal*), the night before Ford was to be sworn in as President, he and Betty reached out for each other in the darkness and began to pray:

> God, give us strength, give us wisdom, give us guidance as the possibility of a new life confronts us. We promise to do our very best, whatever may take place. You have sustained us in the past. We have faith in Your guiding hand in the difficult and challenging days ahead. In Jesus' name we pray.[2]

Ford writes further that as a child in Sunday school fifty years earlier he had learned the preceding prayer and that he also prayed the same words during other times of confusion and concern: the night he found out his stepfather was not his real father, and the many frightening times during his service in World War II. At yet another dark time in his life, Ford claimed to turn to prayer again. About to deliver a policy speech, Ford was informed that Betty's routine lumpectomy revealed a malignant tumor—resulting in the doctors performing a radical mastectomy; Ford left immediately (without delivering the speech) and flew to the hospital in Bethesda, Maryland, with a son and daughter-in-law: "During the flight, the three of us prayed and read passages from the Bible. Betty was in the recovery room by then. She tried to smile and gave my hand a gentle squeeze, but she was too tired and sedated to talk. I reassured her that with God's help she would have a full recovery."[3]

Those who knew Ford best, the aides and staff members surrounding him throughout his long political career, consistently tell of a man who was exactly as he seemed—honest and straightforward, one even claiming that Ford was the only person for whom he had worked who had "never strayed" (concerning marital fidelity, specifically).[4] Others remember his consistency with civil rights issues (helping usher in the major Civil Rights reforms during the Johnson administration, despite little backing from his own party), and Ford suggested that his views toward minorities were shaped by his having spent so much time with men of color during his collegiate athletic career.

Perhaps we rarely think about Ford and religion because of the two men who succeeded him who seemed to be so overtly religious—Carter and Reagan. In contrast to those two politicians and presidents, Ford was, indeed, quiet about his faith. During the 1976 election season, Ford seemed a little stunned by the religious rhetoric during his primary battle with Reagan (which Ford saw as a partial lack of integrity on Reagan's part, especially when Betty's comparatively progressive views on abortion rights and women's rights became an issue of derision for the Reagan campaign). In the general election, Ford was particularly shocked by Jimmy Carter's openly discussing his being "born again" and his sinning to *Playboy*, of all places. Ford recalls in his autobiography:

> Throughout the campaign, Carter had talked about his religious convictions in a way that I found discomfiting. I have always felt a closeness to God and have looked to a higher being for guidance and support, but I didn't think it was appropriate to advertise my religious beliefs. Carter, I was sure, had made a serious mistake.[5]

One thing is clear regarding Ford's views on religion and the American presidency—he was out of touch with what America seemed to want in a president: a man who was overtly "Christian." Indeed, Ford was shocked that in the next election cycle Reagan won the presidency, since he never regarded Reagan as a serious challenger.

A Time to Heal: The Autobiography of Gerald R. Ford begins with an epigraph from Abraham Lincoln that Ford uses to connect his transitional presidency with the presidency during another time of national crisis: "I know there is a God. I see the storm coming, and I know His hand is in it. If He has a place for me, and I think He has, I believe I am ready; with God's help I shall not fail." Ford chooses to begin his religiously titled autobiography with scripture and a reference to another president's hopes in an active Providence. The end of Ford's life (in 2006) is marked by this statement from The Episcopal News Service:

> The former President, a faithful Episcopalian, was a man known for his great integrity and his firm belief in God. He never sought the Presidency, yet when it was thrust upon him he led wisely, guiding our nation well during a time of high inflation, fuel shortages, and the complex foreign policy challenges presented by the Cold War. A kind man who worked hard at building bridges and shaping consensus, he will be remembered for his dignity, his humility and his devotion to healing a divided nation.

JAMES EARL CARTER, JR.
1977-1981

★ ★ ★ ★ ★ ★ ★ ★ ★ ★ ★ ★

President Jimmy Carter's "style of leadership was and is more religious than political in nature," wrote Hendrik Hertzberg, who was the chief speechwriter for the President from 1979 to 1981. "He was and is a moral leader more than a political leader. And I think this helps explain not only some of his successes as President but also some of his failures." Hertzberg also adds, "He spoke openly and convincingly about his Christian faith—and he managed to do this in a way that was inclusive and tolerant. Nowadays every politician," Hertzberg contends, "seems to feel obligated to talk about being born again, just as in decades past, politicians seemed to feel obligated to have themselves photographed wearing an Indian chief's war bonnet. But Carter was Christian before Christian was cool."[1]

Jimmy Carter made presidential campaign history (and perhaps modern American cultural history as well) in 1976 when he used two particular (and for more than a few folks, confusing) words to describe himself, words that most Christians, especially Protestants, recognized but were taken by others as clear and convincing evidence that Carter was some kind of alien creature. When this lifelong Southern Baptist from Plains, Georgia, declared that he was a "born again" Christian, many journalists and pundits scrambled to find someone (anyone?) who could explain what Carter meant and why he now was NOT disqualified from being taken seriously. As Garry Wills writes of Carter's statement, "It seemed vaguely Dogpatchish for him to say he was 'born again'—though all baptized Christians are, in some sense, born again according to Scripture passages like John 3:3-7."[2] According to Randall Balmer, a noted scholar of religion in American public life, "Jimmy Carter's declaration in 1976 that he was a 'born again' Christian had simultaneously energized evangelicals and sent every journalist in New York to his Rolodex to figure out what in the world he meant."[3] As Balmer concludes, in the eyes of this scholar, "Carter's candidacy reintroduced religion into presidential politics."[4]

A native of Georgia, Jimmy Carter was born on October 1, 1924, in Plains, Georgia, to a Baptist father and a Methodist mother. In his autobiography *Living Faith*, Carter writes, "Religious faith has always been at the core of my existence. It has been a changing and evolving experience, beginning when I was a child of three, memorizing Bible verses in Sunday school."[5] When he was nine, he began attending a Sunday school class taught by his father, and he writes that "even as a child, I was dismayed to find myself becoming skeptical about some aspects of my inherited faith."[6] In particular, Carter writes, he began to doubt the orthodox account of Jesus' death and resurrection. "By the time I was twelve or thirteen years old, my anxiety about this became so intense that at the end of every prayer, until after I was an adult, before 'Amen' I added the words, 'And, God, please help me believe in the resurrection.' What made it worse was that I thought I was the only person with such concerns."[7]

Carter was active in numerous aspects of religious and social life centered on Plains Baptist Church. He writes of accepting Christ at age eleven and being baptized with others who also made their professions of faith. He participated in the Baptist Young People's Union, and learned about

Baptist missions around the world, especially in China. When he attended the Naval Academy at Annapolis, Carter attended church regularly and also taught Sunday school to children of enlisted personnel. Upon his return to Georgia after his service in the military, primarily as a submarine officer, Carter was active again in Plains Baptist Church along with his wife, Rosalynn, who had been raised a Methodist but became a Baptist after her marriage to Carter. At the Plains church, both Carters, among other things, taught Sunday school; Carter also became a church deacon, took part in local church governance, gave lay sermons, and when the church deacons voted to prohibit African Americans from attending the local worships services (a vote taken at a meeting when Carter was absent, at the next meeting), Carter moved that they reverse their decision. A vote was taken, and Carter's idea was defeated by a large margin. Around the same time, Carter refused to join the White Citizens' Council, the "respectable" (as opposed to the Klan) organization that had emerged in the contentious civil rights years in the South, even when he was urged to do so by a local Baptist minister and when he was threatened with economic reprisals against his peanut business. Carter also was responsible for the showing of a religious film sponsored by the Billy Graham ministry, a showing that produced the first integrated audience in Sumter County, Georgia, in the twentieth century.[8]

When Carter ran for the presidency in 1976, a year proclaimed by *Newsweek* to be "The Year of the Evangelical," most voters (even though he announced his candidacy in December 1974) had next to no idea who he was, and when he declared his being "born again" and having a personal relationship with Jesus Christ, they probably thought he was a character conjured by the late writer (and fellow Georgian) Flannery O'Connor. Decades ago, one noted student of the American presidency, Clinton Rossiter, argued that one had next to no chance of being elected president if voters thought you were "a freak." Surely, more than a few thought that of Carter, for here was a candidate who, while not necessarily wearing his religion on his sleeve, did not shrink from discussing it. For those who cared to look closely and carefully and, to some degree at least, took Carter at his word, they came to realize that his faith was deep and genuine. As Carter stated during the campaign, "The most important thing in my life is Jesus Christ."[9]

Carter had demonstrated the depth of his religious faith on several occasions prior to his race for the White House. For instance, in his inaugural address as governor of Georgia in 1971, he declared that it was past time for the abolition of racism, and he ordered the hanging of Dr. Martin Luther King, Jr.'s, portrait in the state capitol. (In his Nobel Peace Prize acceptance speech in Oslo on December 10, 2002, Carter would refer to Dr. King as "the greatest leader my native state has ever produced. On a personal note, it is unlikely that my political career beyond Georgia would have been possible without the changes brought about by the civil rights movement in the American south and throughout our nation.")[10] While governor of Georgia, as he would do after entering the White House in 1977, Carter attended church faithfully, often taught Sunday school, prayed, and read the Bible daily. Almost without fail, he and Rosalynn would read at least a chapter from the Bible each night, often in Spanish to each other. And, as Carter biographer Douglas Brinkley has written, "On January 4, 1981, Jimmy Carter taught his last Sunday school class as president of the United States from the balcony of the First Baptist Church in Washington, D.C. His lesson was taken from Luke 9:46-48, and he began by addressing the nature of accomplishment."[11]

Jimmy Carter, according to presidential scholar Erwin Hargrove, "saw politics as a moral activity. Carter was a New Testament rather than an Old Testament Christian. He practiced humility, charity, forgiveness, and tolerance as political virtues. He did not see the world as inherently evil and sought peace through understanding rather than confrontation."[12] As Carter himself stated in Oslo, "I worship Jesus Christ, whom we Christians consider to be the Prince of Peace. As a Jew, he taught us to cross religious boundaries in service and in love. He repeatedly reached out and embraced Roman conquerors, other Gentiles, and even the more despised Samaritans." He noted that "the present era is a challenging and disturbing time for those whose lives are shaped by religious faith based on kindness toward each other. We have been reminded that cruel and inhuman acts can be derived from distorted theological beliefs . . . In order for us human beings to commit ourselves personally to the inhumanity of war, we find it necessary first to dehumanize our opponents, which is in itself a violation of the beliefs of all religions. Once we characterize our adversaries as beyond the scope of God's mercy and grace, their lives lose all value."[13] It is this denial of humanity that Carter attempted to pursue during his presidency, especially with regard to peace in the Middle East but also with regard to other policies concerning energy use and environmental protection.

Carter realized that practicing one's faith in the political arena was challenging, seldom easy, and always open to question and regular misinterpretation. One American Protestant theologian whom Carter studied closely was Reinhold Niebuhr; one insight of Niebuhr's always resonated with Carter: "To establish justice in a sinful world is the whole sad duty of the political order."[14] Carter knew one could not be, as he once put it, a "religious purist" and be president. He stated often that he was elected president, not pastor-in-chief. Nonetheless, Carter also argued that his political behavior and most of the policies he pursued ultimately could not be divorced from his own personal, long-standing religious faith. He once told a gathering of federal employees that he saw himself as "First Servant" rather than "First Boss,"[15] and he truly believed that he could and should take certain political risks as president because of his faith. Most evident in this regard was his commitment to human rights, which he unequivocally put on the nation's political agenda during the 1976 campaign and made a cornerstone of his presidency. As he stated in his January 14, 1981, Farewell Address, "America did not invent human rights. In a very real sense, it's the other way around. Human rights invented America."[16]

Carter suffered the political fate of being only the second incumbent of the White House in the twentieth century to seek and be denied a second term in office. Economic woes, perceptions of his inadequacies as a leader, and especially the Iranian hostage crisis and failed rescue attempt were key reasons for his defeat. As Douglas Brinkley has written, however, Jimmy and Rosalynn Carter returned to Plains with their souls intact. At Carter's presidential inauguration, his Bible had been turned to Micah 6:8, "He hath showed thee, O man, what is good; and what doth the Lord require of thee, but to do justly, and to love mercy, and to walk humbly with thy God." Carter's defeat, as one scholar argues, "turned into one of the greatest gains for God's world, as the thirty-ninth president's post-White House years have been a model of Christ-like love and service."[17]

Central to that love, that Christian love, which Carter actually addressed in speeches during his presidential campaign and White House years, is Carter's focus on peace and serving others. For instance, Carter concludes his memoirs, *Keeping Faith*, with an account of his last official visitor to the Oval Office, Max Cleland, a fellow Georgian, Administrator of Veterans Affairs, a Vietnam veteran and triple amputee, who later would serve one term in the U.S. Senate from Georgia (having lost reelection in part because he was accused of being weak on national security issues!). Cleland brought Carter a plaque with a quote from Thomas Jefferson: "I have the consolation to reflect that during the period of my administration not a drop of the blood of a single citizen was shared by the sword of war." Carter recounts that he wrote in his diary of January 20, 1981, "This is something I shall always cherish."[18]

RONALD WILSON REAGAN
1981-1989

★ ★ ★ ★ ★ ★ ★ ★ ★ ★ ★ ★

Ronald Reagan came to the presidency after one of the most outspokenly evangelical
presidents in U.S. history, Jimmy Carter,
and, understandably, Reagan seemed even
more Christian to many conservative Christians than did Carter. Talk with many conservative Evangelical Christians even today
and one will hear language surrounding
Reagan's legacy that borders on the language
of beatification—much like the hallowed
language that one would have heard from
progressives regarding FDR after his death.
With the glow of historical narrative already
tinting Reagan's tenure in American political life, it is tempting to imagine Reagan as
the last holy crusader against the evil east-
ern empire of godless communism, whose
beliefs in spiritual warfare and the rightness
of American capitalism helped him to deal

the fateful blows against the Soviet Union. While there is no doubt that Reagan identified himself as a Christian and that the Christian Right claimed him as one of its own, and that he did tend to view the world in terms of good versus evil, it is also true that he was above all a skillful politician who dealt very pragmatically with the Soviets, with Congress, and with the law—a Christian, yes; an American president who did whatever it takes to carry out his policy, definitely.

From most reports of his childhood, there are two consistent influences that shaped the future president: his mother's devout faith and commitment to the Disciples of Christ, and his father's alcoholism. While we will not discuss all the scars that alcoholism can leave on a young man, many have argued that Reagan's experiences with his father shaped significantly his response to sin, redemption, right, and wrong. But most centrally to this book, Ronald Reagan was reared in a deeply religious home in which a spiritual, strong mother was the guiding intellectual and religious influence in his life—much like his predecessors Eisenhower and Jackson. In his work *God and Ronald Reagan: A Spiritual Life*, Paul Kengor summarizes the statements from many of Reagan's childhood acquaintances by saying that many of them saw Reagan as being very advanced spiritually, that he was destined to become a preacher, that he had "a stirring evangelical zeal they interpreted as guiding him toward a church pulpit."[1] Unlike any other twentieth-century president, Reagan even graduated from Christian college: the Disciples of Christ's Eureka College. Those who knew Reagan during his long entertainment career consistently recall his integrity and his devotion to his faith, though not always to the point of attending church religiously even before the presidency. One of his radio co-workers recalls Reagan was "not the kid who went to church every Sunday, [but was] a man with a strong inner faith. Whatever he accomplished was God's will—God gave it to him and God could take it away."[2] Through almost his entire adult life Reagan was a member of the Hollywood Beverly Christian Church (DOC) (where his first wife, Jane Wyman, taught Sunday school), and where, to this day, his widow, Nancy, still sends a tithe check in both their names.[3] By 1963, however, Reagan began attending the Bel Air Presbyterian Church and eventually joined the church after he left Washington in 1989.

One of the things that makes writing about Reagan's religious life fairly difficult is that there are no secrets; his faith was completely out in the open, and there appears to be no smoking guns or closeted skeletons. Therefore, there is little here to reveal, especially after Kengor's fairly definitive book. We know from common knowledge about Reagan's speeches before gatherings of American Evangelical Christians, about his concerns regarding Soviet oppression of Christians, and about his tendency to understand and explain the world as being divided into good and evil spheres. On the personal level, Reagan still appeared to be a consistent Christian, even to the point of arguing for the divinity of Christ, the existence of the Trinity, and eternal rewards.[4]

Most of today's American Evangelical Christians would recognize Reagan as one of their own, especially in his view that one must not only believe in Jesus as God's son for redemption (as John 3:16 states it), but one must "accept" Christ personally into one's life, which is a fairly modern way of explaining the religious conversion as some form of accepting right doctrine—as A. W. Tozer puts it, to "take up the cross" is far more demanding than merely believing the right things. Kengor recalls that Reagan had these sort of "born again" or "accepting Christ" beliefs, to the point that in his first meeting with Soviet Premier Mikhail Gorbachev Reagan talked with the politically atheist leader of the "Evil Empire" about his concern for Reagan's son's immortal soul.[5] Further evidence of Reagan's personal religiosity are comments from Reagan's former pastor Rev. Moomaw, who asserts that Reagan had a "knowledgeable faith . . . [and was] very intelligent in his knowledge of the Scriptures." Moomaw also talks about Reagan being very involved in public worship (Moomaw's knowledge of this more than likely came from his friendly conversations with Reagan, rather than having witnessed this, since these churches were not known as being particularly demonstrative), feeling every aspect of the worship experience.[6]

One of the ways we have been attempting to understand the faiths of presidents throughout this book is by scrutinizing the ways individual presidents react to and address crises with moral and religious repercussions that affect their lives and presidencies. While history will most likely remember the Reagan years as a time of Cold War diplomatic battles and nuclear posturing, for the Iran-Contra affair, or even for economic deregulation, millions of Americans think first of Reagan and AIDS. Take a few minutes and look around for articles addressing President Reagan's response to the AIDS epidemic, and one will be overwhelmed with the anger and suspicion vented about the six years between the first diagnoses of AIDS and the first time Reagan said the word "AIDS" in a major speech; if not for the creation of what eventually became known as "AIDS earmarks" by the Democratic-controlled Congress that began in 1986, all NIH funding would have declined during the decade after adjustment for inflation;[7] in other words, very little attention was given to the AIDS crisis by Reagan or his administration. One writer for *Salon* even details in some length that Reagan spent more time speaking about UFOs in his speeches than he did about AIDS,[8] which seems to speak to how little importance this epidemic held for the Reagan administration. Many writers have speculated that part of Reagan's lack of response to the thousands of AIDS-related deaths was due to his religious beliefs—especially since AIDS, at that time, was seen as being an entirely gay-male disease, that it might be some sort of punishment from God, and that the punishment was somehow deserved. In the 2003 CBS mini-series *The Reagans*, for instance, an original scene had Reagan telling his wife that AIDS patients deserved their fates and that "They who live in sin shall die in sin."[9] Yet the Reagans' daughter, Patti Davis (who has been very critical of her father's policies and beliefs over the years), states unequivocally that this was not her father's character, claiming that her father had never said those suffering from AIDS deserved their fate, and further arguing that her father's "compassion for other people is deep and earnest, and whose spiritual life is based on faith in a loving God, not a vengeful one."[10] Anyone who paid much attention as the AIDS crisis unfolded in the 1980s would remember that actor Rock Hudson's death from the disease was one of the first moments when the disease had a real face for the vast number of Americans, and apparently Hudson's death deeply affected the Reagans who had been longtime friends of Hudson's. Davis recounts a time as a child when she and her father were watching a movie in which Hudson was kissing a woman and it seemed to the young Davis that the actor was not very comfortable in the scene, and her father responded in a way that seems to contradict, or at least complicate, the view that Reagan was categorically hateful toward gays:

My father gently explained that Mr. Hudson didn't really have a lot of experience kissing women; in fact, he would much prefer to be kissing a man. This was said in the same tone that would be used if he had been telling me about people with different colored eyes, and I accepted without question that this whole kissing thing wasn't reserved just for men and women.[11]

Considering the dramatically divergent feelings about AIDS and the Reagan legacy, it is difficult to conclude with any certainty how Reagan's faith informed the president's silence and inaction toward one of the major cultural-shaping tragedies for an entire generation. But it might not be a stretch to suggest that a visible lack of compassionate action toward the victims of AIDS (obviously among the "least of these," in terms of public opinion and civil rights, in the 1980s) by the American Church and by the Reagan administration (which fostered close ties with the American Evangelical movement) was a failure of faith and morality.

Many interested in Reagan's legacy, however, consider his policies toward the Soviet Union to be remarkably successful, and at least in the first part of his administration, Reagan's actions and rhetoric toward the Soviet Union seem to be influenced by his religious views. One of the most compelling and memorable of Reagan's speeches (and often vilified) was his 1983 address to the National Association of Evangelicals during which he warned American Christians to support the arms race because the Soviet Union was an "evil empire" with "aggressive impulses" which needed to be guarded against by increasing America's nuclear defenses; for Christians to dismiss this evil, Reagan suggests, was just the sort of sin that the demon Screwtape (of C. S. Lewis's *Screwtape Letters*) would try to lure Christians into committing. Reagan's views regarding the Soviet Union as being an evil entity opposed to American Christian values come directly from his Evangelical Christian upbringing and from his beliefs (dating back at least to his time as governor of California) that the world was coming to its end following now-dated interpretations of the book of Revelations that saw the Soviet Union as being one of the great nations in the battle of Armageddon. Besides this view of biblical prophecy's influence on Reagan, there was also his determination to combat philosophies or governments that made a practice of persecuting Christians (though one could make the argument that he was most concerned if these governments were Communist), so the Soviet Union was certainly evil in this regard, deserving his negative attentions and opposition. And yet Reagan was still the President of the United States, and his allegiance was to this nation and to its safety. Therefore, despite his belief that the world would end in a fiery, nuclear apocalypse that was the will of God, Reagan worked with several Soviet premiers to curb the arms race (always arguing from a position of aggression and strength) and to avert that same apocalypse Reagan thought might not only be inevitable, but even be preordained.

As a scholar of American international affairs Michael B. Oren explains in his work *Power, Faith, and Fantasy: America in the Middle East 1776 to the Present*, Reagan's background in the "restorationist-minded" Disciples of Christ (much more so than with his later affiliation and membership in the Presbyterian Church) inclined him to associate himself with pro-Zionist American Evangelicals, to the extent that he worked diligently to support the country of Israel and Jewish immigrants militarily, politically, and economically.[12] To a significant group of American Evangelical Christians, any American President's stance on Israel and Middle-Eastern issues is one of the critical hallmarks of his Christianity (which marked presidents Carter, Clinton, and now Obama with suspicion since they have worked toward peace accords between Israel and its traditional enemies), and Reagan was a friend to pro-Zionists.

A pro-Zionist, anti-Communist, pro-life, small-government politician, Reagan's presidential record for many Evangelical Christians indicate clearly that he was a Christian made in their image. A family man, church member, graduate of a Christian college, and preacherly speaker, Reagan seemed also to be an Evangelical Christian in his private life. Though he was not a regular church attendee during his presidency (Reagan and those around him said he was concerned with the congregations' safety, especially after the 1981 assassination attempt), there is little reason to doubt Reagan's religious sincerity. Most Christian of his legacy, though, may have been his ability to hold at bay the monster of nuclear war through his personal style of diplomacy, especially with Soviet Premier Gorbachev.

GEORGE HERBERT WALKER BUSH
1989-1993

★ ★ ★ ★ ★ ★ ★ ★ ★ ★ ★ ★

"Heavenly Father, we bow our heads and thank You for Your love. Accept our thanks for the peace that yields this day and the shared faith that makes its continuance likely. Make us strong to do Your work, willing to heed and hear Your will, and write on our hearts these words: 'Use power to help people.' For we are given power not to advance our own purposes, nor to make a great show in the world, nor a name. There is but one just use of power, and it is to serve people. Help us to remember it, Lord. Amen."[1]

With these words, just four brief paragraphs into his January 20, 1989, inaugural address, President George Herbert Walker Bush began his presidency. Bush was the first sitting vice president since Martin Van Buren to go directly from being a heartbeat away from President and elected Commander in Chief, and like Van Buren, his would be a one-term presidency. Virtually no one doubted that Bush was a decent, humane individual, but perhaps his singular political misfortune was to follow in the footsteps of "The Great Communicator," Ronald Reagan. Suffering by comparison, Bush would be turned out of office less than a year after peaking at around 90 percent in popular approval polls following the first Gulf War.

Bush became president at a truly historic moment. The Cold War was coming to a close, the Soviet Union was imploding, and we were witnessing the emergence of what Bush called a "new world order." As he put it in his 1992 State of the Union Address, "We gather tonight at a dramatic and deeply promising time in our history and in the history of man on Earth. For in the past twelve months, the world has known changes of almost Biblical proportions."[2] And then Bush declared, "But the biggest thing that has happened in the world in my life, in our lives, is this: By the grace of God, America won the Cold War."[3] And, in the president's eyes, God not only was blessing America; He was providing this favored nation the opportunity to lead the entire world. "A world once divided into two armed camps," Bush argued on January 28, 1992, "now recognizes one sole and preeminent power, the United States of America. And they regard this with no dread. For the world trusts us with power, and the world is right. They trust us to be fair and restrained. They trust us to be on the side of decency. They trust us to do what's right."[4]

This rhetoric from Bush is very revealing, for throughout his presidency Bush linked closely and consistently freedom and religion, America's values and God's values. In a speech to the National Association of Evangelicals on March 3, 1992, Bush stated, "Americans are the most religious people on Earth. And we have always instinctively sensed that God's purpose was bound up with the cause of liberty . . . Our government was founded on faith. Government must never promote a religion, of course, but it is duty bound to promote religious liberty. And it must never put the believer at a disadvantage because of his belief."[5] On this occasion Bush would reiterate his call for a constitutional amendment concerning school prayer, which in essence would overturn the United States Supreme Court's ruling in *Engel v. Vitale* from 1962 that prohibited government-mandated or sponsored prayer in public schools.

A few months later, at a prayer breakfast in Houston, Texas, on August 20, 1992, Bush said, "More than ever, I believe with all my heart that one cannot be President of our great country without a belief in God, without the truth that comes on one's knees. For me, prayer has always been important but quite personal. You know us Episcopalians. And yet, it has sustained me at every point of my life."[6]

George Herbert Walker Bush was raised in an Episcopalian home, one where faith, family, athletic competition, and public service were stressed constantly. His father, Prescott Bush, was a wealthy Republican, Eisenhower confidant, and U.S. Senator from 1953 to 1963, and he was one of the founders of Planned Parenthood. Bush would follow his father into public service; his first major act that revealed his patriotism was when, on his graduation day from Phillips Academy, he joined the Navy and became the Navy's youngest fighter pilot during World War II. He established an impressive war record: he flew fifty-eight missions and had four planes shot out from under him, including a rescue by submarine in the Pacific Ocean. In spite of such feats, during the political battles of the 1980s, Bush would have to deal with what one publication simply called "the wimp factor." As the historian and public scholar Garry Wills succinctly puts it, "Some wimp."[7]

Prior to his failed presidential bid in 1980, Bush established a resume that was the envy of many other candidates. He served two terms in the U.S. House of Representatives from Houston; ambassador to the United Nations; Republican National Committee chairman; special envoy to the People's Republic of China; director of the Central Intelligence Agency, and then, of course, two terms as vice-president under Ronald Reagan.

What George Bush especially wanted was a good, faithful, decent, tolerant country, one that, in essence, looked like him in large measure. Lyndon Johnson had envisioned a Great Society. George Bush, in his commencement address at the University of Michigan (where LBJ had unveiled his Great Society vision in 1964 in his commencement speech there) on May 4, 1991, called for a Good Society, one "built upon the deeds of the many, a society that promotes service, selflessness, action . . . Dare to serve others, and future generations will never forget the example you set."[8] Ronald Reagan stated once that he dreamed of an America where everyone could get rich. In his 1989 inaugural address, George

Bush argued, "America is never wholly herself unless she is engaged in high moral principle. We as a people have such a purpose today. It is to make kinder the face of the nation and gentler the face of the world. My friends, we have work to do. There are the homeless, lost and roaming. There are the children who have nothing, no love, no normalcy." According to Bush, "We are not the sum of our possessions. They are not the measure of our lives."[9]

Also in his inaugural address Bush declared, "A President is neither prince nor pope, and I don't seek a window on men's souls. In fact, I yearn for a greater tolerance, an easy-goingness about each other's attitudes and way of life."[10] Faith and family were essential for President Bush and central to his image of himself and the country he was chosen to lead. As he once stated, "I believe that family and faith represent the moral compass of the nation."[11] These convictions flowed from Bush's own faith, one he was reticent to address in depth, and one he practiced during his presidency, for he often worshiped at St. John's Episcopal Church in Washington, D.C. After his years in the White House, he and his wife, Barbara, have been active members at St. Martin's Episcopal Church in Houston, Texas, the largest Episcopal Church in the country.

What exactly Bush believes about critical aspects of Christianity in particular and broader theological issues is largely a matter of conjecture. During the 1988 campaign he stated in South Carolina, "Jesus is my personal Savior."[12] In the same campaign season he also stated that he was born again, which is language one doesn't normally associate with High Church Episcopalianism. We do know that Bush worshiped regularly, claimed to pray daily, and truly believed that faith matters personally and socially. As he paraphrased St. Augustine in his 1989 inaugural address, "I take as my guide the hope of a saint: In crucial things, unity; in important things, diversity; in all things, generosity."[13]

WILLIAM JEFFERSON CLINTON
1993—2001

★ ★ ★ ★ ★ ★ ★ ★ ★ ★ ★

The American public seems to enjoy placing its presidents into all sorts of camps—liberal, conservative, pro-life, pro-choice, pro-business, pro-union, Christian, heretic—but particularly we seem to enjoy the pastime of determining whether our presidents are heretics or Christians. Of course we have our favorites over which to battle: Washington, Jefferson, Lincoln. And there are still others with whom most Americans are comfortable labeling as being clearly Christian: Carter, Reagan, George W. Bush; but mostly we choose to avoid saying any president was not a Christian (perhaps begrudgingly acknowledging a president's nominal Christianity), though there are often musings, murmurs, and accusations to the contrary. One such man whose name sparks these conversations is President Bill Clinton, only the second president of the United States to be impeached and certainly the only president to be brought to trial over what were, essentially, attempts of a statesman to use his public power to cover his private sins.

The basic story of Bill Clinton's religious life is simple and clear. As a young boy his single mother took him to the local Baptist church's Sunday School, and from that point until he left for college, Bill Clinton attended that same Park Place Baptist Church in Hot Springs, Arkansas, most often on his own. It was in this church that he was baptized and that he began learning so much of the scripture he would quote throughout his political life. While stories abound regarding the young Clinton's slick, politicking behavior, calling into question, for many, Clinton's religious sincerity (in the world of politics, it seems, every action is open for scrutiny; how many of our own "noble" actions could withstand this scrutiny?), at least the majority of his high school classmates and school's administrators in Hot Springs saw him as being Christian, since he was chosen to give the benediction at their graduation. In Clinton's autobiography he remembers his benedictory prayer as an important event in his life:

> I prayed that God would "leave within us the youthful idealism and moralism which have made our people strong. Sicken us at the sight of apathy, ignorance, and rejection so that our generation will remove complacency, poverty, and prejudice from the hearts of free men. . . . Make us care so that we will never know the misery and muddle of life without purpose, and so that when we die, others will still have the opportunity to live in a free land." I know that some nonreligious people may find all this offensive or naive but I'm glad I was so idealistic back then, and I still believe every word I prayed.[1]

Clinton writes that throughout his life, especially during his time in Arkansas politics, he was drawn not only to his Southern Baptist tradition, but also to the worship cadences of the Pentecostal tradition, at one point attending revival services on a yearly basis.

We could write in detail about Clinton's religious life, his consistent church attendance, his many speeches referencing the Bible and the words of religious leaders, but this would really prove nothing to those who see Bill Clinton as a chameleon, a charlatan, and a philanderer. Some of these feelings about Clinton come from his pro-choice policies, some from the rumors and facts of his marital infidelity, and some from his beliefs regarding gay rights. Dr. Richard Land (president of the Ethics and Religious Liberties Commission of the Southern Baptist Convention) stated in a 2004 *Frontline* interview that although Clinton sounded like a good Southern Baptist Christian, many Evangelicals didn't trust him and even "hated" when he used religious imagery and language because "they were in fundamental disagreement with him about so many very important social issues."[2] It is fascinating that a man can bear all the hallmarks of Christianity—personal testimony, assurances from those closest to him, religious education, belonging to a body of faith—and still members of his own faith will reject him as one of their own because his political beliefs are outside what is considered to be "Christian" by the majority. We could say that Clinton was rejected because of his behaviors, his infidelities, but these only came to full light later. Influential and prolific Evangelical Christian author Philip Yancey acknowledges in a 1994 issue of *Christianity Today* that many evangelicals were "unimpressed" by Clinton's religious testimony and that Clinton may even have intentionally used his (apparently false) Christian testimony to "confuse conservative Christians and divide the body of Christ;"[3] this is akin to calling Clinton the antichrist. Yancey, however, counters with his own conviction that Clinton is, indeed, a Christian and that other prominent Evangelicals were also convinced and that he had "not met a single Christian leader who, after meeting with Clinton, comes away questioning his sincerity."[4]

Like many presidents before and after him, Clinton organized a prayer service before his first inauguration that included Clinton's choice of clergy from among Methodists, Catholics, Orthodox Greek, Baptists, Jews, and Pentecostals. Clinton even went so far as to choose the singers and songs that would be part of the service; in his biography Clinton recounts how significant the service was for him, and we have little reason to believe that his religious expressions are not sincere.[5] Others who watched from the sidelines during Clinton's presidency also comment on his religious sincerity especially when matched to the unbiased memory of magnetic tapes from the Oval Office tape recorder. William Doyle points out in his work *Inside the Oval Office: The White House Tapes from FDR to Clinton* that when Clinton was preparing for his first speech addressing the Republican takeover of the House of Representatives in the 1994 elections, "Clinton closed his eyes, took a deep breath, sighed heavily, and muttered softly, 'Dear God, help me'"—the unbiased tape alone capturing the sigh and murmur while the camera caught the closed eyes.[6] Yet another, and much more visible, example of Clinton's personal beliefs during his time in the White House was his work during the peace accords between Israel and the Palestinians. As a child Clinton had been told by one of his Baptist pastors to support Israel always, and this was certainly on Clinton's mind as he helped to broker the peace negotiations, according to Michael B. Oren. Oren writes that Clinton spent the night before the peace ceremony reading in the book of Joshua about Israel's breaching of Jericho's walls; on Clinton's mind were the words, "Now the horns would herald the coming of a peace that would return Jericho to the Palestinians," and the next morning for the ceremony Clinton wore a tie "adorned with golden horns to remind him of those Joshua blew to topple Jericho's walls."[7] So from his inauguration to his policies, Clinton seemed to be influenced by his significantly Christian background (though, like other presidents, Clinton's political record is cluttered with the flotsam of hurtful policies, such as the welfare reform that moved many of the country's mentally ill [the least of the least of these] out of state-run hospitals and into the streets and poorly-run day programs).

And then came Monica Lewinsky, lying under oath, parsing of words, and loss of integrity. No other American president has fallen so publicly, with such burning shame, as Bill Clinton. Other presidents had been embroiled in scandal, of course, but those scandals were usually covered in the operations of state, in the intrigues of politics, not the tastelessness of sexual innuendo and infidelity. We will not go into any particulars about those years of Kenneth Starr and impeachment, but these years, the end of the twentieth century, define for many Christians the Clinton presidency, proving in their minds that they were always right, that Clinton was unredeemed and irredeemable.

The term "Puritanism" is often used to describe various aspects of the American mind, and one aspect of Puritanism is particularly pertinent regarding Clinton and his sexual scandals: the true American Puritans (the ancestors of Jonathan Edwards) believed that the only way to know whether a person was one of God's chosen was by that person's blessings or curses. It was clear for us American Puritans that the fruit of Clinton's actions proved that he had never been what he had claimed and that everything was just words and images. Today, those who continue to view the world in that way believe that Clinton was never a Christian in anything other than word.

But then there was the confession, the spiritual awakening (another great American tradition) of that fallen man, and a renewed hope for that lost sheep. Clinton actually admitted in public, at a Presidential prayer breakfast, that he had sinned and that he had repented, saying,

> But I believe that to be forgiven, more than sorrow is required—at least two more things. First, genuine repentance—a determination to change and to repair breaches of my own making. I have repented. Second, what my Bible calls a "broken spirit"; an understanding that I must have God's help to be the person that I want to be; a willingness to give the very forgiveness I seek; a renunciation of the pride and the anger which cloud judgment, lead people to excuse and compare and to blame and complain. . . . I will continue on the path of repentance, seeking pastoral support and that of other caring people so that they can hold me accountable for my own commitment. . . . I ask you to share my prayer that God will search me and know my heart, try me and know my anxious thoughts, see if there is any hurtfulness in me, and lead me toward the life everlasting. I ask that God give me a clean heart, let me walk by faith and not sight.

It might be hubris on the part of Christian Americans to say Clinton's words of repentance were not heartfelt, that we know they were lies and that Clinton was not a Christian, that his sins were greater than his repentance. Probably intentionally, Clinton chooses to remind us in those last few sentences of another fallen, yet still loved, leader, King David; for the words "give me a clean heart" come from one of David's own prayers for forgiveness for infidelity and murder.

President Clinton went on to keep his word about seeking spiritual counsel and guidance from Christian leaders, among them Phil Wogaman (pastor of Foundry United Methodist Church, where the Clintons attended most of the time they spent in Washington), Tony Campolo (evangelist and sociologist), Gordon MacDonald (minster and one who recovered his ministry after an extramarital affair), and Bill Hybels of Willow Creek Church. Clinton recalls that these meetings were not easy, that these men "were often tough on me, the pastors took me past the politics into soul-searching and the power of God's love."[8] During this same time of shame, hiding, and recovery, Clinton read two to three hours alone each day in his office, concentrating on works like *The Imitation of Christ, Meditations, Seventy Times Seven,* and a series of sermons by Rabbi Menachem Genack of Englewood, New Jersey.[9] President Bill Clinton, if his words and the words of those who know him best are to be trusted, is a Christian of the most orthodox stripes and the American President carrying the most visible of self-inflicted wounds. We cannot know the state of his soul, and we should be glad we are not the judges. Further, we can be glad that other humans are not the judges of our immortal souls.

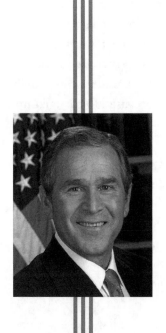

GEORGE WALKER BUSH
2001-2009

★ ★ ★ ★ ★ ★ ★ ★ ★ ★ ★ ★

"God's signs are not always the ones we look for. We learn in tragedy that His purposes are not always our own, yet the prayers of private suffering, whether in our homes or in this great cathedral, are known and heard and understood. There are prayers that help us last through the day or endure the night. There are prayers of friends and strangers that give us strength for the journey, and there are prayers that yield our will to a will greater than our own. This world He created is of moral design. Grief and tragedy and hatred are only for a time. Goodness, remembrance and love have no end, and the Lord of life holds all who die and all who mourn."[1]

President George W. Bush shared these sentiments at the National Cathedral in Washington, D.C., during the National Day of Prayer and Remembrance following the terrorist attacks of September 11, 2001. The tragedy that occurred that day was a turning point for the country, and for the former Texas governor who, at the time of the attacks, had been president for fewer than nine months. And yet, these words should have come as no surprise to Americans, as George W. Bush had campaigned for the presidency as a man of faith; in Iowa in 2000 he answered, "Christ, because He changed my heart," in response to the question, "Who is your favorite philosopher."[2] His campaign biography of that year, *A Charge to Keep*,[3] emphasized his religious faith journey, and journalists and scholars soon would declare that Bush's presidency was "a faith-based presidency" unlike any other in generations. Yet, throughout his presidency, while few doubted the sincerity of Bush's faith, a vital question lingered: Just what does George W. Bush believe? With respect to the religious faith of George W. Bush, as one writer puts it, "It is here that we come to one of the most unique characteristics of the Bush presidency and very possibly to one of the most defining issues of our time."[4]

George W. Bush was born on July 6, 1946, in New Haven, Connecticut; he was the first child of George Herbert Walker and Barbara Bush. His father was attending Yale University after his distinguished, even heroic, service in the Navy in World War II, and before too long the family would strike out for Texas, particularly west Texas, where Bush senior sought his future in oil and politics. George W. was baptized in a New Haven Episcopal Church, attended the First Presbyterian Church in Midland, Texas, with his parents and siblings, and then when the family later moved to Houston, attended St. Martin's Episcopal Church in Houston. After his early public school days in Texas, Bush followed his father's path by attending Phillips Andover Academy and then Yale University, and later would receive his MBA degree from Harvard Business School. When Bush married in 1977 he began attending the United Methodist Church of his wife, Laura; soon after he became United Methodist himself and also taught Sunday school classes at the First United Methodist Church of Midland.

Bush and his wife soon would welcome twin daughters into the family, and while he tried his hand in the oil business in Texas and ran unsuccessfully for a congressional seat in west Texas, Bush entered what are often referred to as "the nomadic years," in which, in part, he would develop a drinking problem and find his longtime marriage in trouble. In the summer of 1985, after his parents summoned the evangelist Billy Graham, the one person in the twentieth century who came the closest to being our national chaplain, Bush and Graham took a life-changing walk along a beach in Maine. Later, Bush would write of the experience, "It was the beginning of a new walk where I would recommit my heart to Jesus Christ."[5]

Back in Midland, Bush took an active part in a local men's weekly Bible study, and in 1986 he quit drinking. (Bush's religious transformation actually began in 1984, when he met an eccentric evangelist, Arthur Blessitt, who was best known for his carrying a 12-foot cross on long walks in the United States and around the world. Bush arranged a private meeting with Blessitt after hearing his sermons on the radio, and he asked Blessitt when they met how to "know Jesus and how to follow him.") But it was the conversation with Graham the following year that gets the bulk of attention.[6] Rather than emphasize or even discuss the Midland moment, the president has focused on his conversations with the more mainstream Graham. In any event, as he would tell a group of religious leaders during his presidency, "You know, I had a drinking problem. Right now I should be in a bar in Texas, not the Oval Office. There is only one reason that I am in the Oval Office and not in a bar. I found faith. I found God. I am here because of the power of prayer."[7]

These words are neither rare nor unusual for Bush, for he often has spoken and written about how faith has significantly altered his life. The language he uses most consistently refers to his "walk," or his "personal walk" after he experienced a "rededication" of his faith. As he said during the second presidential debate in 2004, "Prayer and religion sustain me. I receive calmness in the storms of my presidency. I love the fact that people pray for me and my family all around the country. Somebody asked me one time, how do you know? I said I just feel it."[8] This language of "self-help evangelism" was central to Bush's public presentation of his religious faith during his two terms as president. Was it, at least in part, calculated for political effect? The answer clearly seems to be "Yes." Was it also, at least as one can judge from a distance, or as recounted by others closer to the president, also genuine? Again, "Yes."

Bush clearly identified himself as an Evangelical Christian, conservative politically, and orthodox theologically but neither a fundamentalist nor one especially interested in or well-versed in denominational distinctions or doctrinal complexities. As president, Bush never really chose a "home church" to attend or in which to establish membership, nor did he attend church regularly in Washington while president; often he would attend religious services at the chapel at Camp David conducted by a Navy chaplain. He read the Bible and prayed daily. Oswald Chambers' *My Utmost for His Highest* was a favorite devotional work of his; he used *The One Year Bible*, published by Tyndale House, and his mother once said that he knew and could quote from the Bible better than anyone else in the family.[9]

As with most if not all evangelicals, Bush would seek God's will for his life after his mid-1980s religious experiences. As reported by Stephen Mansfield, before he publicly declared his candidacy for the presidency while in his second term as governor of Texas (Bush was elected in 1994 and reelected in 1998), he confided in friends, "I feel like God wants me to run for president. I can't explain it, but I sense my country is going to need me. Something is going to happen and, at that time, my country is going to need me. I know it won't be easy on me or my family, but God wants me to do it."[10] Bush echoed these sentiments in his first Inaugural Address, "We are not this story's author, who fills time and eternity with His purpose. Yet His purpose is achieved in our duty, and our duty is fulfilled in service to one another."[11] In this sense two things central to Bush's presidency, particularly in terms of social policy, were his faith-based initiatives program and his call for "compassionate conservatism," both of which were largely aborted following the September terrorist attacks on American soil.

This "theology of vocation" Bush applied not just to himself or his presidential administration; he applied it to the nation itself. During the 2000 presidential primary season, speaking at the Simon Wiesenthal Center in Los Angeles, he argued, "For all its flaws, I believe our nation is chosen by God and commissioned by history to be a model to the world of justice and inclusion and diversity without division. These are American convictions. Defending them is America's calling."[12] This awareness of and commitment to "America's calling" on Bush's part became especially ensconced in the Bush presidency following 9/11. As Professors Clyde Wilcox and Carin Robinson put it, "The attacks fit Bush's prediction that he was called to be president in a time when something important would happen, and his country would need him." The attacks refocused Bush's presidency, and he actually seemed to relish being a wartime chief executive. His "religious worldview," according to Wilcox and Robinson, "is widely credited for the stark way he depicted the world post 9-11 as divided into forces of good and evil."[13] We see this Manichean view of the array of global power throughout numerous statements by the president, including his 2002 State of the Union Address where he described "an axis of evil,"[14] and in his 2003 State of the Union Address where he famously (and somewhat controversially) proclaimed, "For so many in our country—the homeless, and the fatherless, the addicted—the need is great. Yet there is power—wonder-working power—in the goodness and idealism and faith of the American people."[15] Bush concluded this January 28, 2003, national address by returning to a fundamental conviction, one at the intersection of his religious faith and political philosophy: God's Providence and America's destiny. According to the president, "America is a strong nation and honorable in the use of our strength. We exercise power without conquest, and we sacrifice for the liberty of strangers. Americans are a free people, who know that freedom is the right of every person and the future of every nation. The liberty we prize is not America's gift to the world; it is God's gift to humanity. We Americans have faith in ourselves, but not in ourselves alone. We do not claim to know all the ways of Providence, yet we can trust them, placing our confidence in the loving God behind all of life and all of history."[16]

Two months later the war in Iraq to depose Saddam Hussein began, and forever more we would associate, in large measure, the presidency of George W. Bush with weapons of mass destruction (WMDs), executive rendition, enhanced interrogation, waterboarding, torture, Gitmo, and Abu Ghraib prison. Virtually forgotten was Bush's exemplary response immediately after 9/11 when he cautioned the nation against viewing Islam as an inherently violent religion and all Muslims as homicidal terrorists (contrary to some Christian Right leaders who spoke quite differently, as in the case of Franklin Graham, son of Billy Graham, who on *NBC Nightly News* denounced Islam as "a very evil and wicked religion"). At the beginning of his second term, Bush was quoted as saying, "I don't see how you can be president . . . without a relationship with the Lord."[17] According to one scholarly account of the faith of George W. Bush, "Bush's critics charge that his administration is filled with men and women who also ask God for guidance, and come away convinced that God has blessed their preferred policies."[18] On the other hand, supporters of Bush, especially prominent leaders of the Religious Right, were convinced that the president was God's divine instrument at a critical juncture in U.S. and world history, and that Providential calling was more evident than evangelical self-righteousness.

The influential presidential scholar Michael Beschloss contends that it takes several decades if not longer to arrive at an accurate accounting of the administration of an American president. The caveat to this clearly includes the presidency of George W. Bush. There is, for instance, the George W. Bush who declares at the 2000 Republican National Convention, "I believe in tolerance, not in spite of my faith, but because of it. I believe in a God who calls us not to judge our neighbors, but to love them."[19] And there's also the George W. Bush who prosecuted a preventive war and jettisoned just war principles in the name not only of national security but also in the name of doing God's will. There is, and probably always will be, a Janus-like quality to the presidency of George W. Bush, and examining it will keep scholars and others busy for decades.

BARACK HUSSEIN OBAMA
2009-

★ ★ ★ ★ ★ ★ ★ ★ ★ ★ ★

Not until the presidency of Barack Obama has any president's religious affiliation been questioned so systematically and severely. Many Americans wondered if presidential candidate John F. Kennedy could be an effective, independent leader since he was a Catholic, perhaps owing his obedience and allegiance to the Pope. An outspoken number of Evangelical Christians doubted President Clinton's religious sincerity, claiming that his Christian identity was merely a political ploy. Presidents throughout the twentieth century and into the next have been called socialists, communists, un-American, crooks—just about everything. But not since the nineteenth century have any serious number of persons or groups claimed a United States President was a religion other than what he had claimed. In fact, even Andrew Johnson's opponent in an earlier senatorial race called him merely a heretic (since Johnson did not necessarily believe in the virgin birth, among other things). But in one of the latest polls of likely American voters, 18 percent of those voters identified President Barack Obama as being a Muslim, while Obama and all who know him maintain that he is a born again, orthodox Christian.

While it should seem that even if Obama were a Muslim (which he is not), his religion would not be a problem for Americans. However, many of those who think that he is "other" than a Christian don't view Islam as a viable religion for an American President; in fact, one of the most influential spokespersons for American Evangelicalism is the evangelist Franklin Graham who has claimed that Obama is a supposed convert from Islam, which he has called "a very evil and wicked religion."[1] With all the preceding presidents in this work we have tried to establish the depth of each man's faith, or even the existence of that Christian faith. Ironically, President Obama is very clear about his Christian faith, his personal experience; there simply is no mystery here, unless we believe in dark conspiracies reminiscent of Masons, all-seeing eyes, hidden national treasures, and the Manchurian Candidate.

From President Obama's own stories we learn that he, like so many Americans, had a hodge podge religious upbringing, with Baptist, Methodist, and Universalist flavors swirled together with doses of Catholicism and Islam for originality. During his time in Indonesia (Obama's mother was then married to an Indonesian man with "a brand of Islam that could make room for the remnants of more ancient and animist Hindu faiths"[2]), Obama attended a Muslim school for two years and a Catholic school for another two years; from both places he remembers more his getting in trouble for not closing his eyes during prayers or making faces during Koranic studies than anything about theology or world views.[3] Throughout his childhood and well into his adulthood, Obama had little concern for religion or spirituality, a skeptic in his own words:

> Unable to confess that I could no longer distinguish between faith and mere folly, between faith and simple endurance; that while I believed in the sincerity I heard in their [persons of faith] voices, I remained a reluctant skeptic, doubtful of my own motives, wary of expedient

conversion, having too many quarrels with God to accept a salvation too easily won.[4]

However, some of that skepticism was to become softened from his first visit to Trinity United Church of Christ while he was working as an organizer in Chicago. The Reverend Jeremiah Wright had just preached a sermon titled "The Audacity of Hope," after which Wright offered a call and prayer for those interested in accepting God's challenge and hope. Obama remembers the two little boys and their mother sitting next to him, and "I looked down to see the older of the two boys sitting beside me, his face slightly apprehensive as he handed me a pocket tissue. Beside him, his mother glanced at me with a faint smile before turning back toward the altar. It was only as I thanked the boy that I felt the tears running down my cheeks."[5]

Lest we think that this instance at Trinity was merely an emotional response to a moving service, Obama writes later that he experienced what Evangelical Christians call a conversion experience:

God's spirit beckoning me. . . . I submitted myself to His will, and dedicated myself to discovering His truth. . . . What was intellectual and what was emotional joined, and the belief in the redemptive power of Jesus Christ, that he died for our sins, that through him we could achieve eternal life—but also that, through good works we could find order and meaning here on Earth and transcend our limits and our flaws and our foibles—I found that powerful.[6]

Perhaps what some Evangelicals (and certainly fundamentalists) find difficult to reconcile is that Obama is also comfortable with ambiguity and with the idea that his view of religion might not be the best one or even the correct one. For many persons of faith, certainty is one of the signs of devotion, while President Obama is clear that he is on his own "faith journey" and is still searching for truths, even to the point of leaving "open the possibility that [he's] entirely wrong."[7]

Like other presidents before him, Obama has not been a regular church attendee; in fact, in the more than two years since he came to office, he and his family have still not found a church to attend regularly. Of course, there are some who see this as proof that his campaign-trail words of faith and religion were just for voters. And, yet, the same thing about church attendance can be said about Ronald Reagan and FDR.

Also, like both Reagan and FDR, Obama has shied from going often to church because of what first-family attendance seems to do to the congregations. According to Jim Wallis (editor of *Sojourners* and a Christian friend of President Obama), the family was "shocked by the circus atmosphere surrounding their attendance and dismayed that some longtime church members couldn't even get into the service" when they attended Washington's Nineteenth Street Baptist Church.[8] Rather than regularly attend a "public" church, Obama and his family (like George W. Bush before him) make a fairly regular practice of attending small services at Camp David led by the Naval chaplain and Evangelical preacher Carey Cash, who is as close to a regular pastor as the Obamas have experienced since they left Chicago. At another military chapel (Marine Corps Base Hawaii) during Christmas 2010, much ado was made of the first family's attendance at the Christmas service, where they seemed to enjoy singing choruses, and where the president took communion through intinction alongside all the other worshippers.[9] (Neither Washington nor Lincoln took communion, at least not publicly.) Among the majority of orthodox Christian denominations, to take communion is to acknowledge, at the very least, that one is a member of the Body of Christ, a member of the Christian Church. So we can say with certainty that President Obama both says he is a Christian and demonstrates such through the sacrament of the body and blood as well as through the sacrament of marriage since he also was married in the Church.

Besides the first family's attendance at the Evergreen Chapel (at Camp David), President Obama has what some have referred to as a "spiritual cabinet," which is made up of some of the most religious members of the executive branch as well as a number of respected Christian leaders. Among that loose cabinet are Rashad Hussain (a White House lawyer and Muslim), Joel Hunter (a Republican and pastor of a 12,000-member non-denominational Florida church), and Sharon Watkins (president and general minister of the Disciples of Christ Christian Church [DOC]).[10] Joshua DuBois (the Obama Faith and Neighborhood Initiatives director) sends a devotional message with Bible passages and reflective thoughts to Obama's Blackberry each morning, and Obama states that he starts each day by going through that devotional reading.[11]

There are many, many persons of faith, indeed Christians, who know President Obama and acknowledge that he is a Christian also. In Obama's own words we have heard about his conversion experience, but he also has spoken clearly about his beliefs. For instance, in 2010 at the Easter Prayer Breakfast, his address is more sermon than anything else. Consider the following excerpts from that address:

And today, I'm particularly blessed to welcome you, my brothers and sisters in Christ, for this Easter breakfast. . . . The young man from Nazareth marched through Jerusalem; object of scorn and derision and abuse and torture by an empire. The agony of crucifixion amid the cries of thieves. The discovery, just three days later, that would forever alter our world—that the Son of Man was not to be found in His tomb and that Jesus Christ had risen. We are awed by the grace He showed even to those who would have killed Him. We are thankful for the sacrifice He gave for the sins of humanity. And we glory in the promise of redemption in the resurrection. . . . But as Christians, we believe that redemption can be delivered—by faith in Jesus Christ. And the possibility of redemption can make straight the crookedness of a character; make whole the incompleteness of a soul. Redemption makes life, however fleeting here on Earth, resound with eternal hope. . . . So, on this day, let us commit our spirit to the pursuit of a life that is true, to act justly and to love mercy and walk humbly with the Lord. And when we falter, as we will, let redemption—through commitment and through perseverance and through faith—be our abiding hope and fervent prayer.[12]

These words do not seem to be words spoken from the outside of a faith to those of a faith one admires, but they are the words of one who belongs to those who are his brothers and sisters—if words are at all to be trusted, that is.

The controversy surrounding President Obama's religious identity comes from at least three sources: his middle name, which is culturally Muslim; his connection with Trinity United Church of Christ; and (as with so many other presidents) policies which some see as being incompatible with Christianity. The first issue needs little attention. The name "Hussein" comes to the president from his culturally Muslim and agnostic father. This name proves he is a Muslim no more than the first names

"Christian" or "Jesús" mean that their bearers are Christians; or that a Morgan is a witch or that a David is a religious Jew. Second is the issue of the Reverend Jeremiah Wright and Trinity United Church of Christ, and this is slightly more complicated. Some loud voices have asserted that the Obamas' previous membership at this church and their close relationship with one of its charismatic pastors is proof that the president is a Black racist/radical, since the church proudly proclaims that it is "Unashamedly Black and Unapologetically Christian." Many Americans believe that the United States is now a colorless society (or should be) and that American Christianity is color-blind. To discuss this issue at length would require a full book on its own, so suffice it to say that churches around the world find their identities in race, language, and culture; further, American Christianity has often been an institution(s) that reinforces segregation and stratification. Trinity Church is a response to that exclusion, as is the African Methodist Episcopal Church and even Greek Orthodox and Romanian Christian Churches (granted, this is an over-simplification). Being an African American and worshipping at Trinity United Christian Church does not make one a racist, but it does mean one is aware of the significance of racial identity and pride.

Finally, there is the issue of religion and politics, which is the elephant lurking in this book. Since this nation's founding (and this is not under-graduate hyperbole) opponents of presidential policy have cried that some parts of those policies are un-Christian, that the policies prove the unredeemed nature of the man. Perhaps these shouts are louder and angrier today, with fights over abortion and same-sex marriage seeming to divide us culturally by what some would say are religiously rigorous lines—pure black and white. No matter what Obama says about Jesus, no matter how many churches the Obama family attends, as long as President Obama is pro-choice and not anti-same-sex marriage (and other issues of significance also), some American Christians will not accept Obama as one of their own. In the August 2010 Pew Research Poll cited above, we see that about 18 percent of Americans believe President Obama is a Muslim (and the poll was taken after he gave the Easter speech referenced above), and we also learn that 30 percent of Republicans believe Obama is a Muslim. Representatives from the Pew Research Center state, "Beliefs about Obama's religion are closely linked to political judgments about him. Those who say he is a Muslim overwhelmingly disapprove of his job performance, while a majority of those who think he is a Christian approve of the job Obama is doing. Those who are unsure about Obama's religion are about evenly divided in their views of his performance."[13] But we must return to what we know of the man and his faith. He describes a personal conversion experience; those who know him best describe him as a praying Christian; he takes communion publicly, and he speaks of Christian beliefs as one from inside the tradition—he is a Christian. He has not made the Hajj (the journey to Mecca); he does not fast or give alms during Ramadan; he does not pray the Salat; and he does not claim Mohammed to be God's messenger—he is not a Muslim. Perhaps there are policies that seem un-Christian, or statements that sound like he is a proponent of a violent civil religion (such as his words after announcing the assassination of Osama Bin Laden: "Let us remember that we can do these things not just because of wealth or power, but because of who we are: one nation, under God, indivisible, with liberty and justice for all. Thank you. May God bless you. And may God bless the United States of America") like so many presidents before him. But we know no man's heart, and we all bear different fruit. Once again, thanks be to God that we do not have to judge one another's hearts and souls.

ENDNOTES

Introduction

1. Skowronek in Philip B. Kunharts, Jr., Philip B. Kunhardt III, and Peter W. Kunhardt, *The American President* (New York: Riverhead Books, 1999), p. 10.

2. Howard Fineman, "Bush and God," *Newsweek* (March 10, 2003).

3. Theodore H. White, *The Making of the President 1960*, (New York: Atheneum Publishers, 1961), p. 64.

4. Michael Novak, *Choosing Our King: Powerful Symbols in Presidential Politics* (New York: Macmillan, 1974) p. 3.

5. Thomas E. Cronin and Michael A. Genovese, *The Paradoxes of the American Presidency*, 3rd ed. (New York: Oxford University Press, 2009), p. 55.

6. Randall Balmer, *God in the White House: A History: How Faith Shaped the Presidency from John F. Kennedy to George W. Bush* (New York: HarperOne, 2008), p. 158.

7. Ibid., (2008), p. 172.

George Washington

1. Daniel L. Dreisbach and Jeffry H. Morrison, "Religion and the Presidency of George Washington," in *Religion and the American Presidency: George Washington to George W. Bush*, ed. by Gastón Espinosa (New York: Columbia UP, 2009), p. 53.

2. Paul F. Boller, *George Washington and Religion* (Dallas: Southern Methodist UP, 1963), p. 29.

3. Ibid., p. 30.

4. Dreisbach and Morrison, "Religion and the Presidency of George Washington," p. 52.

5. Ibid., p. 91.

6. Ibid., p. 89.

7. Ibid., pp. 82-86.

8. Tobias V. Lear, *Letters and Recollections of George Washington: Being Letters to Tobias Lear and Others Between 1790 and 1799, Showing the First American in the Management of His Estate and Domestic Affairs. With a Diary of Washington's Last Days, Kept by Mr. Lear.* The Papers of George Washington, University of Virginia. Online. Gwpapers.virginia.edu.

John Adams

1. David McCullough, *John Adams* (New York: Simon and Schuster, 2001), p. 650.

2. Ibid., p. 19.

3. See, Page Smith, *John Adams*, 2 vols. (New York: Doubleday and Company, 1962).

4. See Joseph J. Ellis, *First Family: Abigail and John* (New York: Alfred A. Knopf, Inc., 2010).

5. Smith, p. 29.

6. Smith, p. 28.

7. McCullough, pp. 83-84.

8. Ibid., p. 84.

9. Smith, p. 31.

10. McCullough, p. 84.

11. Jon Meacham, *American Gospel: God, The Founding Fathers, and The Making of a Nation* (New York: Random House, 2007), pp. 17-18.

12. Smith, p. 1078.

13. Ibid.

14. Ellis, p. 236.

15. Meacham, p. 30.

16. Edmund Fuller and David E. Green, *God in the White House: The Faiths of American Presidents* (New York: Crown Publishers, 1968), p. 27.

17. Smith, p. 1049

18. Philip B. Kunhardt, Jr., Philip B. Kunhardt III, and Peter W. Kunhardt, *The American President* (New York: Riverhead Books, 1999), p. 138.

19. Meacham, p. 8.

20. McCullough, p. 650.

Thomas Jefferson

1. Joseph J.,Ellis, *American Sphinx: The Character of Thomas Jefferson* (New York: Knopf, 1997), p. 215.

2. Daniel L. Dreisbach and Jeffry H. Morrison, "Religion and the Presidency of George Washington," in *Religion and the American Presidency: George Washington to George W. Bush*, ed. by Gastón Espinosa (New York: Columbia UP, 2009), p. 48.

3. Edwin S. Gaustad, *Sworn on the Altar of God: A Religious Biography of Thomas Jefferson* (Grand Rapids, MI: Eerdmans, 1996), p. 216.

4. Ibid., pp. 7-8.

5. Ibid., p. 8.

6. Ibid., p. 13.

7. John Sutherland Bonnell, *Presidential Profiles: Religion in the Life of American Presidents* (Philadelphia: Westminster Press, 1971), p. 33.

8. Gaustad, *Sworn on the Altar of God,* p. 27.

9. Ibid., p. 33.

10. Ibid., p. 33.

11. Gastón Espinosa, ed., *Religion and the American Presidency: George Washington to George W. Bush* (New York: Columbia UP, 2009), p. 15.

12. Gaustad, *Sworn on the Altar of God,* p. 168.

13. Ibid., p. 112.

14. Ellis, *American Sphinx,* p. 259.

15. Thomas Jefferson, *The Jefferson Bible* (Boston: Beacon Press, 1989), p. 147.

16. Thomas E. Buckley, "Religion and the Presidency of Thomas Jefferson," in *Religion and the American Presidency: George Washington to George W. Bush,* ed. Gastón Espinosa (New York: Columbia UP, 2009), p. 88.

17. Edwin S. Gaustad, *Sworn on the Altar of God,* p. 124.

James Madison

1. The Library of America, *James Madison: Writings* (New York: The Library of America, 1999), p. 763.

2. John T. Noonan, Jr., *The Lustre of Our Country: The American Experience of Religious Freedom* (Berkeley, CA: University of California Press, 1998), p. 4.

3. Ralph Ketcham, *James Madison: A Biography* (Charlottesville, VA: University Press of Virginia, 1990), p. 46.

4. Ibid., p. 47.

5. Victor Phillip Munoz, "Religion in the Life, Thought, and Presidency of James Madison," in Mark J. Rozell and Gleaves Whitney, *Religion and the American Presidency* (New York: Palgrave Macmillan, 2007), p. 52.

6. William Lee Miller, *The Business of May Next: James Madison and the Founding* (Charlottesville, VA: University Press of Virginia, 1992), p. 106.

7. Munoz, p. 57

8. See Ketcham, and Irving Brant, *James Madison: The Virginia Revolutionist*. (Indianapolis, IN: The Bobbs-Merrill Company, 1941).

9. See Munoz.

10. Lance Banning, *The Sacred Fire of Liberty: James Madison and the Founding of the Federal Republic* (Ithaca, NY: Cornell University Press, 1995).

11. See Ketcham, and Miller.

12. James Hutson, "James Madison and the Social Utility of Religion: Risks vs. Rewards," paper presented as part of the symposium James Madison: Philosopher and Practitioner of Liberal Democracy at The Library of Congress, Washington, D.C., March 16, 2001, http://www.loc.gov/loc/madison/huston-paper.

13. Ibid.

14. Miller, p. 105

15. Noonan, p. 88.

16. Drew McCoy, *The Last of the Fathers: James Madison and the Republican Legacy* (Cambridge, UK: Cambridge University Press, 1989), p. 19.

17. Library of America

18. Ibid., p. 7.

19. Ibid., p. 30

20. Noonan, p. 4

21. Ibid.

22. The American Presidency Project, accessed May 11, 2011, www.presidency.ucsb.edu,

23. See Library of America, and Ketcham.

24. McCoy, p. 8.

James Monroe

1. David L. Holmes, "The Religion of James Monroe," *The Virginia Quarterly Review* (Autumn 2003): 589-606.

2. John Sutherland Bonnell, *Presidential Profiles: Religion in the Life of American Presidents* (Philadelphia: Westminster Press, 1971), p. 46.

3. Holmes, "The Religion of James Monroe."

4. Ibid.

5. Ibid.

6. Ibid.

7. Miles P. DuVal, *James Monroe: An Appreciation, Highlights of His Life and the Monroe Doctrine* (Orange, VA: James Monroe Memorial Foundation, 1982), p. 9.

8. Daniel C. Gilman, *James Monroe* (Boston: Houghton Mifflin, 1898), p. 241.

9. Ibid., p. 220.

10. Ibid., p. 212.

11. DuVal, p. 56.

12. Emphasis mine.

13. Holmes, "The Religion of James Monroe."

14. Bonnell, John Sutherland, *Presidential Profiles: Religion in the Life of American Presidents*, p. 46.

John Quincy Adams

1. Philip B. Kunhardt, Jr., Philip B. Kunhardt III, and Peter W. Kunhardt, *The American President* (New York: Riverhead Books, 1999), p. 168.

2. Jon Meacham, *American Gospel: God, The Founding Fathers, and The Making of a Nation* (New York: Random House, 2006), p. 13.

3. Paul C. Nagel, *John Quincy Adams: A Public Life, A Private Life.* (New York: Alfred A. Knopf, 1998), p. 203.

4. Fred Kaplan, *Lincoln: The Biography of a Writer* (New York: Harper, 2008), p. 14.

5. Meacham, p. 126

6. See Nagel, and Meacham.

7. Nagel, p. 296.

8. See Nagel.

9. Meacham, p. 27.

10. Meacham, p. 127; see William Lee Miller, *Arguing About Slavery: The Great Battle in the United States Congress* (New York: Alfred A. Knopf, 1995).

11. Nagel, p. 407.

12. Nagel, p. 256.

Andrew Jackson

1. H. W. Brands, *Andrew Jackson: His Life and Times* (New York: Random House, 2005), p. 18.

2. Ibid., 451.

3. Ibid., 450.

4. John Sutherland Bonnell, *Presidential Profiles: Religion in the Life of American Presidents* (Philadelphia: Westminster Press, 1971), p. 60.

5. Brands, p. 449.

6. Ibid., 549.

7. Marquis James, *The Life of Andrew Jackson: Complete in One Volume* (New York: Bobbs-Merrill Company, 1938), p. 733.

8. Brands, p. 536.

Martin Van Buren

1. Major L. Wilson, *The Presidency of Martin Van Buren* (Lawrence, KS: University Press of Kansas, 1984).

2. Ted Widmer, *Martin Van Buren* (New York: Times Books, 2004), p. 4.

3. Daniel Walker Howe, *What God Hath Wrought: The Transformation of America, 1815-1848* (New York: Oxford University Press, 2007), p. 505.

4. Widmer, p. 5.

5. See Wilson.

6. Edmund Fuller and David E. Green, *God in the White House: The Faiths of American Presidents* (New York: Crown Publishers, 1968), pp. 68, 69.

7. Davis Newton Lott, *The Presidents Speak: The Inaugural Addresses of the American Presidents, from Washington to Clinton* (New York: Henry Holt, 1994), p. 80.

William Henry Harrison

1. John Sutherland Bonnell, *Presidential Profiles: Religion in the Life of American Presidents* (Philadelphia: Westminster Press, 1971), p. 70.

2. James Albert Green, *William Henry Harrison: His Life and Times* (Richmond, Virginia: Garrett and Massie, 1941), p. 11.

3. Ibid., 444.

4. Ibid., 443.

5. Bonnell, 71.

6. Green, p. 63.

7. Ibid., 400.

8. Bonnell, p. 70-71.

9. Green, p. 400.

John Tyler

1. Philip B. Kunhardt, Jr., Philip B. Kundhart III, and Peter W. Kunhardt, *The American President* (New York: Riverhead Books, 1999), p. 211.

2. Daniel Walker Howe, *What God Hath Wrought: The Transformation of America, 1815-1848* (New York: Oxford University Press, 2007), p. 589.

3. Jon Meacham, *American Gospel: God the Founding Fathers, and the Making of a Nation* (New York: Random House, 2007), p. 589

4. Ibid., p. 133.

5. Ibid., pp. 134-135.

6. Ibid., p. 135.

7. Gary May, *John Tyler* (New York: Times Books, 2008), p.95.

8. Meacham, pp. 133-134.

James Knox Polk

1. Charles Sellers, *James K. Polk: Jacksonian, 1795-1843* (Princeton: Princeton UP, 1957), p. 25.

2. Ibid., p. 24.

3. Ibid., pp. 210-221.

4. Charles Allan McCoy, *Polk and the Presidency* (Austin: U of Texas P, 1960), p. 54.

5. Ibid., p. 55.

6. Ibid., p. 54.

7. John Sutherland Bonnell, *Presidential Profiles: Religion in the Life of American Presidents* (Philadelphia: Westminster Press, 1971), p. 81.

8. Ibid., pp. 82-83.

Zachary Taylor

1. Edmund Fuller and David E. Green, *God in the White House: The Faiths of American Presidents* (New York: Crown Publishers, 1968), p. 88. See John S. D. Eisenhower, *Zachary Taylor* (New York: Times Books, 2008).

2. Ibid., p. 87.

3. Davis Newton Lott, *The Presidents Speak: The Inaugural Addresses of the American Presidents, from Washington to Clinton* (New York: Henry Holt, 1994), p. 116.

4. The American Presidency Project, accessed June 6, 2011, www.presidency.ucsb.edu.

5. Ibid. See Daniel Walker Howe, *What Hath God Wrought: The Transformation of America, 1815-1848* (New York: Oxford University Press, 2007).

Millard Fillmore

1. John Sutherland Bonnell, *Presidential Profiles: Religion in the Life of American Presidents* (Philadelphia: Westminster Press, 1971), p. 93.

2. W. L. Barre, *The Life and Public Services of Millard Fillmore* (Buffalo, NY: Wanzer, McKim, and Co, 1856), p. 78.

3. Robert J. Rayback, *Millard Fillmore: Biography of a President* (Buffalo, NY: Buffalo Historical Society, 1959), pp. 45-46.

4. Ibid., p. 46.

5. Barre, p. 320.

6. Dorothea Lynde Dix and Millard Fillmore, *The Lady and the President: The Letters of Dorothea Dix and Millard Fillmore,* ed. Charles M. Snyder (Lexington: UP of Kentucky, 1975), p. 150.

7. Bonnell, pp. 93-94.

Franklin Pierce

1. Philip B. Kunhardt, Jr., Philip B. Kunhardt III, and Peter W. Kunhardt, *The American President* (New York: Riverhead Books, 1999).

2. Ibid.

3. Edmund Fuller and David E. Green, *God in the White House: The Faith of American Presidents* (New York: Crown Publishers, 1968), p. 92.

4. Ibid., p. 93.

5. Ibid.

6. See Larry Gara, *The Presidency of Franklin Pierce* (Lawrence, KS: University Press of Kansas, 1988).

7. Ibid.

8. Davis Newton Lott, *The Presidents Speak: The Inaugural Addresses of the American President, from Washington to Clinton* (New York: Henry Holt, 1994), pp. 125, 126.

9. See Mary E. Stuckey, *Defining Americans: The Presidency and National Identity* (Lawrence, KS: University Press of Kansas, 2004).

10. Kunhardt, p. 55.

James Buchanan

1. John Sutherland Bonnell, *Presidential Profiles: Religion in the Life of American Presidents* (Philadelphia: Westminster Press, 1971), p. 105.

2. Ibid., p. 140.

3. Ibid., p. 105.

4. Elbert B. Smith, *The Presidency of James Buchanan* (Lawrence: UP of Kansas, 1975), p. 15.

Abraham Lincoln

1. Martin E. Marty, *Pilgrims in Their Own Land* (New York: Penguin, 1984), p. 220.

2. Reinhold Niebuhr, quoted in Stephen Shaw, "Lincoln and Civil Religion: The President and the Prophetic Stance," in *Abraham Lincoln Contemporary: An American Legacy,* ed. Frank J. Williams and William D. Pederson (Campbell, CA: Savas Woodbury Publishers, 1995), p. 189.

3. Richard Carwardine, *Lincoln: A Life of Purpose and Power* (New York: Alfred A. Knopf, 2006), p. 325.

4. Michael Burlingame, *Abraham Lincoln: A Life,* vol. 1, (Baltimore, MD: The Johns Hopkins University Press, 2008).

5. Allen Guelzo, *Abraham Lincoln: Redeemer President* (Grand Rapids, MI: William B. Eerdmans Publishing, 1999), p. 325.

6. William E. Barton, *The Soul of Abraham Lincoln* (New York: George H. Doran Company, 1920).

7. Mark Noll, *The Civil War as a Theological Crisis* (Chapel Hill, NC: University of North Carolina Press, 2006), p. 14.

8. Shaw, p. 186.

9. Ronald C. White, Jr., *Lincoln's Greatest Speech: The Second Inaugural* (New York: Simon and Schuster, 2002).

10. See Shaw, Guelzo, and Carwardine, e.g.

11. Library of America, *Abraham Lincoln: Speeches and Writings 1832-1858* (New York: Library of America, 1989).

12. Noll, p. 434.

13. White, Jr., p. 208.

14. Noll, p. 431.

15. White, Jr., chap. 5.

16. Ibid., pp. 197-198.

17. Harold Holzer, ed., *The Lincoln Anthology: Great Writers on His Life and Legacy from 1860 to Now* (New York: Library of America, 2009), p. 109.

18. Ibid., p. 386.

19. Ibid., p. 442.

20. Shaw, p. 184.

21. Ted Widmer, "Christmas With Lincoln," accessed December 28, 2010, www .opinionator.blogs.nytimes.com/2010/12/24.

Andrew Johnson

1. John Sutherland Bonnell, *Presidential Profiles: Religion in the Life of American Presidents* (Philadelphia: Westminster Press, 1971), p. 118.

2. Andrew Johnson, *The Papers of Andrew Johnson: Vol. 1, 1822-1851,* eds. Leroy P. Graff and Ralph W. Haskins (Knoxville: U of Tennessee P, 1967), p. 40.

3. Hans L. Trefousse, *Andrew Johnson: A Biography* (New York: Norton, 1989), pp. 60-161.

4. Bonnell, p. 119.

Ulysses Simpson Grant

1. Philip Hamburger, *Separation of Church and State* (Cambridge, MA: Harvard University Press, 2002), p. 247.

2. Hamburger, pp. 322-324.

3. Jean Edward Smith, *Grant* (New York: Simon and Schuster, 2002).

4. Davis Newton Lott, *The Presidents Speak: The Inaugural Addresses of the American Presidents, from Washington to Clinton* (New York: Henry Holt, 1994), pp. 151, 153.

5. Smith, p. 14.

6. Smith, pp. 17, 18.

7. Lott, p. 153.

8. Smith, p. 18; See also William S. McFeeley, *Grant: A Biography* (New York: W. W. Norton, 2002).

9. Smith, p. 653.

Rutherford Birchard Hayes

1. Roger Finke and Rodney Stark, "Turning Pews into People: Estimating 19th Century Church Membership," *Journal for the Scientific Study of Religion* (2001), pp. 180-192.

2. Charles Richard Williams and William Henry Smith, *The Life of Rutherford Birchard Hayes, Nineteenth President of the United States*, vol. 1 (Columbus, Ohio State Archeological and Historical Society: 1928), p. 72.

3. Ibid., p. 70.

4. Ibid., p. 79.

5. John Sutherland Bonnell, *Presidential Profiles: Religion in the Life of American Presidents* (Philadelphia: Westminster Press, 1971), p. 133.

6. Charles Richard Williams and William Henry Smith, *The Life of Rutherford Birchard Hayes, Nineteenth President of the United States*, vol. 2 (Columbus, Ohio State Archeological and Historical Society: 1928), pp. 436-437.

7. Ibid., p. 437.

James Abram Garfield

1. Ira Rutkow, *James Garfield* (New York: Times Books, 2006).

2. Edmund Fuller and David E. Green, *God in the White House: The Faiths of American Presidents* (New York: Crown Publishers, 1968), p. 139.

3. See Ira Rutkow.

4. Fuller and Green, p. 181.

5. Davis Newton Lott, *The Presidents Speak: The Inaugural Addresses of the American Presidents, from Washington to Clinton* (New York: Henry Holt, 1994), p. 167.

6. Sarah Barringer Gordon, *The Mormon Question: Polygamy and Constitutional Conflict in Nineteenth-Century America* (Chapel Hill, NC: University of North Carolina Press, 2001).

7. Ibid.

8. Lott, p. 170.

Chester Alan Arthur

1. Thomas C. Reeves, *Gentleman Boss: The Life of Chester Alan Arthur* (New York: Knopf, 1975), p. 6.

2. Ibid., p. 34.

3. Ibid., p. 34.

4. John Sutherland Bonnell, *Presidential Profiles: Religion in the Life of American Presidents* (Philadelphia: Westminster Press, 1971), p. 143.

5. Ibid., p. 143.

6. Reeves, p. 357.

Grover Cleveland

1. Matthew Algeo, *The President is a Sick Man* (New York: Chicago Review Press, 2011).

2. Philip B. Kunhardt, Jr., Philip Kunhardt, III, and Peter W. Kunhardt, *The American President* (New York: Riverhead Books, 1999), p. 362.

3. Edmund Fuller and David E. Green, *God in the White House: The Faiths of American Presidents* (New York: Crown Publishers, 1968), p. 148.

4. Ibid.

5. See Henry F. Graff, *Grover Cleveland* (New York: Times Books, 2002).

6. Davis Newton Lott, *The Presidents Speak: The Inaugural Addresses of the American Presidents, from Washington to Clinton* (New York: Henry Holt, 1994), p. 195.

7. Ibid., p. 193.

8. The American Presidency Project, accessed May 31, 2011, www.presidency.ucsb.edu.

9. Ibid.

10. Mary E. Stuckey, *Defining Americans: The Presidency and National Identity* (Lawrence, KS: University Press of Kansas, 2004), chap. 3.

Bejamin Harrison

1. Harry Joseph Seivers, *Benjamin Harrison: Hoosier Warrior, 1833-1865* (Chicago: Henry Regnery Company, 1952), p. 28.

2. John Sutherland Bonnell, *Presidential Profiles: Religion in the Life of American Presidents* (Philadelphia: Westminster Press, 1971), p. 153.

3. Seivers, pp. 112-113.

William McKinley

1. The American Presidency Project, accessed June 2, 2011, www.presidency.ucsb.edu.

2. Davis Newton Lott, *The Presidents Speak: The Inaugural Addresses of the American Presidents, from Washington to Clinton* (New York: Henry Holt, 1994), p. 199.

3. Ibid., p. 207.

4. Ibid., pp. 206, 209. See Richard V. Pierard and Robert D. Linder, *Civil Religion and the Presidency* (Grand Rapids, MI: Zondervan Publishing House, 1988), chap. 5.

5. Lewis Gould, *The Spanish American War and President McKinley* (Lawrence, KS: University Press of Kansas, 1982), p. 41.

6. The American Presidency Project, accessed May 31, 2011, www. presidency.ucsb. edu.

7. Ibid.

8. Reinhold Niebuhr, *The Irony of American History* (New York: Charles Scribners Sons, 1952), p. 70.

9. The American Presidency Project, accessed June 2, 2011, www.presidency.ucsb.edu.

10. Ibid.

11. Ibid.

12. Pierard and Linder, p. 131.

13. Gould, p. 54.

14. Pierard and Linder, chap. 5.

15. The American Presidency Project, accessed June 2, 2011, www.presidency.ucsb.edu.

16. Pierard and Linder, p. 134.

Theodore Roosevelt

1. Corinne Roosevelt Robinson, *My Brother Theodore Roosevelt* (New York: Charles Scribner's Sons, 1921), p. 17.

2. John Sutherland Bonnell, *Presidential Profiles: Religion in the Life of American Presidents* (Philadelphia: Westminster Press, 1971), p. 167.

3. Theodore Roosevelt, *Theodore Roosevelt: An Autobiography* (New York: Charles Scribner's Sons, 1920), p. 42.

4. Stefan Lorant, *The Life and Times of Theodore Roosevelt* (New York: Garden City, 1959), p. 629.

5. Robinson, p. 235.

6. Ibid., pp. 335-336.

7. Roosevelt, p. 534.

8. Ibid.

9. Bonnell, p. 170.

William Howard Taft

1. See Lewis L. Gould, *The William Howard Taft Presidency* (Lawrence, KS: University Press of Kansas, 2009).

2. Edmund Fuller and David E. Green, *God in the White House: The Faiths of American Presidents* (New York: Crown Publishers, 1968), pp. 171-172.

3. Ibid., p. 170; See Gould, and Jon Meacham, *American Gospel: God, the Founding Fathers, and the Making of a Nation* (New York: Random House, 2006).

4. www.americanunitarian.org/taftconvictions, accessed January 6, 2011. See Gould, and Fuller and Green.

Woodrow Wilson

1. George C. Osborn, *Woodrow Wilson: The Early Years* (Baton Rouge: Louisiana State UP, 1968), pp. 12-13.

2. John Milton Cooper, Jr., *The Warrior and the Priest: Woodrow Wilson and Theodore Roosevelt* (Cambridge, MA: Harvard UP, 1983), p. 19.

3. John Milton Cooper, Jr., *Woodrow Wilson: A Biography* (New York: Knopf, 2009), p. 4.

4. John Milton Cooper, Jr., *The Warrior and the Priest,* p. 93.

5. John Sutherland Bonnell, *Presidential Profiles: Religion in the Life of American Presidents* (Philadelphia: Westminster Press, 1971), p. 182.

6. John Milton Cooper, Jr., *Woodrow Wilson: A Biography,* p. 279.

7. Ibid., p. 464.

8. Ibid., p. 4.

9. John Milton Cooper, Jr., *The Warrior and the Priest,* p. 171.

10. Ibid., p. 171.

11. Ibid., p. 124.

12. Cooper, *Woodrow Wilson: A Biography,* p. 411.

13. Ibid., p. 411.

14. Ibid., p. 489.

Warren Gamaliel Harding

1. Samuel Hopkins Adams, quoted in John Dean, *Warren G. Harding,* New York: Times Books, 2004.

2. See, Eugene P. Trani and David L. Wilson, *The Presidency of Warren G. Harding,* Lawrence, KS: University Press of Kansas, 1977.

3. John Dean, *Warren G. Harding,* New York: Times Books, 2004, p. 9.

4. Edmund Fuller and David E. Green, *God in the White House: The Faiths of American Presidents,* New York: Crown Publishers, 1968, p. 189.

5. Ibid., pp. 186-187.

6. Dean, p. 51.

7. Ibid. pp. 3-4.

8. William J. Ridings, Jr., and Stuart B. McIver, *Rating the Presidents: A Ranking of U.S. Leaders, From the Great and Honorable to the Dishonest and Incompetent,* Seacacus, NJ: Citadel Press,1997, p. 183.

9. Davis Newton Lott, *The Presidents Speak: The Inaugural Addresses of the American Presidents, from Washington to Clinton,* New York: Henry Holt, 1994, pp. 49-250.

10. Ibid.

11. Ibid.

Calvin Coolidge

1. Charles Allan McCoy, *Polk and the Presidency* (Austin, Texas: U of Texas P, 1960), p. 50.

2. Ibid., p. 50.

3. Ibid., p. 148.

4. Ibid., p. 397.

5. Robert A. Woods, *The Preparation of Calvin Coolidge: An Interpretation* (Boston: Houghton Mifflin, 1924), pp. 234-235.

6. Ibid., p. 6.

7. McCoy, p. 291.

8. Woods, p. 235.

Herbert Clark Hoover

1. Martin L. Fausold, "Quaker President Herbert C. Hoover and American Foreign Policy," in *Herbert Hoover and World Peace*, ed. Lee Nash (Lanham, MD: University Press of America, Inc., 2010), p. 2.

2. David Burner, *Herbert Hoover: A Public Life* (New York: Alfred A. Knopf, 1979).

3. Herbert C. Hoover, *The Memoirs of Herbert Hoover, vol. 1, Years of Adventure, 1874-1920* (New York: Macmillan, 1952), p. 8.

4. Ibid., p. 7.

5. Ibid., p. 8.

6. Ibid., p. 10.

7. Burner, p. 9.

8. Hoover, *Memoirs, vol. 1*, p. 13.

9. Ibid., p. 15.

10. Burner, p. **x.**

11. Ibid., p. 254.

12. Davis Newton Lott, *The Presidents Speak: The Inaugural Addresses of the American Presidents, from Washington to Clinton* (New York: Henry Holt, 1994), p. 265.

13. Ibid.

14. Ibid., p. 270.

15. Herbert C. Hoover, *The Memoirs of Herbert Hoover, vol. 2, The Cabinet and the Presidency, 1920-1933* (New York: Macmillan, 1952).

16. John R. M. Wilson, "Herbert Hoover's Military Policy," in *Herbert Hoover and World Peace, ed. Lee Nash* (Lanham, MD: University Press of America, 2010), p. 116. See Burner, p. 296.

17. Ibid., p. 116.

18. Ibid., p. 117.

19. The American Presidency Project, accessed June 3, 2011, www.presidency.ucsb.edu.

20. Burner, p. 206.

21. Ibid., p. 253.

22. William J. Ridings, Jr., and Stuart B. McIver, *Rating the Presidents: A Ranking of U.S. Leaders, From the Great and Honorable to the Dishonest and Incompetent* (Secaucus, NJ: Citadel Press, 1997), p. 195.

Franklin Delano Roosevelt

1. John Sutherland Bonnell, *Presidential Profiles: Religion in the Life of American Presidents* (Philadelphia: Westminster Press, 1971), p. 208.

2. Kenneth S. Davis, *FDR: The Beckoning of Destiny, 1882-1928* (New York: History Book Club, 2003), pp. 200-201.

3. Francis Perkins, *The Roosevelt I Knew* (New York: Viking Press, 1946), pp. 144-145.

4. Gary Scott Smith, "Religion and the Presidency of Franklin Delano Roosevelt," in *Religion and the American Presidency: George Washington to George W. Bush, ed. Gastón Espinosa* (New York: Columbia UP, 2009), p. 187.

5. Davis, p. 200.

6. Perkins, p. 141.

7. Ibid., p. 141.

8. Davis, p. 83.

9. Smith, p. 188.

10. Perkins, p. 144.

11. Ibid., p. 146.

12. Smith, p. 188.

13. Perkins, p. 333.

14. Smith, p. 199.

15. Perkins, pp. 139-140.

16. Ibid., p. 146.

17. Ibid., p. 29.

18. Bonnell, p. 209.

Harry S. Truman

1. Davis Newton Lott, *The Presidents Speak: The Inaugural Addresses of the American Presidents, from Washington to Clinton* (New York: Henry Holt, 1994), p. 293.

2. Alonzo L. Hamby, *Man of the People: A Life of Harry S. Truman* (New York: Oxford University Press, 1995), p. 7.

3. Ibid.

4. Elizabeth Edwards Spalding, "We Must Put on the Armor of God," in *Religion and the American Presidency*, ed. Mark J. Rozell and Gleaves Whitney (New York: Palgrave Macmillan, 2007), p. 98.

5. Robert H. Ferrell, ed., *Off the Record: The Private Papers of Harry S. Truman* (New York: Harper and Row, 1980), p. 40.

6. Ibid., pp. 251-252.

7. David McCullough, *Truman* (New York: Simon and Schuster, 1992), p. 360.

8. Ferrell, p. 23.

9. Ibid., p. 188.

10. Ibid.

11. Ibid., pp. 196-197.

12. Spalding, p. 102.

13. Ibid.

14. Ibid., p. 97.

15. Ibid., p. 98.

16. Ferrell, p. 313.

17. Harry S. Truman, *Memoirs, vol 1, Year of Decisions* (Garden City, NY: Doubleday and Company, Inc., 1955), p. 452.

18. The American Presidency Project, accessed June 7, 2011, www.presidency.ucsb.edu.

19. Ibid.

20. Thomas E. Cronin and Michael A. Genovese, *The Paradoxes of the American Presidency*, 3rd ed. (New York: Oxford University Press, 2011), p. 13.

Dwight David Eisenhower

1. Bergman, "Religion and the Presidency of Dwight D. Eisenhower," in *Religion and the American Presidency: George Washington to George W. Bush,* edited by Gastón Espinosa (New York: Columbia UP, 2009), p. 252.

2. Stephen E. Ambrose, *Ike: Abilene to Berlin* (New York: Harper and Row, 1973).

3. Bergman, p. 257.

4. John Sutherland Bonnell, *Presidential Profiles: Religion in the Life of American Presidents* (Philadelphia: Westminster Press, 1971), p. 221.

5. Bergman, p. 258.

6. Ibid., p. 264.

7. Ibid., p. 265.

8. Arthur Larson, *Eisenhower: The President Nobody Knew* (New York: Scribner, 1968), pp. 124-125.

9. Ibid., p. 127.

10. Bergman, p. 258.

John Fitzgerald Kennedy

1. Jon Meacham, *American Gospel: God, The Founding Fathers, and The Making of A Nation* (New York: Random House, 2007), pp. 181-82.

2. Gary Scott Smith, *Faith and the Presidency: From George Washington to George W. Bush* (New York: Oxford University Press, 2006), p. 260.

3. Richard Reeves, *President Kennedy: Profile of Power* (New York: Simon and Schuster, 1993), p. 24.

4. See James MacGregor Burns, *John Kennedy: A Political Profile* (New York: Harcourt, Brace and World, 1960); Robert Dallek, *An Unfinished Life: John F. Kennedy 1917-1963* (New York: Little, Brown, 2003).

5. Davis Newton Lott, *The Presidents Speak: The Inaugural Addresses of the American Presidents, from Washington to Clinton* (New York: Henry Holt, 1994), p. 313.

6. Philip Kunhardt, Jr., Philip B. Kunhardt, III, and Peter W. Kunhardt, *The American President* (New York: Riverhead Books, 1999), p. 198.

7. See Reeves; Dallek.

8. Lott, p. 312.

9. Ibid., p. 315.

10. See Shaun A. Casey, *The Making of a Catholic President: Kennedy Vs. Nixon 1960* (New York: Oxford University Press, 2009); and Theodore H. White, *The Making of the President 1960* (New York: Atheneum Publishers 1961).

11. White, p. 391.

12. Sorensen, pp. 188-193; Herbert S. Parmet, *JFK: The Presidency of John F. Kennedy* (New York: The Dial Press, 1983), p. 43.

13. Lawrence H. Fuchs, *John F. Kennedy and American Catholicism* (New York: Meredith Press, 1967), p. 1; Parmet, p. 43.

14. Sorensen, p. 190.

15. See Casey; Thomas J. Carty, *A Catholic in the White House? Religion, Politics, and John F. Kennedy's Presidential Campaign* (New York: Palgrave Macmillan, 2008); and Fuchs.

16. Sorensen, p. 190.

17. White, p. 393.

18. Burns, pp. 85-86.

19. White, p. 392.

20. Sorensen, p. 191

21. White, p. 393
22. See Fuchs, p. 163.
23. Garry Wills, *Bare Ruined Choirs: Doubt, Prophecy, and Radical Religion* (New York: Doubleday and Company, 1972), pp. 80-81.
24. Sorensen, p. 19.
25. Meacham, p. 182.
26. Sorensen, p. 19.
27. Meacham, p. 187.
28. The American Presidency Project, accessed June 9, 2011, www.presidency.ucsb.edu.
29. Ibid.
30. Dallek, p. 619.
31. The American Presidency Project, accessed June 9, 2011, www.presidency.ucsb.edu. See Bruce J. Dierenfield, The Battle over School Prayer: How Engel v. Vitale Changed America (Lawrence, KS: University Press of Kansas 2007), pp. 149-150.
32. Fuchs, p. 222
33. The American Presidency Project, accessed June 9, 2011, www.presidency.ucsb.edu.

Lyndon Baines Johnson

1. Merle Miller, *Lyndon: An Oral Biography* (New York: Ballantine Books, 1980), p. 28.
2. John Sutherland Bonnell, *Presidential Profiles: Religion in the Life of American Presidents* (Philadelphia: Westminster Press, 1971), p. 234.
3. Joseph A. Califano, Jr., *The Triumph and Tragedy of Lyndon Johnson: The White House Years* (New York: Simon and Schuster, 1991), p. 56.
4. Ibid., pp. 10-11.
5. Robert L. Hardesty, "The LBJ the Nation Seldom Saw," (1983), Lyndon Baines Johnson Library and Museum website, www.lbjlibrary.org.
6. Califano, pp. 155-156.
7. Bonnell, pp. 235-236.
8. Miller, pp. 485-486.
9. Califano, p. 334.
10. Ibid., p. 335.
11. Ibid., p. 335.

Richard Milhous Nixon

1. See Taylor Branch, *At Canaan's Edge: America in the King Years 1965-1968* (New York: Simon and Schuster, 2006).
2. See Roger Morris, *Richard Milhous Nixon: The Rise of An American Politician* (New York: Henry Holt, 1990).
3. Richard Nixon, *Six Crises* (Garden City, NY: Doubleday and Company, 1962), p. 295.
4. Charles P. Henderson, Jr., *The Nixon Theology* (New York: Harper and Row, 1972), pp. 179-180.
5. Ibid., p. 187.
6. Davis Newton Lott, *The Presidents Speak: The Inaugural Addresses of the American Presidents, from Washington to Clinton* (New York: Henry Holt, 1994), p. 326.
7. Ibid.
8. Ibid., p. 329.
9. Ibid., p. 329.
10. Ibid.

11. Fawn M. Brodie, *Richard Nixon: The Shaping of His Character* (New York: W. W. Norton, 1981), p. 23.

12. Gene Healy, *The Cult of the Presidency* (Washington, DC: Cato Institute, 2008), p. 109.

13. Henderson, p. 167.

14. Richard Nixon, *The Memoirs of Richard Nixon* (New York: Warner Books, 1979).

15. Ibid., p. 120.

16. Stephen E. Ambrose, *Nixon: The Education of a Politician 1913-1962* (New York: Simon and Schuster, 1987), p. 11.

17. The American Presidency Project, accessed July 8, 2011, www.presidency.ucsb.edu.

18. Brodie, p. 161.

19. Nixon, *The Memories*, p. 16.

20. Ambrose, p. 58.

21. Ibid., p. 14.

22. Ibid.

23. See Morris; Ambrose; and Richard Reeves, *President Nixon: Alone in the White House* (New York: Simon and Schuster, 2001).

24. Lott, p. 334.

25. Leonard Garment, *Crazy Rhythm* (New York: Times Books), p. 57.

26. Reeves, pp. 21, 22, and 25.

27. See H. R. Haldeman, *The Haldeman Diaries: Inside the Nixon White House* (New York: G. P. Putnam's Sons, 1994).

Gerald Rudolph Ford

1. Gerald R. Ford, *A Time to Heal: The Autobiography of Gerald R. Ford* (New York: Harper and Row, 1979), p. 45.

2. Ibid., p. 10.

3. Ibid., p. 191.

4. Thomas M. DeFrank, *Write It When I'm Gone: Remarkable Off-the-Record Conversations with Gerald R. Ford* (New York: Putnam, 2007), p. 184.

5. Ford, p. 417.

James Earl Carter, Jr.

1. Hendrick Hertzberg, "Jimmy Carter 1977-1981," in *Character Above All*, ed. Robert A. Wilson (New York: Simon and Schuster, 1995), p. 180.

2. Garry Wills, *Under God: Religion and American Politics* (New York: Simon and Schuster, 1990), p. 19.

3. Randall Balmer, *God in the White House: A History: How Faith Shaped the Presidency from John F. Kennedy to George W. Bush* (New York: HarperOne, 2008), p. 155.

4. Ibid., p. 156.

5. Jimmy Carter, *Living Faith* (New York: Times Books, 1996), p. 16.

6. Ibid., pp. 16-17.

7. Ibid., p. 17.

8. See Carter, *Living Faith*; and Jimmy Carter, *Our Endangered Values: America's Moral Crisis* (New York: Simon and Schuster, 2005).

9. Gary Scott Smith, *Faith in the Presidency: From George Washington to George W. Bush* (New York: Oxford University Press, 2006), p. 295.

10. The Nobel Prize website, accessed June 27, 2011, Nobelprize.org/nobel_prizes/peace/laureates/2002/carter-lecture.

11. Douglas Brinkley, *The Unfinished Presidency: Jimmy Carter's Journey Beyond the White House* (New York: Viking Press, 1998), p. 30.

12. Erwin C. Hargrove, *Jimmy Carter as President: Leadership and the Politics of the Public Good* (Baton Rouge, LA: Louisiana State University Press, 1988), p. 8.

13. The Nobel Prize website, accessed June 27, 2011, Nobelprize.org/nobel_prizes/peace/laureates/2002/carter-lecture.

14. Harry R. Davis and Robert C. Good, eds., *Reinhold Niebuhr on Politics* (New York: Charles Scribners Sons, 1960), p. 180.

15. Wesley G. Pippert, ed., *The Spiritual Journey of Jimmy Carter in His Own Words* (New York: Macmillan, 1978), p. 16.

16. The American Presidency Project, accessed June 16, 2011, www. presidency.ucsb.edu.

17. Brinkley, p. 47.

18. Jimmy Carter, *Keeping Faith: Memoirs of a President* (New York: Bantam Books, 1982), p. 596. See Carter, *Living Faith*, p. 106.

Ronald Wilson Reagan

1. Paul Kengor, *God and Ronald Reagan: A Spiritual Life* (New York: Regan Books, 2004), p. 31.

2. Ibid., p. 43.

3. Ibid., p. 49.

4. Ibid., p. 127.

5. Ibid., p. 118.

6. Ibid., pp. 119-120.

7. Committee to Study the AIDS Research Program of the National Institutes of Health. The AIDS Research Program of the National Institutes of Health. National Academies Press, 1991. p. 96.

8. Alex Pareene, "Ronald Reagan Cared More about UFOs than AIDS," February 4, 2011, Salon, www.salon.com.

9. Patti Davis, "The Reagans, from One of Them," *Time* (November 4, 2003), website accessed June 2, 2011.

10. Ibid.

11. Ibid.

12. Michael B. Oren, *Power, Faith, and Fantasy: America in the Middle East 1776 to the Present.* (New York: W. W. Norton, 2007), p. 552.

George Herbert Walker Bush

1. Davis Newton Lott, *The Presidents Speak: The Inaugural Addresses of the American Presidents, from Washington to Clinton* (New York: Henry Holt, 1994), p. 358.

2. The American Presidency Project, accessed July 19, 2011, www.presidency.ucsb.edu.

3. Ibid.

4. Ibid.

5. Mary E. Stuckey, *Defining Americans: The Presidency and National Identity* (Lawrence, KS: University Press of Kansas, 2004), see chap. 7.

6. Ibid., p. 320.

7. Garry Wills, *Under God: Religion and American Politics* (New York: Simon and Schuster, 1990), p. 78.

8. Stuckey, p. 299; See www.michigandaily.com, May 4, 1991, accessed July 21, 2011.

9. Lott, pp. 359-360.

10. Ibid., p. 362.

11. Stuckey, p. 320.

12. The American Presidency Project, accessed July 20, 2011, www.presidency.ucsb.edu. Also, see Wills, p. 80.

13. Lott, p. 359.

William Jefferson Clinton

1. Bill Clinton, *My Life* (New York: Knopf, 2004), p. 67.

2. "The Jesus Factor: Religion in the White House: Then and Now." Frontline, (April 29, 2004), accessed June 30, 2011, http://www.pbs.org/wgbh/pages/frontline/shows/jesus/president/religion.html.

3. Philip Yancey, "The Riddle of Bill Clinton's Faith," *Christianity Today*, vol. 38, no. 5 (April 25, 1994), p. 24.

4. Ibid., p. 26.

5. Clinton, pp. 475-475.

6. William Doyle, *Inside the Oval Office: The White House Tapes from FDR to Clinton.* (New York: Kodanasha America, Inc. 1999), p. 300.

7. Michael B. Oren, *Power, Faith, and Fantasy: American in the Middle East 1776 to the Present* (New York: W. W. Norton, 2007), p. 575.

8. Clinton, pp. 810-811.

9. Ibid., pp. 846-847.

George Walker Bush

1. The American Presidency Project, accessed May 12, 2011, www.presidency.ucsb.edu.

2. Carin Robinson and Clyde Wilcox, "The Faith of George W. Bush: The Personal, Practical, and Political," in *Religion and the American Presidency, ed. Mark J. Rozell and Gleaves Whitney* (New York: Palgrave Macmillan, 2007), p. 220.

3. George W. Bush, *A Charge to Keep: My Journey to the White House* (New York: William Morrow and Co., 1999).

4. Stephen Mansfield, *The Faith of George W. Bush* (New York: Jeremy Tarcher/Penguin, 2003), p. xiv.

5. Bush, p. 136.

6. Guy Lawson, "George W's Personal Jesus," *Gentlemen's Quarterly* (September, 2003).

7. David Frum, *The Right Man: The Surprise Presidency of George W. Bush* (New York: Random House, 2003), pp. 3-4.

8. Quoted in Robinson and Wilcox, p. 218.

9. See Mansfield; and, Bush.

10. Quoted in Robinson and Wilcox, p. 224.

11. The American Presidency Project, accessed May 12, 2011, www.presidency.ucsb.edu.

12. Ibid.

13. Robinson and Wilcox, p. 230.

14. The American Presidency Project.

15. Ibid.

16. Ibid.

17. Robinson and Wilcox, p. 221.

18. Ibid.

19. The American Presidency Project.

Barack Hussein Obama

1. David Corn, "Franklin Graham's New Obama-Muslim Conspiracy Theory," *Mother Jones* (March 22, 2011), accessed online July 6, 2011.

2. Barack Obama, *Dreams from My Father: A Story of Race and Inheritance* (New York: Three Rivers Press, 1995, 2004), p. 37.

3. Ibid., p. 154.

4. Ibid., pp. 286-287.

5. Ibid., p. 295.

6. Lisa Miller, "Finding His Faith," *Newsweek* (July 12, 2008), accessed online August 19, 2010.

7. Ibid.

8. Devin Dwyer, "Holy Blackberry! Obama Finds Ways to Keep the Faith During First Year in Office," *ABC News* (January 29, 2010), accessed online July 5, 2011.

9. Mark Niesse, "Obamas Make Rare Trip to Church While in Hawaii," *AP* (December 27, 2010), accessed online December 27, 2010.

10. Daniel Burke, "Obama's 'Spiritual Cabinet' Offers Advice and Prayer," *Christian Century*, vol. 27, issue 7 (April 6, 2010), pp. 13-15.

11. See Dwyer.

12. Lynn Sweet, "Obama at Easter Prayer Breakfast. Transcript," *The Scoop from Washington.* (blog), *Chicago Sun Times,* April 6, 2010, accessed online July 6, 2011.

13. Pew Research Center, "Growing Number of Americans Say Obama Is a Muslim: Religion, Politics, and the President," Pew Research Center Publications (August 19, 2010), accessed online July 6, 2010.

BIBLIOGRAPHY

?Skowronek in *Kunhardt* (1999), p. 10.

?Reinhold Niebuhr, quoted in Stephen Shaw, "Lincoln and Civil Religion: The President and the Prophetic Stance," in Frank J. Williams and William D. Pederson (eds.), *Abraham Lincoln Contemporary: An American Legacy* (Campbell, CA: Savas Woodbury Publishers, 1995), p. 189.

Algeo, Matthew. *The President is a Sick Man.* New York: Chicago Review Press, 2011.

Ambrose, Stephen E. Ike: *Abilene to Berlin.* New York: Harper and Row, 1973.

———. *Nixon: The Education of a Politician 1913-1962.* New York: Simon and Schuster, 1987.

The American Presidency Project. www.presidency.ucsb.edu.

Balmer, Randall. *God in the White House: A History: How Faith Shaped the Presidency from John F. Kennedy to George W. Bush.* New York: HarperOne, 2008.

Banning, Lance. *The Sacred Fire of Liberty: James Madison and the Founding of the Federal Republic.* Ithaca, NY: Cornell University Press, 1995.

Barre, W. L. T*he Life and Public Services of Millard Fillmore.* Buffalo, NY: Wanzer, McKim, and Co, 1856.

Barton, William E. *The Soul of Abraham Lincoln.* New York: George H. Doran Company, 1920.

Bergman "Religion and the Presidency of Dwight D. Eisenhower" In *Religion and the American Presidency: George Washington to George W. Bush,* edited by Gastón Espinosa. New York: Columbia UP, 2009.

Boller, Paul F. *George Washington and Religion.* Dallas: Southern Methodist UP, 1963.

Bonnell, John Sutherland. *Presidential Profiles: Religion in the Life of American Presidents.* Philadelphia: Westminster Press, 1971.

Branch, Taylor. *At Canaan's Edge: America in the King Years 1965-1968.* New York: Simon and Schuster, 2006.

Brands, H. W. *Andrew Jackson: His Life and Times.* New York: Random House, 2005.

Brant, Irving. *James Madison: The Virginia Revolutionist.* Indianapolis, IN: The Bobbs-Merrill Company, 1941.

Brinkley, Douglas. *The Unfinished Presidency: Jimmy Carter's Journey Beyond the White House.* New York: Viking Press, 1998.

Brodie, Fawn M. *Richard Nixon: The Shaping of His Character.* New York: W.W. Norton, 1981.

Buckley, Thomas E. "Religion and the Presidency of Thomas Jefferson." In *Religion and the American Presidency: George Washington to George W. Bush.* Edited by Gastón Espinosa. New York: Columbia UP, 2009.

Burke, Daniel. "Obama's 'Spiritual Cabinet' Offers Advice and Prayer." *Christian Century Vol. 27, Issue 7 (April 6, 2010): pp.* 13-15.

Burlingame, Michael. *Abraham Lincoln: A Life.* Vol. 1. Baltimore, MD: The Johns Hopkins University Press, 2008.

Burner, David. *Herbert Hoover: A Public Life.* New York: Alfred A. Knopf, 1979.

Burns, James MacGregor. *John Kennedy: A Political Profile.* New York: Harcourt, Brace and World, 1960.

Bush, George W. *A Charge to Keep: My Journey to the White House*. New York: William Morrow and Co., 1999.

Califano, Joseph A., Jr. *The Triumph and Tragedy of Lyndon Johnson: The White House Years*. New York: Simon and Schuster, 1991.

Carter, Jimmy. *Keeping Faith: Memoirs of a President*. New York: Bantam Books, 1982.

————. *Living Faith*. New York: Times Books, 1996.

————. *Our Endangered Values: America's Moral Crisis*. New York: Simon and Schuster, 2005.

Carty, Thomas J. *A Catholic in the White House? Religion, Politics, and John F. Kennedy's Presidential Campaign*. New York: Palgrave Macmillan, 2008.

Carwardine, Richard. *Lincoln: A Life of Purpose and Power*. New York: Alfred A. Knopf, 2006.

Casey, Shaun A. *The Making of a Catholic President: Kennedy Vs. Nixon 1960*. New York: Oxford University Press, 2009.

Clinton, Bill. *My Life*. New York: Knopf, 2004.

Committee to Study the AIDS Research Program of the National Institutes of Health. *The AIDS Research Program of the National Institutes of Health*. National Academies Press, 1991.

Cooper, John Milton, Jr. *The Warrior and the Priest: Woodrow Wilson and Theodore Roosevelt*. Cambridge, MA: Harvard UP, 1983.

————. *Woodrow Wilson: A Biography*. New York: Knopf, 2009.

Corn, David. "Franklin Graham's New Obama-Muslim Conspiracy Theory." Mother Jones (22 March 2011).

Cronin, Thomas E. and Michael A. Genovese. *The Paradoxes of the American Presidency*. 3rd ed. New York: Oxford University Press, 2009.

Dallek, Robert. *An Unfinished Life: John F. Kennedy 1917-1963*. New York: Little, Brown, 2003.

Davis, Harry R. and Robert C. Good, eds. *Reinhold Niebuhr on Politics*. New York: Charles Scribners Sons, 1960.

Davis, Kenneth S. *FDR: The Beckoning of Destiny 1882-1928*. New York: History Book Club, 2003.

Davis, Patti. "The Reagans, from One of Them." *Time* (4 Nov 2003). Website accessed June 2, 2011.

DeFrank, Thomas M. *Write It When I'm Gone: Remarkable Off-the-Record Conversations with Gerald R. Ford*. New York: Putnam, 2007.

Dierenfield, Bruce J. The Battle over School Prayer: How Engel v. Vitale Changed America. Lawrence, KS: University Press of Kansas, 2007.

Dix, Dorothea Lynde and Millard Fillmore. *The Lady and the President: The Letters of Dorothea Dix and Millard Fillmore*. Edited by Charles M. Snyder. Lexington: UP of Kentucky, 1975.

Doyle, William. *Inside the Oval Office: The White House Tapes from FDR to Clinton*. New York: Kodanasha America, Inc. 1999.

Dreisbach, Daniel L. and Jeffry H. Morrison. "Religion and the Presidency of George Washington." In *Religion and the American Presidency: George Washington to George W. Bush*. Edited by Gastón Espinosa. New York: Columbia UP, 2009.

DuVal, Miles P. *James Monroe: An Appreciation, Highlights of His Life and the Monroe Doctrine*. Orange, VA: James Monroe Memorial Foundation, 1982.

Dwyer, Devin. "Holy Blackberry! Obama Finds Ways to Keep the Faith During First Year in Office." ABC News (January 29, 2010), Accessed online July 5, 2011.

Eisenhower, John S. D. *Zachary Taylor.* New York: Times Books, 2008.

Ellis, Joseph J. *American Sphinx: The Character of Thomas Jefferson.* New York: Knopf, 1997.

———. *First Family: Abigail and John.* New York: Alfred A. Knopf, Inc., 2010.

Espinosa, Gastón, ed., *Religion and the American Presidency: George Washington to George W. Bush.* New York: Columbia UP, 2009.

Fausold, Martin L. "Quaker President Herbert C. Hoover and American Foreign Policy." In *Herbert Hoover and World Peace, edited by Lee Nash,* Lanham, MD: University Press of America, Inc., 2010.

Ferrell, Robert H., ed. *Off the Record: The Private Papers of Harry S. Truman.* New York: Harper and Row, 1980.

Fineman, Howard. "Bush and God." *Newsweek,* March 10, 2003.

Finke, Roger and Rodney Stark. "Turning Pews into People: Estimating 19th Century Church Membership." *Journal for the Scientific Study of Religion,* (2001): 180-192.

Ford, Gerald R. *A Time to Heal: The Autobiography of Gerald R. Ford.* New York: Harper and Row, 1979.

Fuchs, Lawrence H. *John F. Kennedy and American Catholicism.* New York: Meredith Press, 1967.

Fuller, Edmund and David E. Green. *God in the White House: The Faiths of American Presidents.* New York: Crown Publishers, 1968.

Frum, David. *The Right Man: The Surprise Presidency of George W. Bush.* New York: Random House, 2003.

Gara, Larry. *The Presidency of Franklin Pierce.* Lawrence, KS: University Press of Kansas, 1988.

Garment, Leonard. *Crazy Rhythm.* New York: De Capo Press, 2001.

Gaustad, Edwin S. *Sworn on the Altar of God: A Religious Biography of Thomas Jefferson.* Grand Rapids, MI: Eerdmans, 1996.

Gould, Lewis. *The Spanish American War and President McKinley.* Lawrence, KS: University Press of Kansas, 1982.

Gilman, Daniel C. *James Monroe.* Boston: Houghton Mifflin, 1898.

Gordon, Sarah Barringer. *The Mormon Question: Polygamy and Constitutional Conflict in Nineteenth-Century America.* Chapel Hill, NC: University of North Carolina Press, 2001.

Gould, Lewis. *The Spanish American War and President McKinley.* Lawrence, KS: University Press of Kansas, 1982.

———. *The William Howard Taft Presidency.* Lawrence, KS: University Press of Kansas, 2009.

Graff, Henry F. *Grover Cleveland.* New York: Times Books, 2002.

Green, James Albert. *William Henry Harrison: His Life and Times.* Richmond, Virginia: Garrett and Massie, 1941.

Guelzo, Allen. *Abraham Lincoln: Redeemer President.* Grand Rapids, MI: William B. Eerdmans Publishing, 1999.

Haldeman, H. R. *The Haldeman Diaries: Inside the Nixon White House.* New York: G. P. Putnam's Sons, 1994.

Hamburger, Philip. *Separation of Church and State.* Cambridge, MA: Harvard University Press, 2002.

Hamby, Alonzo L. *Man of the People: A Life of Harry S. Truman*. New York: Oxford University Press, 1995.

Hargrove, Erwin C. *Jimmy Carter as President: Leadership and the Politics of the Public Good*. Baton Rouge, LA: Louisiana State University Press, 1988.

Healy, Gene. *The Cult of the Presidency*. Washington, DC: Cato Institute, 2008.

Henderson, Charles P., Jr. *The Nixon Theology*. New York: Harper and Row, 1972.

Hertzberg, Hendrick. "Jimmy Carter 1977-1981." In *Character Above All, edited by* Robert A. Wilson. New York: Simon and Schuster, 1995.

Holmes, David L. "The Religion of James Monroe." *The Virginia Quarterly Review* (Autumn 2003): 589-606.

Holzer, Harold, ed. *The Lincoln Anthology: Great Writers on His Life and Legacy from 1860 to Now*. New York: Library of America, 2009.

Hoover, Herbert C. *The Memoirs of Herbert Hoover. Vol. 1, Years of Adventure, 1874-1920*. New York: Macmillan, 1952.

———. *The Memoirs of Herbert Hoover. Vol. 2, The Cabinet and the Presidency, 1920-1933*. New York: Macmillan, 1952.

Howe, Daniel Walker. *What God Hath Wrought: The Transformation of America, 1815-1848*. New York: Oxford University Press, 2007.

Hutson, James. "James Madison and the Social Utility of Religion: Risks vs. Rewards." Paper presented as part of the symposium James Madison: Philosopher and Practitioner of Liberal Democracy at The Library of Congress, Washington, D.C., March 16, 2001. http://www.loc.gov/loc/madison/huston-paper.

James, Marquis. *The Life of Andrew Jackson: Complete in One Volume*. New York: Bobbs-Merrill Company, 1938.

Jefferson, Thomas. *The Jefferson Bible*. Boston: Beacon Press, 1989.

Johnson, Andrew. *The Papers of Andrew Johnson:* Vol. 1, 1822-1851. Edited by Leroy P. Graff and Ralph W. Haskins. Knoxville: U of Tennessee P, 1967.

Kaplan, Fred. *Lincoln: The Biography of a Writer*. New York: Harper, 2008.

Kengor, Paul. *God and Ronald Reagan: A Spiritual Life*. New York: Regan Books, 2004.

Ketcham, Ralph. *James Madison: A Biography*. Charlottesville, VA: University Press of Virginia, 1990.

Kunhardt, Philip B., Jr., Philip B. Kunhardt III, and Peter W. Kunhardt, *The American President*. New York: Riverhead Books, 1999.

Larson, Arthur. *Eisenhower: The President Nobody Knew*. New York: Scribner, 1968.

Lawson, Guy. "George W's Personal Jesus." *Gentlemen's Quarterly* (September, 2003).

Lear, Tobias V. Letters and Recollections of George Washington: Being Letters to Tobias Lear and Others Between 1790 and 1799, Showing the First American in the Management of His Estate and Domestic Affairs. With a Diary of Washington's Last Days, Kept by Mr. Lear. The Papers of George Washington, University of Virginia. Online. Gwpapers.virginia.edu.

The Library of America. *Abraham Lincoln: Speeches and Writings 1832-1858*. New York: Library of America, 1989.

The Library of America. *James Madison: Writings*. New York: The Library of America, 1999.

Lorant, Stefan. *The Life and Times of Theodore Roosevelt*. New York: Garden City, 1959.

Lott, Davis Newton. *The Presidents Speak: The Inaugural Addresses of the American Presidents, from Washington to Clinton*. New York: Henry Holt, 1994.

Mansfield, Stephen. *The Faith of George W. Bush*. New York: Jeremy Tarcher/Penguin, 2003.

Marty, Martin E. *Pilgrims in Their Own Land*. New York: Penguin, 1984.

May, Gary. *John Tyler.* New York: Times Books, 2008.

McCoy, Charles Allan. *Polk and the Presidency.* Austin: U of Texas P, 1960.

McCoy, Drew. *The Last of the Fathers: James Madison and the Republican Legacy.* Cambridge, UK: Cambridge University Press, 1989.

McCullough, David. *John Adams.* New York: Simon and Schuster, 2001.

———. *Truman.* New York: Simon and Schuster, 1992.

McFeeley, William S. *Grant: A Biography.* New York: W.W. Norton, 2002.

Meacham, Jon. *American Gospel: God, The Founding Fathers, and The Making of a Nation.* New York: Random House, 2007.

Miller, Lisa. "Finding His Faith." *Newsweek* (July 12, 2008). Online.

Miller, Merle. *Lyndon: An Oral Biography.* New York: Ballantine Books, 1980.

Miller, William Lee. *Arguing About Slavery: The Great Battle in the United States Congress.* New York: Alfred A. Knopf, 1995.

———. *The Business of May Next: James Madison and the Founding.* Charlottesville, VA: University Press of Virginia, 1992.

Morris, Roger. *Richard Milhous Nixon: The Rise of An American Politician.* New York: Henry Holt, 1990.

Munoz, Victor Phillip. "Religion in the Life, Thought, and Presidency of James Madison." In Mark J. Rozell and Gleaves Whitney, *Religion and the American Presidency.* New York: Palgrave Macmillan, 2007.

Nagel, Paul C. *John Quincy Adams: A Public Life, A Private Life.* New York: Alfred A. Knopf, 1998.

Nash, Lee, ed. *Herbert Hoover and World Peace.* Lanham, MD: University Press of America, Inc., 2010.

Niebuhr, Reinhold. *The Irony of American History.* New York: Charles Scribners Sons, 1952.

Niesse, Mark. "Obamas Make Rare Trip to Church While in Hawaii." AP (December 27, 2010). Accessed online December 27, 2010.

Nixon, Richard. *The Memoirs of Richard Nixon.* New York: Warner Books, 1979.

———. *Six Crises.* Garden City, NY: Doubleday and Company, 1962.

The Nobel Prize website. Nobelprize.org/nobel_prizes/peace/laureates/2002/carter-lecture

Noll, Mark. *The Civil War as a Theological Crisis.* Chapel Hill, NC: University of North Carolina Press, 2006.

Noonan, John T., Jr. *The Lustre of Our Country: The American Experience of Religious Freedom.* Berkeley, CA: University of California Press, 1998.

Novak, Michael. *Choosing Our King: Powerful Symbols in Presidential Politics. New York: Macmillan,* 1974.

Obama, Barack. *Dreams from My Father: A Story of Race and Inheritance.* New York: Three Rivers Press, 1995, 2004.

Oren, Michael B. Power, *Faith, and Fantasy: America in the Middle East 1776 to the Present.* New York: W. W. Norton, 2007.

Osborn, George C. *Woodrow Wilson: The Early Years.* Baton Rouge: Louisiana State UP, 1968.

Pareene, Alex. "Ronald Reagan Cared More about UFOs than AIDS." February 4, 2011. Salon. www.salon.com.

Parmet, Herbert S. *JFK: The Presidency of John F. Kennedy.* New York: The Dial Press, 1983.

Perkins, Francis. *The Roosevelt I Knew.* New York: Viking Press, 1946.

Pew Research Center. "Growing Number of Americans Say Obama Is a Muslim: Religion, Politics, and the President." Pew Research Center Publications (August 19, 2010). Accessed online July 6, 2010.

Pierard, Richard V. and Robert D. Linder. *Civil Religion and the Presidency*. Grand Rapids, MI: Zondervan Publishing House, 1988, chap. 5.

Pippert, Wesley G., ed. *The Spiritual Journey of Jimmy Carter in His Own Words*. New York: Macmillan, 1978.

Rayback, Robert J. *Millard Fillmore: Biography of a President*. Buffalo, NY: Buffalo Historical Society, 1959.

Reeves, Thomas C. *Gentleman Boss: The Life of Chester Alan Arthur*. New York: Knopf, 1975.

Reeves, Richard. *President Kennedy: Profile of Power*. New York: Simon and Schuster, 1993.

———. *President Nixon: Alone in the White House*. New York: Simon and Schuster, 2001.

Ridings, William J., Jr. and Stuart B. McIver *Rating the Presidents: A Ranking of U.S. Leaders, From the Great and Honorable to the Dishonest and Incompetent*. Secaucus, NJ: Citadel Press, 1997.

Robinson, Carin and Clyde Wilcox. "The Faith of George W. Bush: The Personal, Practical, and Political." In *Religion and the American Presidency, edited by* Mark J. Rozell and Gleaves Whitney. New York: Palgrave Macmillan, 2007.

Robinson, Corinne Roosevelt. *My Brother Theodore Roosevelt*. New York: Charles Scribner's Sons, 1921.

Roosevelt, Theodore. *Theodore Roosevelt: An Autobiography*. New York: Charles Scribner's Sons, 1920.

Rozell, Mark J. and Gleaves Whitney. *Religion and the American Presidency*. New York: Palgrave Macmillan, 2007.

Rutkow, Ira. *James Garfield*. New York: Times Books, 2006.

Sellers, Charles. *James K. Polk: Jacksonian, 1795-1843*. Princeton: Princeton UP, 1957.

Shaw, Stephen. "Lincoln and Civil Religion: The President and the Prophetic Stance." In *Abraham Lincoln Contemporary: An American Legacy, edited by* Frank J. Williams and William D. Pederson, p. 189. Campbell, CA: Savas Woodbury Publishers, 1995.

Seivers, Harry Joseph. *Benjamin Harrison: Hoosier Warrior, 1833-1865*. Chicago: Henry Regnery Company, 1952.

Smith, Elbert B. *The Presidency of James Buchanan*. Lawrence: UP of Kansas, 1975.

Smith, Gary Scott. *Faith and the Presidency: From George Washington to George W. Bush*. New York: Oxford University Press, 2006.

Smith, Gary Scott. "Religion and the Presidency of Franklin Delano Roosevelt." In *Religion and the American Presidency: George Washington to George W. Bush, edited by* Gastón Espinosa. New York: Columbia UP, 2009, pp. 184-217.

Smith, Jean Edward. *Grant*. New York: Simon and Schuster, 2002.

Smith, Page. *John Adams*. 2 vols. New York: Doubleday and Company, 1962.

Spalding, Elizabeth Edwards. "We Must Put on the Armor of God." In *Religion and the American Presidency, edited by* Mark J. Rozell and Gleaves Whitney. New York: Palgrave Macmillan, 2007.

Stuckey, Mary E. *Defining Americans: The Presidency and National Identity*. Lawrence, KS: University Press of Kansas, 2004.

Sweet, Lynn. "Obama at Easter Prayer Breakfast. Transcript." The Scoop from Washington (blog). *Chicago Sun Times*, April 6, 2010. Accessed online July 6, 2011.

Trefousse, Hans L. *Andrew Johnson: A Biography*. New York: Norton, 1989.

Truman, Harry S. *Memoirs, Vol. 1, Year of Decisions*. Garden City, NY: Doubleday and Company, Inc., 1955.

White, Ronald C., Jr. *Lincoln's Greatest Speech: The Second Inaugural*. New York: Simon and Schuster, 2002.

White, Theodore H. *The Making of the President 1960*. New York: Atheneum Publishers, 1961.

Widmer, Ted. "Christmas With Lincoln." www. opinionator.blogs.nytimes. com/2010/12/24. Accessed December 28, 2010.

———. *Martin Van Buren*. New York: Times Books, 2004.

Williams, Charles Richard and William Henry Smith. *The Life of Rutherford Birchard Hayes, Nineteenth President of the United States*. 2 vols. Columbus, Ohio State Archeological and Historical Society: 1928.

Williams, Frank J. and William D. Pederson, eds. *Abraham Lincoln Contemporary: An American Legacy*. Campbell, CA: Savas Woodbury Publishers, 1995.

Wills, Garry. *Bare Ruined Choirs: Doubt, Prophecy, and Radical Religion*. New York: Doubleday and Company, 1972.

———. *Under God: Religion and American Politics*. New York: Simon and Schuster, 1990.

Wilson, John R. M. "Herbert Hoover's Military Policy." In *Herbert Hoover and World Peace, edited by Lee Nash*, Lanham, MD: University Press of America, 2010.

Wilson, Major L. *The Presidency of Martin Van Buren*. Lawrence, KS: University Press of Kansas, 1984.

Wilson, Robert A., ed. *Character Above All*. New York: Simon and Schuster, 1995.

Woods, Robert A. *The Preparation of Calvin Coolidge: An Interpretation*. Boston: Houghton Mifflin, 1924.

Yancey, Philip. "The Riddle of Bill Clinton's Faith." *Christianity Today Vol. 38, no. 5 (April 25, 1994)*.

INDEX

ACKNOWLEDGMENTS

I'd like to thank our publisher, Mark Russell, for his incredible patience and teasing sense of humor, which made his requests (demands) for making deadlines much more palatable. You're a great man to work with.

A special thank you is also in order to our editor, Anna McHargue, for her close and attentive reading. I would not have wanted your task of editing an English professor's writing; you handled it with aplomb and grace, and you even put up with my pedantic punctuation rants.

Finally, thanks to the library staff at Northwest Nazarene University, who ordered so many books for me and who maintain such a pleasant place to read and write (and thank you for not getting after me when I ate my lunch in the back of the stacks).

Darrin Grinder

This book grew out of an unexpected encounter with Mark Russell in San Diego in the spring of 2010 as we were attending a conference at Point Loma Nazarene University concerning "the prophetic imagination." Talk about prophetic! We began talking and he asked if I knew anyone who knew much about the American presidency, and especially presidents and their religious faith. Before I could answer, another colleague there, Professor Brent Peterson, friend and fellow faculty member at Northwest Nazarene University, pointed at me, told Mark how much I knew, and I then had to try to come through and not embarrass myself or Brent or our employer. The seed was sown, and you have the result in your hands.

My co-author, Professor Darrin Grinder, deserves so much credit, along with Mark Russell and Anna McHargue, for bringing this book to fruition. Darrin's endless encouragement, necessary and proper persistent prodding, and sage counsel have helped to keep me somewhat on track and complete this project, which took a good deal longer to complete than perhaps anyone expected or desired.

This book has been, in large measure, a labor of love, and yet at times the labor pains seemed quite daunting. Studying the American presidency is not for the faint of heart; writing a book on the religious faith of American presidents may test one's own faith, such that one vacillates between Dante and Don Quixote. In any event, the journey has been worth it—personally and professionally, and I am thankful for having such guides along the way as Mark, Anna, Darrin, Brent, and many other colleagues, students, family members, and friends.

Steve Shaw